T0399666

Rhinencephalon, Tabes dorsalis and Elpenor's Syndrome

This book is a fascinating collection of various neuroscience terms coined over the last centuries. Each of the 45 chapters in this book dives deep into the etymologies, vernacular subtleties and historical anecdotes relating to these terms.

This book illustrates the rich and diverse history of neuroscience, which has borrowed and continues to borrow terms and concepts from across cultures, literature and languages. The ever-increasing number of terms that needed to be coined with the mushrooming of the field required neuroscientists to show astonishing imagination and creativity, leading them to draw inspiration from Graeco-Roman mythology (Elpenor's syndrome), literature (Lasthenie de Ferjol's syndrome), theatre (Ondine's curse), Japanese folklore (Kanashibari) and even the Bible (Matthew effect). This book will be of immense interest to scholars and researchers studying neuroscience, history of science, anatomy, psychology and linguistics. It will also appeal to any reader interested in learning more about neuroscience and its history.

All the chapters included in this book were originally published in a column that appeared from 1997 to 2020 in the *Journal of the History of the Neurosciences*.

Régis Olry, MD, MSC (France), is Professor of Anatomy at the University of Québec, Trois-Rivières, Canada, and has previously held faculty positions in Germany (Heidelberg and Marburg). He has published numerous articles and three books on the history of anatomical terminology, and has received awards for university teaching and his articles on the origins of words and phrases in the neurosciences.

Duane E. Haines, PhD, has held faculty positions at Wake Forest, Mississippi, West Virginia (Professor and Chairman), and at Medical College of Virginia. He is the author of numerous scientific papers and 15 books, including a brain atlas and a neuroscience text. He has held offices in scientific organisations and participated in the writing of *Nomina Anatomica*.

Rhinencephalon, Tabes dorsalis and Elpenor's Syndrome

The Fascinating Stories Behind These and Other Neuroscience Terms

Régis Olry and Duane E. Haines

LONDON AND NEW YORK

First published 2022
by Routledge
2 Park Square, Milton Park, Abingdon, Oxon, OX14 4RN

and by Routledge
605 Third Avenue, New York, NY 10158

Routledge is an imprint of the Taylor & Francis Group, an informa business

© 2022 Taylor & Francis

All rights reserved. No part of this book may be reprinted or reproduced or utilised in any form or by any electronic, mechanical, or other means, now known or hereafter invented, including photocopying and recording, or in any information storage or retrieval system, without permission in writing from the publishers.

Trademark notice: Product or corporate names may be trademarks or registered trademarks, and are used only for identification and explanation without intent to infringe.

British Library Cataloguing-in-Publication Data
A catalogue record for this book is available from the British Library

ISBN13: 978-0-367-64651-6 (hbk)
ISBN13: 978-0-367-64653-0 (pbk)
ISBN13: 978-1-003-12566-2 (ebk)

DOI: 10.4324/9781003125662

Typeset in Times New Roman
by codeMantra

Publisher's Note
The publisher accepts responsibility for any inconsistencies that may have arisen during the conversion of this book from journal articles to book chapters, namely the inclusion of journal terminology.

Disclaimer
Every effort has been made to contact copyright holders for their permission to reprint material in this book. The publishers would be grateful to hear from any copyright holder who is not here acknowledged and will undertake to rectify any errors or omissions in future editions of this book.

Contents

	Citation Information	viii
	Preface	xiv
1	Rhinencephalon: a Brain for the Nose?	1
2	Fornix and Gyrus fornicatus: Carnal Sins?	3
3	Cerebral Mythology: A Skull Stuffed With Gods	5
4	The Three Musketeers and the Twelve Cranial Nerves	7
5	Just What *is* the Inferior Cerebellar Peduncle?	9
6	Vague, Uncertain, Ambiguous, Obscure: Imprecision or Modesty?	12
7	Vater, Pacini, Wagner, Meissner, Golgi, Mazzoni, Ruffini, Merkel and Krause: Were their nerves all on edge?	14
8	The Subfornical and Subcommissural Organs: Never-Ending Rediscoveries	17
9	Arachnophobia: Spiders and Spider's Webs in the Head	20
10	Claustrum: A Sea Wall Between the Island and the Shell?	23
11	Phantom Limb: Haunted Body?	26
12	Lasthénie de Ferjol's Syndrome: A Tribute Paid by Jean Bernard to Jules Amédée Barbey D'Aurevilly	28
13	Ansa Hypoglossi or Ansa Cervicalis? That is the Question …	30
14	Reissner's Fibre: The Exception Which Proves the Rule, or the Devil According to Charles Baudelaire?	33

vi   CONTENTS

15 If There are "Deep" Cerebellar Nuclei, Where are the
    "Superficial" Ones?   36

16 "James Parkinson did not die of his own personal disease ... he died
    of a stroke" Eponyms: Possessive or Nonpossessive?   39

17 Give a Kiss to a Frog and it Will Turn into ... A Neuropeptide: The
    Genealogy of the Bombesin-Like Family   42

18 Nomenclature of Persistent Carotid Vertebrobasilar Anastomoses   45

19 Interthalamic Adhesion: Scruples About Calling a Spade a Spade?   48

20 Herophilus' Press, Torcular and Confluens Sinuum: A Triple Mistake 51

21 From Dante Alighieri's First Circle To Paul Donald MacLean's
    Limbic System   54

22 Elpenor's Syndrome: The Link Between One of Ulysses'
    Companions and the Tenth President of the Third French Republic   57

23 Munchausen Syndrome By Proxy: Karl Friedrich Hieronymus,
    Baron von Münchhausen, Hasn't Got Anything To Do With It   60

24 Oedipus Complex: A Confession to a Berlin Otorhinolaryngologist
    that Became a Cornerstone of Psychoanalysis   63

25 The Brain in its Birthday Suit: No More Reason to be Ashamed   67

26 The Pen Nib and the Bolt: The Rhomboid Fossa of the Fourth
    Ventricle or the Symbol of the Censorship of the Press?   71

27 A Concert Hall for Stringed Musical Instruments Under
    the Splenium of the Corpus Callosum   75

28 The Cerebellum, the Earthworm and the Freshwater Crayfish: An
    Unpublished Fable of Jean de La Fontaine?   78

29 Korbinian Brodmann: The Victor Hugo of Cytoarchitectonic Brain Maps 81

30 Brain Heraldic Tinctures and Evolution Theory: A Sensational Turn
    of Events That Should Have Been Kept Secret   85

31 Renfield's Syndrome: A Psychiatric Illness Drawn from Bram
    Stoker's *Dracula*   88

32 "Matthew Effect" in Neurosciences   92

33 Is Poetry a Disease of the Brain, as Alfred de Vigny Said?   96

CONTENTS vii

34 Between André Du Laurens' Horse Tail and William Cadogan's Pony Tail 100

35 Kanashibari (金縛り): A Ghost's Business 105

36 "Magic Mirror in my Hand, Who is the Fairest in the Land ... and, Incidentally, Are You Transparent or Shining?" 111

37 Trigeminal Neuralgia: Pleonasm and Miscalculation 114

38 Hallervorden-Spatz Disease: Did One Set the Fox to Mind the Geese? 121

39 The sleeping brain: Extenuating circumstances of the Marquis de La Fayette on October 6, 1789 127

40 The devil always experienced malicious pleasure in imposing himself in neuropsychiatric nosology 131

41 *Tabes dorsalis*: Not, at all, "Elementary my dear Watson!" 138

42 Ondine's curse: With Jean Giraudoux's finishing touches 144

43 *Moyamoya* (もやもや): When cerebral arteries go up in smoke 150

44 Migraine: Between headache, pomegranate, seed of cochineal, and unidentified fish 155

45 Phrenology: Scheherazade of etymology 160

Index 169

Citation Information

The following chapters were originally published in various issues of the *Journal of the History of the Neurosciences*. When citing this material, please use the original citations and page numbering for each article, as follows:

Chapter 1
Rhinencephalon: a Brain for the Nose
Régis Olry and Duane E. Haines
Journal of the History of the Neurosciences, volume 6, issue 2 (1997) pp. 217–218

Chapter 2
Fornix and Gyrus fornicatus: Carnal Sins?
Régis Olry and Duane E. Haines
Journal of the History of the Neurosciences, volume 6, issue 3 (1997) pp. 338–339

Chapter 3
Cerebral Mythology: A Skull Stuffed With Gods
Régis Olry and Duane E. Haines
Journal of the History of the Neurosciences, volume 7, issue 1 (1998) pp. 82–83

Chapter 4
The Three Musketeers and the Twelve Cranial Nerves
Régis Olry and Duane E. Haines
Journal of the History of the Neurosciences, volume 7, issue 3 (1998) pp. 248–249

Chapter 5
Just What is the Inferior Cerebellar Peduncle?
Régis Olry and Duane E. Haines
Journal of the History of the Neurosciences, volume 8, issue 1 (1999) pp. 74–76

Chapter 6
Vague, Uncertain, Ambiguous, Obscure: Imprecision or Modesty?
Régis Olry and Duane E. Haines
Journal of the History of the Neurosciences, volume 8, issue 3 (1999) pp. 294–295

Chapter 7
Vater, Pacini, Wagner, Meissner, Golgi, Mazzoni, Ruffini, Merkel and Krause: Were their nerves all on edge?
Régis Olry and Duane E. Haines
Journal of the History of the Neurosciences, volume 9, issue 3 (2000) pp. 311–313

Chapter 8
The Subfornical and Subcommissural Organs: Never-Ending Rediscoveries
Régis Olry and Duane E. Haines
Journal of the History of the Neurosciences, volume 10, issue 1 (2001) pp. 108–110

Chapter 9
Arachnophobia: Spiders and Spider's Webs in the Head
Régis Olry and Duane E. Haines
Journal of the History of the Neurosciences, volume 10, issue 2 (2001) pp. 198–200

Chapter 10
Claustrum: A Sea Wall Between the Island and the Shell?
Régis Olry and Duane E. Haines
Journal of the History of the Neurosciences, volume 10, issue 3 (2001) pp. 321–322

Chapter 11
Phantom Limb: Haunted Body?
Régis Olry and Duane E. Haines
Journal of the History of the Neurosciences, volume 11, issue 1 (2002) pp. 67–68

Chapter 12
Lasthénie de Ferjol's Syndrome: A Tribute Paid by Jean Bernard to Jules Amédée Barbey D'Aurevilly
Régis Olry and Duane E. Haines
Journal of the History of the Neurosciences, volume 11, issue 2 (2002) pp. 181–182

Chapter 13
Ansa Hypoglossi or Ansa Cervicalis: That is the Question …
Régis Olry and Duane E. Haines
Journal of the History of the Neurosciences, volume 11, issue 3 (2002) pp. 302–304

Chapter 14
Reissner's Fibre: The Exception Which Proves the Rule, or the Devil According to Charles Baudelaire?
Régis Olry and Duane E. Haines
Journal of the History of the Neurosciences, volume 12, issue 1 (2003) pp. 73–75

Chapter 15
If there are "Deep" Cerebellar Nuclei, Where are the "Superficial" Ones?
Régis Olry and Duane E. Haines
Journal of the History of the Neurosciences, volume 12, issue 2 (2003) pp. 203–205

Chapter 16

"James Parkinson did not die of his own personal disease ... he died of a stroke" Eponyms: Possessive or Nonpossessive?
Régis Olry and Duane E. Haines
Journal of the History of the Neurosciences, volume 12, issue 3 (2003) pp. 305–307

Chapter 17

Give a Kiss to a Frog and it Will Turn into ... A Neuropeptide: The Genealogy of the Bombesin-Like Family
Régis Olry and Duane E. Haines
Journal of the History of the Neurosciences, volume 12, issue 4 (2003) pp. 411–412

Chapter 18

Nomenclature of Persistent Carotid Vertebrobasilar Anastomoses
Régis Olry and Duane E. Haines
Journal of the History of the Neurosciences, volume 13, issue 2 (2004) pp. 190–192

Chapter 19

Interthalamic Adhesion: Scruples About Calling a Spade a Spade?
Régis Olry and Duane E. Haines
Journal of the History of the Neurosciences, volume 14, issue 2 (2005) pp. 116–118

Chapter 20

Herophilus' Press, Torcular and Confluens Sinuum: A Triple Mistake
Régis Olry and Duane E. Haines
Journal of the History of the Neurosciences, volume 14, issue 3 (2005) pp. 235–237

Chapter 21

From Dante Alighieri's First Circle To Paul Donald MacLean's Limbic System
Régis Olry and Duane E. Haines
Journal of the History of the Neurosciences, volume 14, issue 4 (2005) pp. 368–370

Chapter 22

Elpenor's Syndrome: The Link Between One of Ulysses' Companions and the Tenth President of the Third French Republic
Régis Olry and Duane E. Haines
Journal of the History of the Neurosciences, volume 15, issue 2 (2006) pp. 159–161

Chapter 23

Munchausen Syndrome By Proxy: Karl Friedrich Hieronymus, Baron von Münchhausen, Hasn't Got Anything To Do With It
Régis Olry and Duane E. Haines
Journal of the History of the Neurosciences, volume 15, issue 3 (2006) pp. 276–278

Chapter 24

Oedipus Complex: A Confession to a Berlin Otorhinolaryngologist that Became a Cornerstone of Psychoanalysis
Régis Olry and Duane E. Haines
Journal of the History of the Neurosciences, volume 16, issue 3 (2007) pp. 337–340

Chapter 25

The Brain in its Birthday Suit: No More Reason to be Ashamed
Régis Olry and Duane E. Haines
Journal of the History of the Neurosciences, volume 17, issue 4 (2008) pp. 461–464

Chapter 26

The Pen Nib and the Bolt: The Rhomboid Fossa of the Fourth Ventricle or the Symbol of the Censorship of the Press?
Régis Olry and Duane E. Haines
Journal of the History of the Neurosciences, volume 18, issue 1 (2009) pp. 76–79

Chapter 27

A Concert Hall for Stringed Musical Instruments Under the Splenium of the Corpus Callosum
Régis Olry and Duane E. Haines
Journal of the History of the Neurosciences, volume 18, issue 2 (2009) pp. 214–216

Chapter 28

The Cerebellum, the Earthworm and the Freshwater Crayfish: An Unpublished Fable of Jean de La Fontaine?
Régis Olry and Duane E. Haines
Journal of the History of the Neurosciences, volume 19, issue 1 (2010) pp. 35–37

Chapter 29

Korbinian Brodmann: The Victor Hugo of Cytoarchitectonic Brain Maps
Régis Olry and Duane E. Haines
Journal of the History of the Neurosciences, volume 19, issue 2 (2010) pp. 195–198

Chapter 30

Brain Heraldic Tinctures and Evolution Theory: A Sensational Turn of Events That Should Have Been Kept Secret
Régis Olry and Duane E. Haines
Journal of the History of the Neurosciences, volume 20, issue 3 (2011) pp. 236–238

Chapter 31

Renfield's Syndrome: A Psychiatric Illness drawn From Bram Stoker's Dracula
Régis Olry and Duane E. Haines
Journal of the History of the Neurosciences, volume 20, issue 4 (2011) pp. 368–371

Chapter 32

"Matthew Effect" in Neurosciences
Régis Olry and Duane E. Haines
Journal of the History of the Neurosciences, volume 21, issue 1 (2012) pp. 115–118

Chapter 33

Is Poetry a Disease of the Brain, as Alfred de Vigny Said?
Régis Olry and Duane E. Haines
Journal of the History of the Neurosciences, volume 21, issue 2 (2012) pp. 228–231

Chapter 34

Between André Du Laurens' Horst Tail and William Cadogan's Pony Tail
Régis Olry and Duane E. Haines
Journal of the History of the Neurosciences, volume 21, issue 3 (2012) pp. 327–331

Chapter 35

Kanashibari (金縛り): A Ghost's Business
Régis Olry and Duane E. Haines
Journal of the History of the Neurosciences, volume 23, issue 2 (2014) pp. 192–197

Chapter 36

"Magic Mirror in my Hand, Who is the Fairest in the Land … and, Incidentally, Are You Transparent or Shining?"
Régis Olry and Duane E. Haines
Journal of the History of the Neurosciences, volume 23, issue 3 (2014) pp. 327–329

Chapter 37

Trigeminal Neuralgia: Pleonasm and Miscalculation
Régis Olry and Duane E. Haines
Journal of the History of the Neurosciences, volume 24, issue 3 (2015) pp. 303–309

Chapter 38

Hallervorden-Spatz Disease: Did One Set the Fox to Mind the Geese?
Régis Olry and Duane E. Haines
Journal of the History of the Neurosciences, volume 24, issue 4 (2015) pp. 420–425

Chapter 39

The sleeping brain: Extenuating Circumstances of the Marquis de La Fayette on October 6, 1789
Régis Olry and Duane E. Haines
Journal of the History of the Neurosciences, volume 26, issue 2 (2017) pp. 224–227

Chapter 40

The devil always experienced malicious pleasure in imposing himself in neuropsychiatric nosology
Régis Olry and Duane E. Haines
Journal of the History of the Neurosciences, volume 26, issue 3 (2017) pp. 329–335

Chapter 41

Tabes dorsalis*: Not, at all, "Elementary my dear Watson!"*
Régis Olry and Duane E. Haines
Journal of the History of the Neurosciences, volume 27, issue 2 (2018) pp. 198–203

Chapter 42

Ondine's curse: With Jean Giraudoux's finishing touches
Régis Olry and Duane E. Haines
Journal of the History of the Neurosciences, volume 27, issue 4 (2018) pp. 390–395

Chapter 43
Moyamoya *(もやもや): When cerebral arteries go up in smoke*
Régis Olry and Duane E. Haines
Journal of the History of the Neurosciences, volume 28, issue 1 (2019) pp. 71–75

Chapter 44
Migraine: Between headache, pomegranate, seed of cochineal, and unidentified fish
Régis Olry and Duane E. Haines
Journal of the History of the Neurosciences, volume 28, issue 3 (2019) pp. 346–350

Chapter 45
Phrenology: Scheherazade of etymology
Régis Olry and Duane E. Haines
Journal of the History of the Neurosciences, volume 29, issue 1 (2020) pp. 150–157

For any permission-related enquiries please visit:
http://www.tandfonline.com/page/help/permissions

Preface

It is a pleasure to see all the NeuroWords columns we wrote for the *Journal of the History of the Neurosciences* since 1997 published together in this volume, and we hope it will be of great use to neuroscientists as well as to those who simply have a passion for language and its roots. The history of the sciences corresponds closely with the history of the terms each scientific discipline coins, and neurosciences are no exception to this rule. When scholars engage with historical documents, one thing that frequently stands out is the quality of the writing when one compares the insights of the work with the lack of sophisticated equipment at the time. But to talk about a newly discovered formation or a newly developed concept naturally leads to the coining of either a new term or at least a more meaningful synonym from an existing term.

The ever-increasing number of terms that needed to be coined with the mushrooming of the field obliged neuroscientists to show astonishing imagination and creativity, leading them on many occasions to draw inspiration from Graeco-Roman mythology (Elpenor's syndrome), literature (Lasthenie de Ferjol's syndrome), theatre (Ondine's curse), Japanese folklore (Kanashibari), and even the Bible (Matthew effect).

Many illustrious forerunners led the way: Rufus of Ephesus (c.70–c.110), Jean Férapied Dufieu (1737–1769), and Joseph Hyrtl (1810–1894), among others. Today, it is our turn to invite you to travel through this marvellous world of strict etymologies, vernacular subtleties and historical anecdotes.

A special thank you is due to Dr Stanley Finger, a noted neurohistorian in his own right, for having had the idea of these columns, entrusting this project to us, and for always showing interest in such publications. Finally, we would like to thank Robinson Raju, our editor at Taylor & Francis, for his enthusiasm for this project.

Régis Olry, Trois-Rivières, Canada
Duane E. Haines, Winston Salem, USA

Rhinencephalon: a Brain for the Nose?

The term "rhinencephalon" has its roots in the teratology of the early nineteenth century. Indeed, this term appears in the writings of the famous French naturalist, Etienne Geoffroy Saint-Hilaire, though its meaning was quite different from that of today. In his 1822 monograph on human monstrosities, the author termed "rhinencephalon" one of the thirteen kinds of acephaly characterized by tube-shaped nasal teguments and the total absence of an olfactory nervous system (1822, pp. 93–96). Therefore, a term which was later to designate that part of the nervous system responsible for olfaction initially denoted a dysgenesis distinguished, paradoxically, by the lack of an olfactory nervous system.

During the second half of the nineteenth century, an increasing number of researchers tended to locate olfactory centres on the medial side of the cerebral hemisphere. Paul Broca described his famous "grand lobe limbique" (1878), and Emil Zuckerkandl lay the semantic foundations for a rhinencephalon (1887) by introducing the term "Riechcentrum" (olfactory centre). A short time later, Sir William Turner termed "rhinencephalon" that part of the cerebral cortex that is separated from the pallium by the rhinal sulcus (1890–1891). This term remained in the nomenclatures of the German anatomists Wilhelm His (1895) and Ludwig Edinger (1905), but its use soon led to controversy. Gustav Retzius, for example, seemed to have had the mistaken impression that Turner's rhinencephalon included the whole of Broca's "grand lobe limbique". The effect of this blurring of distinction between two different concepts was an ambiguity in the definition of a rhinencephalon which has persisted to the present day.

In 1913, Paul de Terra suggested the term "osphrencephalon" in place of "rhinencephalon" but did not cite a reason for his choice (1913, p. 484). In a 1923 monograph, Maurice Mutel devoted less than a page to explaining the origin of the term, which he used nevertheless in the title of a 236-page book. He then went on to develop a concept of the rhinencephalon without ever stopping to consider the appropriateness of the word. The emergence in neuroanatomical language of a visceral brain, and afterwards of a limbic system (MacLean, 1949 and 1952, respectively), only complicated the issue by leading to an overlapping of two very different concepts. In spite of its ambiguity, the term "rhinencephalon" remained in the Nomina anatomica of Basel (1895) and Jena (1935); it would be defined as an "unofficial didactic term" only in the 1955 revision of the work (Donath, 1960).

In 1963, Alf Brodal organized a debate on the terminology of the rhinencephalon which included the participation of Lammers, Crosby, Droogleever Fortuyn,

Arien Kappers, Stephan and Szentagothai, among others. Since no agreement could be reached in spite of heated arguments on both the anatomical and physiological sides of the issue, Brodal concluded that the term should always be accompanied by a footnote explaining the author's particular understanding of its meaning.

Most modern authors avoid using the term "rhinencephalon" because of its inexactness. The prefix had been chosen ostensibly to emphasize the functional aspect of that part of the brain, but its effect was to render the term too all-encompassing and therefore inadequate. This issue has been further complicated by the tendency of some authors to define the rhinencephalon as the "olfactory brain" while, at the same time, including structures under this heading that have little, or nothing, to do with olfaction. The trend in contemporary textbooks is to describe olfactory structures in their own right and not use the term rhinencephalon. It is likely that this term will disappear from official lists of anatomical terminology in the future.

References

Brodal A (1963): General Discussion on the Terminology of the Rhinencephalon. In Bargmann W, Schadé J P (Eds) *The rhinencephalon and related structures*. Amsterdam, London, New York: Elsevier Publishing Company, pp. 237–244.

Broca P (1878): Le grand lobe limbique et la scissure limbique dans la série des mammifères. *Revue d'Anthropologie, 2e série, t. 1*, pp. 385–498.

De Terra P (1913): *Vademecum anatomicum. Kritisch-etymologisches Wörterbuch der systematischen Anatomie, mit besonderer Berücksichtigung der Synonymen*. Jena: G. Fischer.

Donath T (1960): *Erläuterndes anatomisches Wörterbuch. Vergleichende Übersicht der Baseler, Jenaer und Pariser Nomenklaturen, gruppiert nach Organen*. Budapest: Verlag Medicina Budapest.

Edinger L (1905): Die Herkunft des Hirnmantels in der Tierreihe. *Umschau* (Frankfurt): 786–789.

Geoffroy Saint-Hilaire E (1822): *Philosophie anatomique. Des monstruosités humaines*. Paris: chez l'Auteur et chez les principaux Libraires pour l'anatomie.

His W (1895): Die Anatomische Nomenclatur. *Arch Anat Physiol, Anat Abt, Suppl*, 80–87, 155–180.

MacLean PD (1949): Psychosomatic Disease and the Visceral Brain. Recent Developments Bearing on the Papez Theory of Emotion. *Psychosom Med* 11: 338–353.

MacLean PD (1952): Some Psychiatric Implications of Physiological Studies on Frontotemporal Portion of Limbic System (Visceral Brain). *Electroenceph Clin Neurophysiol* 4: 407–418.

Mutel M (1923): *Etudes morphologiques sur le rhinencéphale de l'homme et des mammifères*. Nancy: A. Humblot et Cie.

Retzius G (1896): *Das Menschenhirn. Studien in der Makroskopischen Morphologie*. Stockholm: Nordstedt & Söhne.

Turner W (1891): The convolutions of the brain. A study in comparative anatomy. *J Anat Physiol* 25: 105–153.

Zuckerkandl E (1887): *Über das Riechcentrum*. Stuttgart: F. Enke.

Fornix and Gyrus fornicatus: Carnal Sins?

The fornix and its surrounding gyrus founicatus are two examples, among the numerous terms with a sexual connotation, that have adorned neuroanatomical terminology in the last several centuries. Others are, as some examples, nates (buttocks), testes for the colliculi of the mesencephalon (Vesale, 1604; Diemerbroeck, 1695), glans for the pineal gland (Vesale, 1604), cerebral vulva between the habenulae (Colombo, 1559), and vulvar triangle between the columns of fornix and the posterior commissure (Vieussens, 1685).

Rather than being related to behavior, as one might conclude, the term "fornix" has its roots in Roman architecture. At the time of Vitruve (first century B.C.) Roman architects used two different terms to describe vaulted-ceilinged rooms (Hyrtl, 1880): either "Camera" (from the Latin camera: vault) if the roof were made of brick, or "Fornix" (from the Latin fornix: arch) if it were constructed of wood. The first of these two terms was widely used in anatomical terminology over the last centuries; for example, camerae cranii (Albinus) and camera pericardiaca (Bauhin) for the cranial recesses and the pericardium, respectively. The second term, fornix, was also used for many anatomical structures, such as fornix conjunctivae, f. pharyngis, f. sacci lacrimalis or f. vaginae (De Terra, 1913). At present, this term belongs mainly to neuroanatomy, and seems to have been used in its current meaning for the first time by Thomas Willis (1664). The third ventricle was therefore compared with a vaulted-ceilinged room, and its roof was called fornix.

The reason why the term "fornix" unaviodably reminds everyone of fornication is quite logical: at the time of ancient Rome, prostitutes exercised their profession in vaulted-ceilinged cellars. Under a fornix shaped roof, they indulged in fornication, that is, in carnal sins (Delaveau, 1995). The real etymology of the term "fornix" is therefore related to the form of the roof of the third ventricle, (a vaulted room), but also to the sexual intercourse which occurred in such rooms, these rooms being compared with this ventricle. Since this time, current neuroanatomy added many other fornicies, such as fornix transversus, f. periphericus, f. longus, f. dorsalis, and f. fimbrialis (Stephan, 1975).

The term "gyrus fornicatus" has a comparable etymology: it means "vaulted convolution", and was described as synonymous with gyrus cinguli by Alexander Ecker (1873). It was also called "fornix periphericus" (Arnold, 1838). But for most early authors, the gyrus fornicatus included both gyrus cinguli and gyrus parahippocampalis (Foville, 1844).

The "Nomina Anatomica" of Basel (1895) and Lena (1935) defined the gyrus fornicatus as incuding the gyrus cinguli, its isthmus and the gyrus parahippocampalis (Donath, 1960). However, the 1955 revision deleted this term from official lists of anatomical terminology. It is by mere chance, that fornix and the gyrus fornicatus received their suggestive names long before the concept of limbic system and its involvement in sexual behavior appeared.

References

Arnold F (1838): Bemerkungen über den Bau des Hirns und Rückenmarks, nebst Beiträgen zur Physiologie des zehnten und elften Hirnnerven, mehreren kritischen Mitteilungen, sowie verschiedene pathologischen und anatomischen Beobachtungen, Zürich, Hoehr.

Colombo R (1559): De re anatomica libri XV, Venetiis, Nicolai Bevilacquae.

Delaveau P (1995): La memoire des mots en medecine, pharmacie et sciences, 2nd ed. Paris, Louis Pariente.

De Terra P (1913): Vademecum anatomicum. Kritisch-etymologisches Wörterbuch der system-atischen Anatomie. Mit besonderer Berücksichtigung der Synonymen. Jena, Gustav Fischer.

Donath T (1960): Erläuterndes anatomisches Wörterbuch. Vergleichende Übersicht der Baseler, Jenaer und Pariser Nomenklaturen, gruppiert nach Organen. Budapest, Verlag Medicina Budapest.

Ecker A (1873): On the circonvolutions of the human brains. London, Smith, Elder & Co.

Foville AL (1844): Traite complet de l'anatomie, de la physiologie et de la pathologie du système nerveux cerebro-spinal. Premiere partie: Anatomie. Paris, Fortin, Masson et Cie.

Hyrtl J (1880): Onomatologia anatomica. Geschichte und Kritik der anatomischen Sprache der Gegenwart, mit besonderer Berücksichtigung ihrer Barbarismen, Widersinnigkeiten, Tropen, und grammatikalischen Fehler. Wien, Wilhelm Braumller.

Stephan H (1975): Allocortex. In: Von Mullendorff W, Bargmann W, eds., Handbuch der mikros-kopischen Anatomie, Band 4, Teil 9. Berlin, Heidelberg, New York, Springer Verlag.

Van Diemerbroeck I (1695): L'anatomie du corps humain. Lyon, Anisson et Posuel (French translation by J. Prost).

Vesale A (1604): De corporis humani fabrica libri septem, Venetiis, et lacobum de Franscicis. loan Anton.

Vieussens R (1685): Neurographia universalis, hoc est, omnium corporis humani nervorum, simul & cerebri, medullaequa spinalis descriptio anatomica...Physico discursu explicata. Editio nave, Lugduni, Joannem Certe.

Willis T (1664): Cerebri anatome: cui accessit nervorum descriptio et usa, Londini, Typis Tho. Roycroft, Impensis Jo. Martyn et Ja. Allestry.

Cerebral Mythology: A Skull Stuffed With Gods

In the image of Mount Olympus, which lodged the most powerfull but also the most mysterious ancient gods, the skull contains structures which have remained mythological for a long time. It is therefore not surprising to recognize in neuronatomical terminology some metaphors which evoke comparisons between the gods and the brain, such as the Ammon's horn, the lyra Davidis, the cornucopia and the nucleus endymalis.

The hippocampus received its name from the Italian Julius Caesar Arantius in the late sixteenth century (1587, chapter III). The author hesitated between hippocampus and silk-worm, but the little sea horse was finally preferred to the mulberry bombyx. Less than two centuries later, the hippocampus was called Ammon's horn by an author whom nobody could identify until now (Lewis, 1922–23; Olry 1991, 1993; Olry & Fischer, 1993). The first reference to this term is probably that found in the book of the French surgeon René Jacques Croissant de Garengeot (1742, vol. 2, pp. 250–251). It is unlikely that this term existed in 1732 because Jacques Bénigne Winslow refered to the ram's horn and not to Ammon's horn. Albrecht von Haller, the great bibliographer of anatomy, does not give any information about this question, but he points out that the term Ammon's horn was already used in a paper of the Oeconomische Abhandlung of 1755 (Haller, 1774–1777, vol. 2, p. 507). The metaphor Ammon's horn refers to the ram-shaped Egyptian God Amon which protects the Pharaoh Taharqa in the temple of Kawa (De Smet, 1995).

The hippocampal commissure, together with the crura of the fornix, is sometimes termed the psalterium or lyra Davidis. Psalterium and lyra are both varieties of harp, but who was David? King David defeated the Ammonites, a Transjordanian tribe which was descended from Ammon, the incestuous son of Loth and his youngest daughter. He also succeeded in treating King Saül's melancholy by playing on a psalterion, as can be seen on an illustration attributed to the Florentians Gherardo and Monte di Giovanni di Miniato (De Smet, 1995).

French neuroanatomists call "corne d'abondance" (cornucopia) the horn-shaped lateral part of the fourth ventricle with its choroid plexus exciting the foramen much like a bunch of flowers. As far back as in 1849, the anatomist Victor Bochdalek compared this part of the rhombencephalon with a "bunch of flowers going out of a vase". The cornucopia has its mythological origin in a battle which Achilles had with Hercules. Achilles, the son of Ocean and Thétys, and Hercules wanted both to wed Déjanire. Both men came to the point of fighting, and Achilles took the shape of a bull to try to defeat his gallant rival. Hercules, however, won the victory and tore a horn out of the vanquished. This horn, left on the field after the battle, was then picked up by the Naiads who filled it with flowers and so created the cornucopia (Commelin, 1960).

The nucleus endymalis belongs to the median thalamic nuclei with the nuclei parataenialis, paramedianus and commissuralis (Rauber & Kopsch, 1987). Though its name probably has nothing to do with Roman mythology, its reminds us of the name of the God Endymion, who obtained from his grandfather Jupiter the right to sleep for the eternity in a grotto of the Latmos mountains (Commelin, 1960). It is note-worthy that the nucleus endymalis is located in the vicinity of the pulvinar which means "cushion for the head to sleep" (Joubert, 1738): the sleepy God is therefore not far away from his pillow.

Mythology and neurosciences will probably continue to go hand-in-hand. The French neurophysiologist Jean-Didier Vincent wrote some ten years ago: "Like limbo of Christian mythology, the limbic system is the intermediary between neocortical sky and reptilian hell" (Vincent, 1986).

References

Arantius JC (1587): *De humano foetu liber... Ejusdem Anatomicarum observationum liber.* Venetiis, J. Brechtanus.

Bochdalek V (1849): *Neue Beobachtungen im Gebiet der physiologischen Anatomie.* Prager Vierteljahrsschrift f. d. practische Heilkunde: 6.

Commelin P (1960): *Mythologie grecque et romaine.* Paris, Garnier Frères.

De Smet Y (1995): *De l'hippocampe à la corne d'Ammon.* Histoire. Anatomie. Embryologie. Louvain, UCB Pharma.

Garengeot, RJ Croissant de (1742): *Splanchnologie, ou l'Anatomie des viscères, avec des figures originales tirées d'après les cadavres, suivie d'une dissertation sur l'origine de la chirurgie.* Paris, Osmont, vol. 2.

Haller, A von (1774–1777): *Bibliotheca anatomica.* Tiguri: apud Orell, Gessner, Fuessli, et Socc., 2 volumes.

Joubert, J (1738): *Dictionnaire français et latin, tiré des auteurs originaux et classiques...* Lyon: Declaustre.

Lewis, FT (1922–23): The significance of the term hippocampus. *J Comp Neurol 35*: 213–230.

Olry R (1989): Le curieux baptême de l'hippocampe. Nancy, Memoir.

Olry R (1991): Métaphores zoologiques au sein des ventricues latéraux du cerveau, ou l'imagination au service de la linguistique. *Hist Sci Med 25*: 221–224.

Olry R, Fischer A (1993): The limbic terminology: natural history of semantic fluctuations. *Acta Belg Hist Med 6*: 220–223.

Rauber AA, Kopsch F (1987): *Anatomie des Menschen.* Band 3. Nervensystem. Sinnesorgane. Edited by H. Leonhardt, G. Töndury and K. Zilles. Stuttgart, New York: Georg Thieme Verlag.

Vincent, JD (1986): *Biologie des passions.* Paris: Odile Jacob.

Winslow, JB (1732): *Exposition anatomique de la structure du corps humain.* Paris, G. Desprez.

The Three Musketeers and the Twelve Cranial Nerves

Surprisingly, the three musketeers and the twelve cranial nerve have at least one thing in common: their numbering is wrong. Indeed, every one knows that the three musketeers (Athos, Aramis and Porthos) were, in reality, four in number and since 1914 everyone should know that the human cranial nerves are not twelve, but thirteen in number.

In 1894, the German researcher Felix Pinkus made an incredible discovery. While the end of the nineteenth century was believed to sound the death knell of discoveries in macroscopic anatomy, he found a new cranial nerve close by the olfactory bulb in *Protopterus annectens*. Protopterus is a dipnoan fish, a group having both gills and lungs, common to central and western Africa. Pinkus therefore called his discovery the "new nerve" (1894), though it had been previously depicted by Fritsch, of Fritsch and Hitzig and the dog motor cortex fame, in the shark (1878) and mentioned by Herrick in the urodeles (1893). However, the significance of this nerve escaped notice in the studies of these authors. In the following years, the occurrence of the new nerve was looked for in many species: Sewertzoff called it the "preoptic nerve" in *Ceratodua forsteri* (also a dipnoan fish, 1902), Locy the "terminal nerve" in Selachians (cartilaginous fish especially sharks, 1903), and van Wijhe the "apical nerve" in Amphioxus (1918). The nerve of Pinkus was found in almost all animals: Actinopterygians (ganoid and teleost fish, Allis, 1897), frog (Herrick, 1909), turtle (Johnston, 1913), chicken (Rubaschkin, 1902), Cyclostomes (lampreys and hagfish, Ayers, 1919), chiropters (bats, Simonetta and Magnoni, 1939), rabbit (Huber and Guild, 1913), cat and dog (McCotter, 1913), porpoise, horse, pig, sheep, and macaque (Johnston, 1914), chimpanzee and gibbon (Nicholas, 1918). Finally, the occurrence of this nerve was proved in human embryos (De Vries, 1905) and in adult man. In 1914 Johnston described the intracranial course of the nerve, and Brookover its ramifications in the nasal septum (Dalcq, 1920). It is interesting to note that the terminal nerve has been described in wide range of animals spanning the gulf from forms regarded as more primitive to those recognized as specialized/advanced both structionally and functionally.

Why is the terminal nerve not yet included in the current classification of cranial nerves, when its existence in many animals and in human and its features as a cranial nerve are unquestionably demonstrated? This classification was proposed by the famous German anatomist Samuel Thomas von Soemmering (1778); it takes into consideration the ventrodorsal axis of the cranial base, and the foramina which are traversed by the different cranial nerves. In Soemmering's view the olfactory nerve is number one for it traverses the most anterior foramina (cribriform plate of the ethmoid bone) of the skull base, and the hypoglossal is number twelve for it traverses the most posterior foramina (hypoglossal canal). This means that the terminal nerve should either be the first cranial nerve, and therefore shift the number of the twelve others, or even replace the olfactory nerve as number one (Lazorthes, 1944). This change seems to be bound to fail, in consideration of over two centuries of habit (Olry, 1995). On the other hand, the central connections and functions of the terminal nerve are still obscure; it is probably connected to hypothalamic nuclei and the interpeduncular region, and may act as a vasomotor or vasosensitive nerve in the nasal septum. It is entirely possible that by gaining a greater understanding of the functional importance of the terminal nerve this question will be revisited.

Its clinical importance is possibly negligible in human neurology, and so long as its function is not be clearly understood, it will remain the fourth (d'Artagnan) of the three musketeers.

Bibliography

Allis EP (1897): The cranial muscles and cranial and first spinal nerves in Amia calva. *J Morph* 12: 487–814.

Ayers H (1919): Vertebrate cephalogenesis IV. Transformation of the anterior end of the head resulting in the formation of the nose. *J Comp Neurol* 30: 323–342.

Brookover C (1914): The nervus terminalis in adult man. *J Comp Neurol* 24: 131–135, 1914.

Dalcq AM (1920): Le nerf terminal. *J Neurol* 5: 1–15.

De Vries E (1905): Note on the ganglion vomeronasale. *Proc kon ned Akad Wet* 7: 704–708, 1905.

Fritsch G (1878): *Untersuchungen über den feineren Bau des Fischgehirns*. Berlin.

Herrick CJ (1893): cited by Lazorthes, 1944.

Herrick CJ (1909): The nervus terminalis (nerve of Pinkus) in the frog. *J Comp Neurol* 19: 175–190.

Huber GC, Guild SR (1913): Observations on the peripheral distribution of the nervus terminalis in Mammalia. *Anat Rec* 7: 253–272.

Johnston JB (1913): Nervus terminalis in reptiles and mammals. *J Comp Neurol* 23: 97–120.

Johnston JB (1914): The nervus terminalis in man and mammals. *Anat Rec* 8: 185–198.

Lazorthes G (1944): *Le nerf terminal... Premier nerf crânien?* Toulouse: Les Frères Douladoure.

Locy WA (1903): A new cranial nerve in Selachians. *Mark Anniversary.*

McCotter RE (1913): The nervus terminalis in the adult dog and cat. *J Comp Neurol* 23: 145–152.

Nicolas (1918): Note sur le nerf terminal. *Bull Acad Med* 79: 250–252.

Olry R (1995): Sémantique anatomique. Un langage pour une science. Trois-Rivières, privately printed.

Pinkus F (1894): Ueber einen noch nicht beschrie-benen Hirnnerven des Protopterus annectens. Anat Anz 9: 562–566.

Rubaschkin W (1902): Ueber die Beziehung des Nervus Trigeminus zur Reichschleimhaut. *Anat Anz* 22: 407.

Sewertzoff AW (1902): Zur Entwickelungsgeschichte des Ceratodus forsteri. *Anat Anz* 21: 592–608.

Simonetta B, Magnoni (1939): Sulla presenza e sullo sviluppo del nervo terminale a del l'organo di Jacobson nei Chirotteri. *Arch Ital Anat* 41: 343.

Soemmering ST (1778): *Dissertatio de basi encephali et orginibus nervorum cranio egredientium libri quinque*. Gottingae: Abr. Vandenhoeck Viduam.

Wihje JW van (1918): On the nervus terminalis from Man to Amphioxus, K *Akad van Weterschappen te Amsterdam 21.*

Just What *is* the Inferior Cerebellar Peduncle?

As indicated in the inaugural NEUROwords column, this forum is designed to explore words and their usage in the neurosciences including '...the revisitation and revision of older terms, now with more precise definitions or use' (Finger, 1997). In the spirit of this mandate two terms are considered both of which have a long, albeit somewhat confused, history; terms that are well-known to most neuromorphologists but frequently, indeed usually, used incorrectly. These terms are the pedunclus cerebellaris inferior (inferior cerebellar peduncle) and the corpus restiforme (restiform body).

The cerebellum of all mammals is attached to the brainstem by three pairs of stalk-like bundles of myelinated fibers, the cerebellar peduncles. The superior cerebellar peduncle relates, in a structural sense, to the midbrain, the middle cerebellar peduncle to the basilar pons, and the inferior cerebellar peduncle to the medulla oblongata and, by extension, to the spinal cord. Over the last 100 years the general definitions of the superior and middle peduncle have changed little. For example Barker (1899), in his elegantly detailed text, described fibers of the superior cerebellar peduncle (brachium conjunctivum) as arising in the dentate nucleus of the cerebellum, crossing in the decussation of the superior peduncle, and entering the contralateral red nucleus and '...ventro-lateral region of the thalamus'. Edinger (1900) clearly described connections from the basilar pons (pontal ganglia in his terminology) to the cerebellum via the middle cerebellar peduncle (*brachium pontis*, 'in the arms of the pons'). However, he incorrectly deduced that fibers passed in both directions in and out of the cerebellum in this peduncle and that the majority of these fibers were probably ipsi-lateral. While the general fiber populations thought to be contained in these two peduncles has changed little, significant details and newly discovered fiber bundles have been added.

The case of the inferior cerebellar peduncle is somewhat different. By the mid 1800's the terms restiform body and inferior cerebellar peduncle were considered synonymous. Dunglison (1860) defined *corpora restiformia* as 'medullary projections, oblong ...whitish... which proceed... from the medulla oblongata, and contribute to the formation of the cerebellum' and he defined the 'peduncles, inferior, of the cerebellum' as 'corpora restiformia-p. of the medulla oblongata'. The lack of a uniform terminology at this time meant that a variety of other terms were also used, such as *crura cerebelli* or *processus cerebelli*. Perhaps the most interesting of these was *processus cerebelli ad testes* referring to the relationship of the superior cerebellar peduncle to the inferior colliculi of the midbrain.

The first attempt to establish a uniform anatomical terminology was made primarily by a group of German scientists in 1895 (Di Dio, 1998). The resulting document, *Basal Nomina Anatomica* (B.N.A.), adopted *corpus restiforme* as the official term. However, 'inferior cerebellar peduncle' was widely used as the unofficial equivalent term. Interestingly enough, the official term was changed to 'inferior cerebellar peduncle' in 1955 (Nomina Anatomica, 1956). The approach of equating these terms was clearly reflected in the major text books of the period (Barker, 1899; Jakob, 1901; Johnston, 1905; Herrick, 1918; Ranson, 1920), where one term was used with the other sometimes following in parenthesis. During the same time frame, there was a growing body of evidence that clearly suggested that these two terms simply did not specify the same structures. The frustration of these inconsistencies was reflected in Edinger's (1900) statement 'Where the inferior cerebellar peduncle enters the cerebellum is the least understood portion of the whole nervous system'.

Barker (1899), while describing major connections to the cerebellum via the restiform body, also described fibers passing to the cerebellum from Deiters nucleus (the lateral vestibular nucleus) via a clearly different route, that being '...through the brachium conjunctivum...' or in his illustrations as medially adjacent to the restiform body. This plan was enlarged by Edinger (1900) who indicated that the inferior cerebellar peduncle actually consisted of a 'median portion having connections with the sensory cranial nerves, especially the acusticus' and the 'corpus restiforme proper, conducting fibers from the opposite olivary body and from the spinal cord'. While incorrect on the acoustic nerve connection, Edinger (1900) set the stage for a division, based on structural/functional criteria, of the inferior cerebellar peduncle into two distinct parts. Ranson (1920) while also equating these two terms, did describe a 'medial part of the restiform body' that contained fibers arising in the vestibular nuclei (vestibulocerebellar fibers) and entering the cerebellum.

Although the description of a medial part of the inferior peduncle was continued for many years (e.g., Walberg & Jansen, 1961; Angaut & Brodal, 1967), others used a more precise terminology to designate this medial portion. Tilney (1927) described large bundles of fibers passing between the lateral vestibular nucleus and cerebellum as the main part of the 'juxtarestiform body' and Dow (1935) used this term to include cerebellar corticovestibular projections of the flocculonodular lobe. Ariëns Kappers et al. (1936), in their comprehensive treatise on the comparative anatomy of the nervous system, stated that the corpus restiforme consisted of a *pars lateralis* (the larger lateral part) and a *pars corpus juxtarestiforme* (a smaller medial part that mainly interconnects vestibular and cerebellar structures). Subsequent studies (Haines, 1975, 1977) have confirmed that the juxtarestiform body is a distinct entity that contains fiber populations clearly different from those found within the restiform body.

So, just what is the inferior cerebellar peduncle? As now stipulated in *Terminologia Anatomica* (1998), the official international anatomical terminology document, the inferior cerebellar peduncle (*pedunculus cerebellaris inferior*) consist of two parts, a restiform body (*corpus restiforme*) and a juxtarestiform body (*corpus juxtarestiforme*). A broader look at the literature reveals that the restiform body is clearly the larger of the two and transmits posterior spinocerebellar fibers, olivocerebellar fibers, trigeminocerebellar fibers, reticulocerebellar fibers, and many others, while the juxtarestiform body is smaller and conducts only vestibulocerebellar and cerebellovestibular interconnections as broadly defined. Consequently, the inferior cerebellar peduncle is *not* the same as the restiform body. Despite a historical clarity that extends back 60–70 years these terms continue to be equated and, therefore, used inappropriately.

References

Angaut P, Brodal A (1967): The projection of the "vestibulocerebellum" onto the vestibular nuclei in the cat. *Arch ital Biol 105*: 441–479.

Ariëns Kappers CV, Huber GC, Crosby EC (1936): *The Comparative Anatomy of the Nervous System of Vertebrates, Including Man.* New York, The MacMillan Company. 2 Volumes.

Barker LF (1899): *The Nervous System and its Constituent Neurones. Designed for...* New York, D. Appleton and Company

Di Dio (1998): History of the anatomical terminology. In: *Terminologia Anatomica.* New York, Thieme.

Dow RS (1938): Efferent connections of the floculonodular lobe in *macaca mulatta. J Comp Neurol 68*: 297–305.

Dunglison R (1860): *A Dictionary of Medical Science; Containing...* Philadelphia, Blanchard and Lea.

Edinger L (1900): *The Anatomy of the Central Nervous System of Man and of Vertebrates in General.* Translated from the fifth German edition by W.S. Hall. Philadelphia, F.A. Davis Company.

Finger S (1997): NEUROwords, A Column devoted to history of words in neuroscience. *J Hist Neurosci 6*: 216.

Haines DE (1975): Cerebellar corticovestibular fibers of the posterior lobe in a prosimian primate, the lesser bushbaby (*Galage senegalensis*). *J Comp Neurol 160*: 363–398.

Haines DE (1977): Cerebellar corticonuclear and corticovestibular fibers of the flocculomodular lobe in a prosimian primate (*Galage senegalensis*). *J Comp Neurol 174*: 607–630.

Herrick CJ (1918): *An Introduction to Neurology.* Philadelphia, W.B. Saunders Company.

Jakob C (1901): *Atlas of the Nervous System Including an Epitome of the Anatomy, Pathology, and Treatment.* Edited by E.D. Fisher. Philadelphia: W.B. Saunders Company.

Johnston JB (1906): The Nervous System of Vertebrates. Philadelphia, P. Blakiston's Son and Co.

Nomina Anatomica (1956), Baltimore, The Williams & Wilkins Co.

Ranson SW (1920): *The Anatomy of the Nervous System From the Standpoint of Development and Function.* Philadelphia, W.B. Saunders Company.

Terminologia Anatomica (1998), New York: Thieme.

Tilney F (1927): The brain stem of *Tarsius*: A critical comparison with other primates. *J Comp Neurol 43*: 371–432.

Walberg F and Jansen J (1961): Cerebellar corticovestibular fibers in the cat. *Exp Neural 3*: 32–52.

Vague, Uncertain, Ambiguous, Obscure: Imprecision or Modesty?

It is stating the obvious to say that neuroanatomy has not yet given away all of its secrets. However, was it necessary to lay stress on this fact even in the terminology itself? It is nevertheless what happened in the last centuries, when some anatomists discovered or named structures, such as the vagus nerve, the zona incerta, the nucleus ambiguus, and the nucleus raphes obscurus.

Unlike most of the cranial nerves which supply a topographically limited region of the head, the vagus nerve is largely responsible for the innervation of numerous cervical, thoracic and abdominal viscera. Though its course seems to have been roughly described as far back as in Praxagoras' time (Lauth, 1815, pp. 83–84), the particulars of its distribution remained enigmatic for a long time. It is therefore its distribution, and not its course, which led an anatomist to call it vague, 'quia non determinatur ad aliquam specialem partem, sed per omnia viscera vagatur' (for it does not restrict itself to some special parts, but it wanders through all viscera) (Rolfinck, 1656, p. 742). The name of this anatomist is unknown, but he must be prior to André Dulaurens who already used this term in 1605 (Dulaurens, 1605, p. 245). The vagus nerve was later called 'Lungen-Magennerv' by Meckel or 'nerf pneumogastrique' by Chaussier, owing to its bronchial and gastric rami (Hyrtl, 1880, p. 596). However, this term was too exhaustive to be introduced into official terminology.

In 1877, the German neurologist, psychiatrist and entomologist August Henri Forel discovered a thin grey lamina in the subthalamus which he called zona incerta (uncertain zone). Some years later, his compatriot Heinrich Obersteiner wrote: 'It should be noted that views with regard to the subthalamic region are still very conjectural' (Obersteiner, 1893, p. 313). According to Jules Dejerine, Forel's zona incerta is part of the thalamus reticular formation located between both thalamic and lenticular fasciculi, and it vanishes into the grey matter of the third ventricle (Dejerine, 1901, vol. 2, pp. 394–396). Some years later, the French anatomist and army physician Charles Debierre (1907) translated 'zona incerta' into 'couche incertaine' (uncertain layer), but this translation was never retained in French anatomical nomenclatures (Debierre, 1907, p. 349).

The nucleus ambiguus (ambiguous nucleus-although this spelling is rarely used) is straddling both the open and the closed portions of the medulla oblongata. It contributes fibers to three cranial nerves: the glossopharyngeal nerve (to the stylopharyngeus), the vagus nerve (to the pharyngeal constrictors and the intrinsic laryngeal muscles), and the cranial roots of the accessory nerve (to continue over the inferior vagal ganglion). It is important to note that axons of neurons of the nucleus ambiguus join the accessory nerve then rejoin the vagus nerve; the nucleus ambiguus does not innervate motor targets of the accessory nerve. According to Jules Dejerine (1901, vol. 2, p. 566), the term nucleus ambiguus was proposed by the English anatomist Jacob Augustus Lockhart Clarke who also discovered the nucleus dorsalis of the posterior grey columns of spinal cord (Clarke, 1851). In Latin, ambiguus means 'doubtful, questionable' but also 'ambivalent' for this nucleus was regarded as being the central origin of motor fibres for both glossopharyngeal and vagus nerves.

The nucleus raphes obscurus (obscure nucleus of the raphe) belongs to the reticular formation of the brain stem. This nucleus was not known when Alf Brodal published his monograph on the reticular formation of the brain stem, but this author acknowledged the complexity of the region: 'Our data on this nucleus (of the raphe) are as yet too incomplete to warrant more than a suggestion' (Brodal, 1958, p. 49). In spite of numerous researches, the nucleus raphe obscurus remains poorly understood: 'Seine Faserverbindungen sind nicht hinreichend bekannt' (its fibre connections are not well-known enough) (Leonhardt and Lange, 1987, vol. 3, p. 280).

We do not know the real reason why authors intentionally chose such strange terms. However, their choice proved to be right: though vague, uncertain, ambiguus and obscure, all these formations have kept their original term in the current international anatomical terminology.

References

Brodal A (1958): *The Reticular Formation of the Brain Stem Anatomical Aspects and Functional Correlations*, Edinburgh, London: Published for The William Ramsay Henderson Trust by Oliver and Boyd.

Clarke JAL (1851): Researches into the structure of the spinal cord. *Phil Trans 141*: 607–621.

Debierre C (1907): *Le cerveau et la moelle épinière avec applications physiologiques et médico-chirurgicales,* Paris, Félix Alcan.

Dejerine J (1901): *Anatomie des centres nerveux*, Paris, J. Rueff, 2 volumes.

Dulaurens A (1605): *Historia anatomica humani corporis partes*, Lyons: Apud Horatium Cardon.

Forel AH (1877): Untersuchungen über die Haubenregion und ihre oberen Verknüpfungen im Gehirne des Menschen und einiger Säugethiere, mit Beiträgen zu den Methoden der Gehirn-untersuchung. *Arch Psychiat Nervenkr 7*: 393–495.

Hyrtl J (1880): Onomatologia anatomica. Geschichte und Kritik der anatomischen Sprache der Gegenwart, mit besonderer Berücksichtigung ihrer Barbarismen, Widersinnigkeiten, Tropen, und grammatikalischen Fehler, Wien: Wilhelm Braumüller.

Lauth T (1815): *Histoire de l'Anatomie*, Strasbourg, F.G. Levrault (Part 1, all published).

Leonhardt H, Lange W (1987): Graue und weisse Substanz des Hirnstammes. In: H Leonhardt, B Tillmann, G Töndury and K Zilles (Eds) *Rauber Kopsch Anatomie des Menschen. Lehrbuch und Atlas*, Stuttgart, New York: Georg Thieme.

Obersteiner H (1893): *Anatomie des centres nerveux. Guide pour l'étude de leur structure à l'état normal et pathologique,* Paris, George Carré (French translation from the second German edition by J.-X. Coroënne).

Rolfinck W (1656): *Dissertationes anatomicae methodo synthetica exaratae, sex libris comprehensa*, Nuremberg, Michael Endterus.

Vater, Pacini, Wagner, Meissner, Golgi, Mazzoni, Ruffini, Merkel and Krause: Were their nerves all on edge?

Classification of sensory endings (Corpuscula nervosa terminalia) includes free nerve endings (without any particular association with other types of cell), encapsulated endings (where specialized non-nervous cells invest neural process), and epidermal endings (where sensory fibres are attached to specific non-nervous cells or tissues) (Bannister, 1976). The terminology for these structures includes many eponyms (Olry, 1995): surprisingly, it appears that all these structures were discovered by German or Italian researchers.

The large lamellated corpuscles of Vater-Pacini (Corpuscula lamellosa) are situated subcutaneously in the ventral aspects of the hand and foot and their digits, the genital organs of both sexes, arm, neck, nipple, periostea, interosseous membranes, near the joints and in the mesentery and pancreas (Williams et al., 1989, p. 911). These are known to be especially sensitive to vibration (Gray and Sato, 1953). According to Morton (1993, p. 201), these corpuscles were described for the first time by the Wittemberg professor of anatomy and botany Abraham Vater in 1717 (dissertation by Joachim Gottlieb Klepperbein). However, their description was again to be found in Johann Gottlob Lehmann' doctoral thesis supervised by Vater in 1741. In this thesis, the corpuscles were depicted on Figure 2 of the plate printed on the back of the frontispiece (Corsi, 1990, pp. 117–118). The importance of this discovery was not lost on the famous bibliographer Albrecht von Haller who summarized the thesis in these terms: "cum nervorum manus icone, ramisque nerveis in papillas deductis" (with an illustration of the nerves of the hand, and nervous rami that join papillae) (Haller, 1777, p. 43). About one century later, the Florence professor of topographical anatomy and histology Filippo Pacini clarified the structure, distribution and connections of these corpuscles (1840).

The tactile corpuscles of Wagner-Meissner (Corpuscula tactus) are found in the dermal papillae of all parts of the hand and foot, the front of the forearm, the lips, palpebral conjunctiva and mucous membrane of the apical part of the tongue (Williams et al., 1989, p. 910). They were discovered in 1851 by Georg Meissner, a pupil of the Göttingen professor of physiology, comparative anatomy and zoology Rudolph Wagner (Lefébure, 1909). The results were published under their two names in 1852. In a later publication, Meissner (1853) acknowledged that Gerber, a prosector in the University of Bern, had generally described these corpuscles about ten years before in his treatise on human and comparative anatomy, but he does not mention the edition of this book (1840 or 1844?). Albert von Kölliker (1852) denied the existence of these corpuscles which he regarded as artifacts since he believed that the afferent nervous fibre had to leave the corpuscle again via an efferent fibre. This opinion was disproved by Wagner (1852), who demonstrated that the efferent fibre was in fact a vessel. In 1889, Louis Antoine Ranvier acknowledged that all the credit was due to Meissner for "the description he made probably less wanders from the truth than those of most histologists who succeeded him" (Ranvier, 1889, p. 709).

The Golgi-Mazzoni endings (Corpuscula lamellosa) are regarded as a subtype of the large lamellated corpuscles (Ruffini, 1905, p. 433; Leonhardt et al., 1987, p. 510). They were discovered in 1880 by the famous Italian pathologist Camillo Golgi in the peritendinous connective tissue and the external perimysium in man. His compatriot Vittorio Mazzoni (1891) focused on the description of their nervous fibre in an "excellent and important study" (Régaud, 1907, p. 676). The occurrence of Golgi-Mazzoni endings in the dermal papillae of digits was first reported by Angelo Ruffini in 1894.

The corpuscles of Ruffini, which are found in the skin, but also in dura mater, iris and ciliary body, were discovered by the Bologna histologist Angelo Ruffini in 1891, and the tactile menisci (Menisci tactus) by the Göttingen anatomist Friedrich Sigismund Merkel in 1875. Finally, The German anatomist Wilhelm Johann Friedrich Krause (1858) gave his name to the currently called end bulbs (Corpuscula bulboidea).

The renowned Marcello Malpighi, who observed the digit dermal papillae after removing of the cuticula by the way of a red-hot iron, outlined some corpuscles as far back as in 1665. These corpuscles were also depicted in Govert Bidloo's Anatomia (1685). However, only eighteenth and nineteenth century researchers found their place in history and anatomical terminology.

References

Bannister LH (1976): Sensory terminals of peripheral nerves. In: Landon DN, ed., *The peripheral nerve*. London, Chapman & Hall, pp. 396–463.

Bidloo G (1685): *Anatomia humani corporis*, Amsterdam, Sumptibus Viduae Joannis à Someren.

Corsi P (1990): *La fabrique de la pensée. La découverte du cerveau de l'art de la mémoire aux neurosciences*, Milan, Electa.

Gerber F (1844): *Handbuch der allgemeinen Anatomie des Menschen und der Haussäugethiere*, Bern, Dalp (the first edition was published in 1840).

Golgi C (1880): Sui nervi nei tendini dell' uomo e di altri vertebrati e di un nuovo organo nervoso terminale muscolo-tendineo. *Mem Accad Sc Torino*, ser. 2, vol. XXXIII.

Gray JAB, Sato M (1953): Properties of receptors potentials in Pacinian corpuscles. *J Physiol 122*: 610–636.

Haller A von (1774–1777): *Bibliotheca anatomica*, Tiguri, Orell, Gessner, Fuessli et Socc., 2 volumes (vol. 2 dated 1777).

Kölliker A (1852): Ueber die Struktur der Cutispapillen und der sogenannten Tastkörper R. Wagner's. *Zeitschr für wiss Zool 4*.

Krause WJF (1858): Ueber Nervenendigungen. *Zeitschr rat Med 5* (3).

Lefébure M (1909): *Les corpuscules de Wagner-Meissner ou corpuscules du tact*, Paris, Masson et Cie. (From Revue générale d'Histologie 3 (11): 571–736).

Leonhardt H, Leuenberger P, Töndury G, Zilles K, Kubik S (1987): Sinnesorgane. In: Leonhardt H, Tillmann B, Töndury G, Zilles K, eds., *Anatomie des Menschen*, vol. 3, Stuttgart, New York, Georg Thieme Verlag.

Malpighi M (1665): *De externo tactus organo anatomica observatio*, Naples, apud Aegidium Longum.

Mazzoni V (1891): Osservazioni microscopiche sopra i cosi dette corpuscoli terminali dei tendini dell' uomo e sopra alcune particolari piastre nervose superficiali che si trovano nei medesimi tendini. *Mem R Accad Sc Istit Bologna 5* (1): 401–408.

Meissner G (1853): *Beiträge zur Kenntnis der Anatomie und Physiologie der Haut*, Leipzig, 1853.

Merkel FS (1875): Tastzellen und Tastkoerperchen bei den Hausthieren und beim Menschen. *Arch mikr Anat 11* (4): 678.

Morton LT (1993): *Morton's Medical Bibliography. Edited by Jeremy M. Norman*, Brookfield, Gower Publishing Company, 5th edition.

Olry R (1995): *Dictionary of anatomical eponyms*, Stuttgart, Jena, New York, Gustav Fischer Verlag.

Pacini F (1840): *Nuovi organi scoperti nel corpo umano*, Pistoja, tipog. Cino.

Ranvier L (1889): *Traité technique d'histologie*, Paris, F. Savy, 2nd edition.

Regaud C (1907): *Les terminaisons nerveuses et les organes nerveux sensitifs de l'appareil locomoteur (Dispositifs nerveux kinesthésiques). Deuxième partie,* Lyon, Paris, A. Storck & Cie. (From Revue générale d'Histologie 2 (7): 587–689).

Ruffini A (1891): *Mem. present. al concorso per il premio Vittorio Emanuele II, nella R. Univers. di Bologna, nell' Ottobre dell' anno 1891.* Bologna: prem. stabil. tipogr. succ. Monti.

Ruffini A (1894): Di un nuovo organo nervoso terminale, e sulla presenza dei corpuscoli Golgi-Mazzoni nel connettivo sotto-cutaneo dei polpastrelli delle dita dell' uomo. *Mem R Accad dei Lincei, cl sc fis, mat e natur*, ser. 4, vol. 7.

Ruffini A (1905): *Les dispositifs anatomiques de la sensibilité cutanée: sur les expansions nerveuses de la peau,* Lyon, Paris, A. Storck & Cie. (From Revue générale d'Histologie 1 (3): 421–540).

Vater A (1717): *Oeconomia sensuum ex speciali organorum sensoriorum & sigillatim ex papillarum nervearum textura mechanice demonstrata*, Wittemberg, lit. A. Kobersteinii.

Vater A (1741): *Dissertatio inauguralis medica de consensu partium corporis humani occasione spasmi singularis in manu eiusque digitis ex hernia observati*, Vitembergae, typis Schlomachianis.

Wagner R (1852): Ueber die Tastkörper (corpuscula tactus). *Müller's Arch Anat Physiol:* 9, 19.

Wagner R, Meissner G (1852): Ueber das Vorhand-sein bisher unbekannten eigenthümlicher Tastkörper (corpuscula tactus) in den Gefühlwärzchen der menschlichen Haut, und über die Endaus-breitung der sensiblen Nerven. *Nachrichten von der Univ. und kgl. Gesellsch. der Wissensch. zu Göttingen.*

Williams PL, Warwick R, Dyson M, Bannister LH (1989): *Gray's Anatomy*, Edinburgh, London, Melbourne and New York, Churchill Livingstone, 37th edition.

The Subfornical and Subcommissural Organs: Never-Ending Rediscoveries

Specialized areas of ependymal cells around the margins of the third ventricle are collectively termed circumventricular organs (Collins & Woollam, 1981), or ependymal organs of the third ventricle (Legait, 1942). The characteristic features of these regions are the presence of three main cell varieties (ciliated ependymal cells, secretory cells, and tanycytes), and the fact that most of them constitute special zones by which substances can pass from the nervous tissue and vascular supply into the cerebrospinal fluid within the ventricles. In most of these areas the blood brain barrier is modified. The circumventricular organs include the subfornical organ, the subcommissural organ, the median eminence, the collicular recess organ, the habenular ependyma and commissural organ, and the organum vasculosum of the lamina terminalis (Williams et al., 1995). By extension, both area postrema and funiculus separans have been sometimes considered as circumventricular organs, in spite of their location around the fourth and not third ventricle. This paper will focus on two of these circumventricular organs: the subfornical and subcommissural organs.

The subfornical organ (Organum subfornicale: Terminologia Anatomica, 1998) is located on the inferior surface of the fornix, between both interventricular foramina. It contains numerous receptors for angiotensin II (Nieuwenhuys, 1985), and is known to be connected with many formations of the limbic system and the hypothalamus (Nieuwenhuys et al., 1988). The subfornical organ received its name from Pines who described it in animal species (dog, mouse, urchin, and lemurs) in 1926. As pointed out in the title of his publication, Pines believed he had discovered an "hitherto unobserved formation in the brain of some mammals". In fact, Pines did not know about a study of Putnam which had been published four years before (Legait, 1942). The latter had described the same formation in man and some species (rat, guinea pig, rabbit, and monkey), which he called intercolumnar tubercle because of its location between both columns of the fornix (Putnam, 1922). Surprisingly, Putnam made the same mistake as Pines: the title of his publication mentioned "an undescribed area in the anterior wall of the third ventricle", whereas this formation had been observed by Spiegel in man and some mammals as early as 1918. About twenty years later, Spiegel, who refered to his discovery as "Ganglion psalterii", confirmed its equivalence with the intercolumnar tubercle and the subfornical organ (Spiegel, 1937). Many other terms have been used in the subsequent literature: subfornical gland of the third ventricle (Pines, 1926), paratrigonal organ (Roussy & Mossinger, 1941), paraseptal or anterior parietal organ (Legait, 1942), the latter being more accurate for this organ develops in the anterior wall of the median telencephalon whether a fornix will be found or not. However, the term created by Pines (1926) prevailed in anatomical terminology.

The subcommissural organ (Organum subcommissurale: Terminologia Anatomica, 1998) was sometimes called the dorsal ependymal column (Poppi, 1929) or the "sling formation" (Turkewitch, 1937). It is located ventral to and below the posterior commissure, i.e near the inferior wall of the pineal recess, close to the junction of the third ventricle with the cerebral aqueduct. Unlike all other circumventricular organs, it constitutes a blood-brain barrier (Leonhardt et al., 1987). Stieda seems to have been the first to describe this patch of ependymal cells in the mouse (Stieda, 1870). In 1902, Dendy refered to this formation in cyclostome by the name of "ciliated grooves", but the subcommissural organ received its current name from Dendy and Nicholls only in 1910, that is to say forty years after its first description. Two reasons probably account for this delay. On the one hand, this region of the posterior commissure was the subject of numerous researches which gave rise to a nearly incomprehensible nomenclature. For example, the "support connective lamella" described by Tartuferi in 1878 (cited by Castaldi, 1926) was not exactly the subcommissural organ, but a region located more caudal: the mesocoelic recess (Sargent, 1903), the dorsal ependymal septum (Sterzi, 1907–1912), or the intermediate recess (Krabbe, 1933). The distinction between all these formations is not easy especially since the subcommissural organ is known to extend to the cerebral aqueduct in early embryonic stages (Chiarugi, 1918), and remnants of this organ are sometimes found along the posterior wall of the aqueduct in adult (Saïtta, 1930). On the other hand, most of these studies focused more on the enigmatic Reissner's fibre (Reissner, 1860) which is attached on the subcommissural organ, than on the subcommissural organ itself. In 1917, Marianne Bauer-Jokl wrote the first monograph devoted to the subcommissural organ in mammals and birds, and ratified the current name of this formation.

In his masterly doctoral thesis, Etienne-Jules Legait wrote that the subcommissural organ "is generally so little known that it is periodically rediscovered; it has therefore some variant names" (Legait, 1942). The subfornical and subcommissural organs perfectly illustrate the phenomenon of never-ending rediscoveries in morphological sciences, a phenomenon that accounts for the inexhaustible richness of the anatomical terminology and its history.

References

Bauer-Jokl M (1917): Ueber das sogenannte Subcommissuralorgan. *Arb Neurol Inst Wien Univ 22*: 41–79.

Castaldi L (1926): Morfogenesi dell' acquedotto cerebrale. *Arch Gen Neur Psich e Psicoanalisi 6*: 151–172.

Chiarugi G (1918): L'organo subcommissurale della Cavia durante lo svilluppo e nell' adulto. *Mon Zool Ital 29*: 163–177.

Collins P, Woollam DHM (1981): *The circumventricular organs*. In: Hamson RJ, Holmes RL (eds) Progress in Anatomy. Vol. 1. Cambridge, Cambridge University Press, pp. 123–139.

Dendy A (1902): On a pair of ciliated grooves in the brain of the ammonoete, apparently serving to promote the circulation of the fluid in the brain cavity. *Proc Roy Soc London 69*: 485–495.

Dendy A, Nicholls GE (1910): On the occurrence of a mesocoelic recess in the human brain and its relations to the subcommissural organ of lower vertebrates; with special reference to the distribution of Reissner's fibre in the vertebrate series and its possible function. *Proc Roy Soc London 82*: 515–529.

Krabbe KH (1933): Anatomy of subcommissural organ of brain; review of literature. *Nordisk Medicinsk Tidskrift 6*: 1030–1035.

Legait EJ (1942): *Les organes épendymaires du troisième ventricule. L'organe sous-commissural. L'organe sub-fornical. L'organe paraventriculaire.* Nancy, Georges Thomas.

Leonhardt H, Krisch B, Zilles K (1987): Graue und weisse Substanz des Zwischenhirns. In: Leonhardt H, Tillmann B, Töndury G, Zilles K (eds) Anatomie des Menschen. Lehrbuch und Atlas. Stuttgart, New York, Georg Thieme, vol. 3.

Nieuwenhuys R (1985): *Chemoarchitecture of the Brain.* Berlin, Heidelberg, New York, Tokyo, Springer-Verlag.

Nieuwenhuys R, Voogd J, van Huijzen C (1985): *The Human Central Nervous System. A Synopsis and Atlas.* Berlin, Heidelberg, New York, London, Paris, Tokyo, Springer-Verlag, 3rd edition.

Pines L (1926): Ueber ein bisher unbeachteter Gebilde im Gehirn einiger Säugetiere: das subfornikale Organ des 3. Ventrikels. *J Psychol Neurol 34*.

Poppi U (1929): Sulla mielinizzazione dei principali sistemi di fibre nel mesencefalo umano e sulla constituzione della guaina mielinica. *Riv Pat Nerv Ment 34*: 260.

Putnam TJ (1922): The intercolumnar tubercle; an undescribed area in the anterior wall of the third ventricle. *Bull J Hopkins Hosp 38*: 181–182.

Reissner E (1860): Beiträge zur Kenntniss vom Bau des Rückenmarkes von Petromyzon fluvialis L. *Arch Anat Physiol*: 545–588.

Roussy G, Mosinger M (1941): Le diencéphale et les mécanismes régulateurs de la vie organique. *Bull Acad Méd Paris 125*: 373–377.

Saïtta S (1930): Subcommissural organ in certain mammals. *Scrit Biol 5*: 419–428.

Sargent PE (1903): The ependymal grooves in the roof of the diencephalon of vertebrates. *Science 17*: 487.

Spiegel E (1937): Zur Frage der Identität von Ganglion psalterii, Intercolumnar tubercle und Subfornikale Organ des dritten Ventrikels. *Zeitschr Anat 107*: 154.

Sterzi G (1907–1912): *Il sistema nervosa centrale dei Vertebrati.* Padova, 2 volumes.

Stieda L (1870): Studien über das centrale Nervensystem der Wirbeltiere. *Zeitsch Wiss Zool 20*: 386–425.

Terminologia Anatomica. International Anatomical Terminology (1998). Stuttgart, New York, Georg Thieme Verlag.

Turkewitsch N (1937): Eigentümlichkeiten der Struktur des Ependyms der Sylvius'schen Wasserleitung bei Embryonen des Stachelschweins (Hystrix hirsutirostris Satuniti Müll.) *Anat Anz 84*: 330–333.

Williams PL, Bannister LH, Berry MM, Collins P, Dyson M, Dussek JE, Ferguson MWJ (1995): *Gray's Anatomy. The Anatomical Basis of Medicine and Surgery.* New York, Edinburgh, London, Tokyo, Madrid and Melbourne, Churchill Livingstone, 38th edition.

Arachnophobia: Spiders and Spider's Webs in the Head

The arachnoid matter is a delicate membrane enveloping the brain and spinal cord between the pial and dural meninges. Its fineness and delicacy account for its ignorance by the ancient anatomists, as stated by the French physician Raphael Bienvenu Sabatier who wrote in the late eighteenth century: "L'arachnoïde est si mince que si on n'étoit pas prévenu de son existence, on pourrait la méconnoître" (the arachnoid matter is so thin that it could escape notice if we were not told of its existence) (Sabatier, 1792). The discovery of the arachnoid matter is usually attributed to Gerardus Blasius (1666) and Andreas Ottomar Goelicke (1697) who called it *tertia cerebri meninge* (third cerebral meninge). However, this membrane had been outlined as far back as 1573 by Constantius Varolius who achieved celebrity for his idea to examine the brain from its base up, in contrast with previous dissections from the top down (Haller, 1774; Cruveilhier, 1871).

Though the arachnoid matter was not discovered before the late Renaissance, the Greek term *arachnoid* (*arachné*: spider, or spider's web, and *eidos*: shape) and its Latin translation (*aranea*) belong to anatomical terminology since the early first millennium. At that time, it was applied to some component parts of the eyeball: about 50 A.D., Rufus Ephesius, one of the very first to have pointed out the importance of the anatomical nomenclature (Olry, 1989), called *arachnoidea* the third tunic of the eyeball (Rufus Ephesius, 1604). Though it is difficult to compare the anatomical descriptions of that time with our current knowledge of the anatomy of the eyeball, it seems likely that this third tunic was the retina. Aurelius Cornelius Celsus called *arachnoidea* the zonular ligament, and four centuries later, Oribasius, the famous physician of Pergamum, used the same term to refer to the ciliary processes of the choroid (Hyrtl, 1880). On the famous plate illustrating Fuchs' booklet on ophthalmology (1538), both Greek and Latin terms are to be found: *Arachnoides*, which refers to a gap interposed between the lens and the aqueous humor of the posterior chamber, and *Aranea retina*, which applies to the extensions of this gap around the lens and the vitreous body. Both terms seem to designate either the posterior chamber of the eye, or the capsule of the lens. One year after (1539), Leonhart Fuchs published another booklet on the same subject, including a plate inspired by John Peckham's *Prospectiva communis* (1482): this time, the term *Arachnoides* became synonymous with *Tela aranea* (spider's web).

In the following decades, Giacomo Berengario da Carpi called *arachnoidea* the anterior part of the retina (Hyrtl, 1880). However, most authors used this term to refer to the capsule of the lens: *Araneae telarum* (Vesalius, 1604), *Aranea* or *Telas aranearum* (Dulaurens, 1605), *Aranea* (Bartholin, 1677). The famous Dutch anatomist Isbrand van Diemerbroeck explained in clear terms the validity of this comparison: "Elle [le cristallin] est environnée d'une tunique transparente, laquelle lui est particulière: on l'appelle tunique cristalloïde, & aussi à raison de sa tissure extrêmement mince, Aranée" (It [the lens] is surrounded with a transparent tunic, which is specific to it: it is called cristalloid tunic, and also owing to its very thin structure, Aranea) (Diemer-broeck, 1695).

From the eighteenth century, the term arachnoid disappeared from the anatomical terminology related to the eyeball, and was only used to refer to the newly discovered arachnoid matter (Verheyen, 1710). Only Lorenz Heister kept on applying this term to a membrane "crystallinum et vitreum corpus cingit" (surrounding the lens and vitreous body) (Heister, 1719).

The arachnoid matter received other names which were never recognized by official anatomical nomenclatures: *Meninx media* by Govard Bidloo, *Meninx mucosa* by Georg Friedrich Hildebrandt (both cited by Hyrtl, 1880), and *Meninx serosa* by de Terra (de Terra, 1913). Langdon (1891) described the arachnoid as consisting of parietal (external) and visceral (internal) layers that enclosed a serous sac, the "arachnoid cavity proper". Subsequent investigators did not corroborate this view of arachnoid structure. Since the passing of the first international anatomical terminology in 1895 (His, 1895), the arachnoid matter was always called *arachnoidea*, except in the 1935 Iena Nomina anatomica where it temporarily became *arachnoides* (Donath, 1960). The officially recognized term in the most recent international anatomical terminology publication (Terminologia Anatomica, 1998) is *Arachnoidea matter* (arachnoid matter) with a further differenciation into cranial arachnoid matter and spinal arachnoid matter.

Based on electron microscopic investigations of the meninges, a contemporary view of the arachnoid has emerged (see Haines 1991, Haines et al. 1993 for reviews). The arachnoid matter consists of cells that are closely apposed, may form a layer several cells thick and are attached to each other by numerous cell junctions especially occluding tight junctions. Recognizing that the structure of this layer precluded the movement of fluid from the subarachnoid space outwardly into the dura, Nabeshma et al. (1975) designated this layer as the arachnoid barrier cell layer. These same investigators (and others, see Haines 1991 for review) also reported that the arachnoid (arachnoid barrier cell layer) was tenuously attached to the inner surface of the dura and that there was no naturally occuring subdural space lined by a mesothelium, as reported early in the 1900's. In addition, and as well known for many years, tendrils of arachnoid cells traverse the subarachnoid space as arachnoid trabeculae to attach to the pia mater on the surface of the brain. While the details have changed, the principals of our understanding of the arachnoid have remained similar for many years.

References

Bartholin T (1677): *Anatome quartum renovata.* Lugduni: sumpt. Joan. Ant. Huguetan, p. 518.
Blasius G (1666): *Anatome medullae spinalis, et nervorum inde provenientium.* Amstelodami: Apud Casparum Commelinum.
Cruveilhier J (1871): *Traité d'anatomie descriptive.* Paris: P. Asselin, 4th edition, vol. 3, p. 345.
Diemerbroeck I van (1695): *L'anatomie du corps humain.* Lyon: chez Anisson & Posuel, vol. 2, p. 371 and Pl. 14, fig. XIII.
Donath T (1960): *Erläuterndes anatomisches wörterbuch. Vergleichende Übersicht der Baseler, Jenaer und Pariser Nomenklaturen, gruppiert nach Organen.* Budapest: Verlag Medicina Budapest, p. 222.

Dulaurens A (1605): *Historia anatomica, humani corporis partes.* Lugduni: apud Horatium Cardon, p. 828.

Fuchs L (1538): *Ein newes hochnutzlichs Büchlin von erkantnus der Kranckheyten der Augen.* Strassburg: Heinrich Vogtherr.

Fuchs L (1539): *Alle Kranckheyt der Augen...* Strassburg: Heinrich Vogtherr.

Goelicke, Andreas Ottomar (1697): *Epistola anatomica, problematica nona... Ad... Fredericum Ruyschium... De cursu arteriarum per piam matrem cerebrum involventem, de tertia cerebri meninge, de arteriis membranarum cavitates ossis frontis supra narium radices...* Amstelaedami: Apud Joannem Wolters.

Haines DE (1991): On the question of a subdural space. *Anat Rec 230*: 3–21.

Haines DE, Harkey HL, Al-Mefty O (1993): The "subdural" space: A new look at an outdated concept. *Neurosurgery 32*: 111–120.

Haller A von (1774): *Bibliotheca anatomica.* Tiguri: apud Orell, Gessner, Fuesslin, et Socc., vol. 1, p. 241.

Heister L (1719): *Compendium anatomicum. Editio altera.* Altorfi et Norimbergae: in Bibliopolio Kohlesiano et Adolphiano, p. 119.

His W (1895): Die anatomische Nomenclatur. Nomina anatomica, Verzeichniss der von der Commission der anatomischen Gesellschaft festgestellten Namen, eingeleitet und im Einverständniss mit dem Redactionsausschuss erläutert. *Arch Anat Physiol (Supplement-Band).*

Hyrtl J (1880): *Onomatologia anatomica. Geschichte und Kritik der anatomischen Sprache der Gegenwart, mit besonderer Berücksichtigung ihrer Barbarismen, widersinnigkeiten, Tropen, und grammatikalischen Fehler.* Wien: Wilhelm Braumüller, pp. 46–48.

Langdon FW (1891): The arachnoid of the brain. *J Comp Neurol 1*: 205–210.

Nabeshima S, Reese TS, Landis DMD, Brightman MW (1975): Junctions in the meninges and marginal glia. *J Comp Neurol 164*: 127–170.

Olry R (1989): Histoire des nomenclatures anatomiques. *Doc Hist Vocab Sci CNRS 9*: 91–98.

Peckham J (1482): *Prospectiva communis.* Milan: Petrus de Corneno.

Rufus Ephesius (1604): *Universa Antiquorum Anatome, Tamossium, quam partium & externarum, & internarum... expicata per Fabium Paulinum.* In: A Vesalius (1604).

Sabatier RB (1792): Sur quelques particularités de la structure de la moëlle de l'Epine, et de ses enveloppes. In *Traité complet d'anatomie, ou description de toutes les parties du corps humain.* Paris: Théophile Barrois, vol. 4, p. 429.

Terminologia Anatomica (1998): New York: Thieme.

Terra P de (1913): *Vademecum anatomicum. Kritischetymologisches wörterbuch der systematischen Anatomie. Mit besonderer Berücksichtigung der Synonymen. Nebst einem Anhang: Die anatomischen Schriftsteller des Altertums bis zur Neuzeit.* Jena: Gustav Fischer, pp. 14–15.

Varoli C (1573): *De Nervis Opticis nonnullisque aliis praeter communem opinionem in Humano capite observatis. Ad Hieronymum Mercurialem.* Patavii: apud Paulum et Antonium Meiettos fratres.

Verheyen P (1710): *Corporis humani anatomiae.* Bruxellis: Apud Fratres t'Serstevens, vol. 1, p. 213 and Pl. 24, fig. 4, E.

Vesalius A (1604): *De corporis humani fabrica libri septem.* Venetiis: apud Ioan. Anton. et Iacobum de Franciscis, p. 497.

Claustrum: A Sea Wall Between the Island and the Shell?

The claustrum is a thin sheet of grey matter that splits the insular subcortical white matter to create the extreme and external capsules. It is thus interposed between the insula, compared with an island by Johann Christian Reil (Reil, 1796), and the putamen, compared with a husk or a shell by Karl Friedrich Burdach (Dejerine, 1895). Its connections and functional significance are unknown in the human brain (Williams et al., 1995). Surprisingly, the claustrum escaped notice up to the late 18th century. One of the 17 plates drawn by Giovanni Battista Piazetta and engraved by Fiorenza Marcello for Giandomenico Santorini depicts a coronal section of the human brain on which we might have expected to see the claustrum: thalamus, putamen and insula are well visible, but there is no trace of the claustrum to be found in the insular subcortical white matter (Santorini, 1775). According to Dejerine, the very first anatomist to have depicted the claustrum on a plate was Félix Vicq d'Azyr (probably in his 1786 masterpiece) who compared this formation with a worm and referred to it as the nucleus taeniaformis (Dejerine, 1895).

The term claustrum was coined by the German anatomist Karl Friedrich Burdach in his famous *Vom Baue und Leben des Gehirns* (Burdach, 1822); it means lock, bolt, fence, barrier or sea wall (Theil, 1855), and was translated into 'Vormauer' (forewall) in the German literature (Burdach, 1822; Henle, 1888), and into 'avantmur' by French anatomists (Féré, 1886; Debierre, 1907). Other terms were used to refer to this formation: nucleus lateralis (lateral nucleus), 'noyau rubanné' (ribbon-shaped nucleus), or 'bandelette vermiculaire' (vermicular band) (Obersteiner, 1893; Poirier and Charpy, 1901; de Terra, 1913) but the term claustrum always prevailed in anatomical literature, including the successive editions of the official anatomical nomenclature (Donath, 1960 Terminologia Anatomica, 1998). Burdach also named the brachium conjunctivum (superior cerebellar peduncle) and the cuneus (Kay, 1970), and his name remained for a long time linked to the fasciculus cuneatus and the cuneate nucleus in French anatomical terminology (Olry, 1995). Surprisingly, Burdach's description of the claustrum seems to have escaped notice during the following decades: Cruveilhier (1837), Bayle (1845), Sappey (1852) and Masse (1858) totally ignored this formation in their treatises.

In the mid-1930s, Landau discovered a continuation of the claustrum in the baboon which he called claustrum parvum (little or small claustrum). In 1938, he could observe the same formation in man and defined his claustrum parvum as 'une chaîne de cellules qui s' approche de l'avantmur en arrière pour s'unir finalement avec ce dernier' (a chain of cells which comes close to the claustrum behind to finally unite with the latter: Landau, 1938). Unlike many anatomists of that time who regarded the claustrum as a detached part of the insular cortex (Duval, 1892, Debierre, 1907) and sometimes referred to it as the claustral layer of the insula, Landau claimed that it belonged to the basal ganglia and was actually related to the rhinencephalon, the amygdaloid nuclear complex and the anterior perforated substance. This question has still not been resolved, for the claustrum may have at least two structurally and functionally distinct zones, the insular claustrum on the one hand, and the prepiriform claustrum on the other hand (Williams et al., 1995).

The claustrum escaped notice for a long time. It remained ignored by most anatomical treatises many decades after Burdach's description. Féré lamented in 1886 to notice that its lesions could not yet be related to any neurological symptomatology: over one century later, we are no further on than he was. The claustrum parvum rapidly sank into oblivion. Obviously, Landau was right when he wrote in 1938: 'L'avant-mur mérite plus d'attention qu'on ne lui en accorde en général' (the claustrum deserves more attention than is generally paid to it).

References

Bayle ALJ (1845): *Traité élémentaire d'anatomie, ou description succincte des organes et des éléments organiques qui composent le corps humain,* 5th ed. Paris, Méquignon-Marvis fils.

Burdach KF (1822): *Vom Baue und Leben des Gehirns.* Leipzig, Dyk.

Cruveilhier J (1837): *Anatomie descriptive,* Vol. 2. Méline, Cans et Compagnie, Bruxelles.

Debierre Ch (1907): *Le cerveau et la moelle épinière avec applications physiologiques et médico-chirurgicales.* Paris, Félix Alcan, p. 357.

Dejerine J (1895): *Anatomie des centres nerveux,* Vol. 1, Paris, Rueff et Cie, pp. 118, 369 and 375.

Donath T (1960): *Erläuterndes anatomisches Wörterbuch. Vergleichende Übersicht der Baseler, Jenaer und Pariser Nomenklaturen, gruppiert nach Organen.* Terra Budapest, Verlag Medicina Budapest, p. 215.

Duval M (1892): *Cours de physiologie,* 7th ed. Paris, J.-B. Baillière et fils, p. 107.

Féré Ch (1886): *Traité élémentaire d'anatomie médicale du système nerveux.* Paris, A. Delahaye et Lecrosnier, p. 149.

Henle J (1888): *Grundriss der Anatomie des Menschen. Herausgegeben von Fr. Merkel,* 3rd ed., Vol. 1 (text), Braunschweig, Friedrich Vieweg und Sohn, p. 374.

Kay AS (1970): Burdach, Karl Friedrich. In: C.C. Gillispie, ed., *Dictionary of Scientific Biography,* Vol. 2. New York, Charles Scribner's Sons, pp. 594–597.

Landau E (1938): Le Claustrum parvum chez l'homme. *Mém Soc Vaudoise Sci Nat 6 (2):* 45–64.

Masse JN (1858): *Traité pratique d'anatomie descriptive mis en rapport avec l'atlas d'anatomie et lui servant de complément.* Paris, J.-B. Baillière et fils.

Obersteiner H (1893): *Anatomie des centres nerveux. Guide pour l'étude de leur structure à l'état normal et pathologique.* French translation by J.-X. Coroënne. Paris, Georges Carré, p. 85.

Olry R (1995): *Dictionary of anatomical Eponyms.* Stuttgart, Jena, New York, Gustav Fischer, p. 29.

Poirier P, Charpy A (1901): *Traité d'anatomie humaine,* Vol. 3, fasc. 1, 2nd édition. Paris, Masson et Cie, p. 334.

Reil JC (1796): *Exercitationum anatomicarum fasciculus primus. De structura nervorum.* Halle, Venalis.

RHINENCEPHALON, TABES DORSALIS, ETC

Santorini G (1775): *Septemdecim tabulae quas nunc primum edit atque explicat.* Parmae: ex Regia Typographia, Plate III, Figure III.

Sappey PC (1852): *Traité d'anatomie descriptive.* Vol. 2, Paris, Victor Masson.

Terminologia Anatomica (1998): New York, Thieme.

Terra P de (1913): Vademecum anatomicum. *Kritischetymologisches Wörterbuch der systematischen Anatomie.* Mit besonderer Berücksichtigung der Synonymen. Jena: Gustav Fischer, p. 82.

Theil N (1855): *Grand dictionnaire de la langue latine,* Vol. 1. Paris: Firmin Didot frères, p. 514.

Williams PL, Bannister LH, Berry MN, Collins P, Dyson M, Dussek JE, Ferguson MWJ (1995): *Gray's Anatomy. The anatomical basis of medicine and surgery,* 38th ed. New York, Edinburgh, London, Tokyo, Madrid and Melbourne, Churchill Livingstone, pp. 1189 and 1197.

Phantom Limb: Haunted Body?

A very simple but accurate definition of the phantom limb phenomenon is to be found in the masterpiece of the French anatomist Xavier Bichat: "Ainsi, quand l'extrémité du moignon fait souffrir le malade qui vient d'éprouver une amputation, le principe qui sent en lui éprouve bien la sensation, mais il se trompe sur l'endroit d'où elle part: il la rapporte au pied qui n'existe plus" (In this way, when the end of the stump makes the patient who underwent an amputation suffer, the principle which feels in him indeed experiences the sensation, but he is mistaken as to the place where it comes from: he relates it to the foot which does not exist any more, Bichat, 1830). Hypotheses concerning etiology of the phantom limb pain include the gate theory (loss of sensory input decreases self-sustaining neural activity of the gate, causing pain), the peripheral theory (nerve endings in the stump represent parts originally innervated by the severed nerve), and the psychologic theory (hostility, guilt, and denial are interpreted as pain) (Krupski et al., 1994).

The term phantom limb was coined by the famous American neurologist Silas Weir Mitchell (1829–1914) who wrote more than 170 medical and scientific papers, on posthemiplegic chorea (1874a), causalgia and traumatic neuralgia (1872a), and various forms of headache (1874b), among others. He also coined the term erythromelalgia (1878) and described the cremasteric reflex (1879) (Bynum, 1974). The term phantom limb appeared in the title of a paper published by Mitchell in 1871 in the *Lippincott's Magazine* of Philadelphia. One year later, the author extended his neurological observations in his *Injuries of Nerves and Their Consequences*: "Nearly every man who loses a limb carries about with him a constant or inconstant phantom of the missing member, a sensory ghost of that much of himself, faintly felt at times, but ready to be called up to his perception by a touch or a change of wind" (Mitchell, 1872). Mitchell could observe this phenomenon in 86 of his 90 patients, which is in accordance with later studies showing that phantom limbs occur in 95–100% of all people who have had a limb or part of a limb amputated (PWN, 1974). Shortly after Mitchell's publication, George Henry Lewes wrote that "the motor feelings are due to states of the centre, and not to states of the muscles or sensory nerves; because *they arise even after the limbs have been amputated*, when, of course, the muscular actions represented in these motor images are absent" (Lewes, 1879).

This strange phenomenon had already been observed in the eighteenth century. In 1778, a certain Lamarier published in Montpellier his comments on the physiopathology of the "pains which one believes to feel in many parts of the body which have been separated from it" (Lamarier, 1778), and 20 years later, the German physician Aaron Lemos devoted the 34 pages of his doctoral thesis to the same question

(Lemos, 1798). In 1861, Guéniot refered to this phenomenon as the "hétérotopie subjective des extrémités" (subjective heterotopia of limbs; Guéniot, 1861), and in the late nineteenth century, the famous French neurologist Jules Bernard Luys wrote about the "reviviscence des sensibilités" (revitalization of sensibilities: Luys, 1894) and the "persistance des impressions sensitives" (persistence of sensory feelings: Luys, 1895). Nowadays, the term phantom limb has been translated in most languages and acknowledged as the most appropriate term to refer to this strange neurological phenomenon: *douleur des membres fantômes* or *algohallucinose* in French, *dolore fantasma* or *allucinosi del moncone* in Italian, *dolor fantasma* in Spanish, *Phantomgliedschmerz* in German (Bossy, 1999; Sliosberg, 1964).

The Scottish dramatist and novelist Sir James Matthew Barrie wrote in his *The Little Minister* that "a house is never quiet in darkness for those who listen carefully. Phantoms have been created when the first human being awoke during the night" (Barrie, 1897, cited in Petit, 1960). It seems that the human body might also put up its own ghosts . . .

References

Bichat X (1830): *Anatomie générale appliquée à la physiologie et à la médecine. Nouvelle édition contenant les additions précédemment publiées par Béclard, et augmentée d'un grand nombre de notes nouvelles par F. Blandin.* J. S. Chaude, Paris. vol. 1, p. 252.

Bossy J (1999): *La grande aventure du terme médical. Filiation et valeurs actuelles.* Montpellier: Sauramps Médical, p. 328.

Bynum WF (1974): Mitchell, Silas Weir. In: Gillispie, CC ed., *Dictionary of Scientific Biography*, New York, Charles Scribner's. Vol. 9, pp. 422–424.

Gueniot (1861): D'une hallucination du toucher (ou hétérotopie subjective des extrémités) particulière à certains amputés. *J Physiol de l'homme, Paris* 4: 416–430.

Krupski WC, Skinner HB, Effeney DJ (1994): Amputation. In: Way, LW ed., *Current Surgical Diagnosis & Treatment.* Norwalk, Connecticut, Appleton & Lange, 10th edition, pp. 772–782.

Lamarier (1778): Mémoire sur l'union qui se fait des artères avec les nerfs après les amputations, pour déterminer la cause méchanique des douleurs que l'on croit sentir dans plusieurs parties du corps qui en ont été séparées. *Hist Soc Roy Sci Montpellier 2* (2): 168–184.

Lemos A (1798): *De dolore membri amputati remanente explicatio.* Halae: in off. Batheana.

Lewes GH (1879): *Problems of Life and Mind.* London, Trübner & Co., pp. 334–341.

Luys J (1894): De la reviviscence de la sensibilité du membre amputé chez un sujet en état hypnotique. *Ann Psychiat Hypnol Paris* 4: 225–227.

Luys J (1895): De la persistance des impressions sensitives après les amputations. *Ann Psychiat Hypnol Paris* 5: 193–198.

Mitchell SW (1871): Phantom limbs. *Lippincott's Mag., Phila.* 8: 563–569.

Mitchell SW (1872a): Clinical lecture on certain painful affections of the feet. *Phila Med Times 3*: 81–82, 113–115.

Mitchell SW (1872b): *Injuries of Nerves and Their Consequences.* J. B. Lippincott & Co., Philadelphia, pp. 348–359.

Mitchell SW (1874a): Post-paralytic chorea. *Am J Med Sci 61*: 342–352.

Mitchell SW (1874b): Headaches, from heat stroke, from fevers, after meningitis, from over use of the brain, from eye strain. *Med Surg Reporter 31*: 67–70.

Mitchell SW (1878): On a rare vaso-motor neurosis of the extremities, and on the maladies with which it may be confounded. *Am J Med Sci 76*: 17–36.

Mitchell SW (1879): The cremaster-reflex. *J Nerv Ment Dis 6*: 577–586.

Petit K (1960): *Le dictionnaire des citations du monde entier.* Verviers, Gérard & Co., p. 157.

PWN (1974): Help for the painful phantom limb? *Nature 248*: 731–732.

Sliosberg A (1964): *Elsevier's Medical Dictionary in Five Languages.* Amsterdam, London, New York, Elsevier Publishing Company, p. 832.

Lasthénie de Ferjol's Syndrome: A Tribute Paid by Jean Bernard to Jules Amédée Barbey D'Aurevilly

Jules Amédée Barbey d'Aurevilly, one of the leading French novelists of the nineteenth century, was born on November 2, 1808, at Saint-Sauveur-le-Vicomte. Much influenced by Sir Walter Scott and by Lord Byron, his novels are "sombre in tone and often strained and melodramatic" (Gould, 1967). He wrote many novels, including *L'Ensorcelée* (1854), *Le Chevalier des Touches* (1864), *Un Prêtre marié* (1865) which inspired the Belgian surrealist painter René Magritte to the title of one of his paintings in 1950 (Blavier, 1979), and his masterpiece *Les Diaboliques* (1874). Barbey d'Aurevilly died in Paris on April 23, 1889. You may wonder why we refer to a French nineteenth century writer in a column devoted to the roots of terms used in neurosciences. The reason is to be found in a novel which Barbey d'Aurevilly wrote in the late 1870s: a strange mental disorder, Lasthénie de Ferjol's syndrome, was named after the heroine of this story titled *Une Histoire sans nom*. Let us shortly summarize the story of this novel.

In the late eighteenth century, the 16-year-old Lasthénie led a cloistered life with her mother, the Baroness of Ferjol, and their old servant Agathe Thousard in a small village of the Cévennes. As usual at that time, they put up for somes weeks a travelling Capuchin, Father Riculf, who shamefully took advantage of Lasthénie's somnambulism to have sexual intercourse with her. As soon as he left, Lasthénie sank into melancholy so much that the trusty servant believed in a bewitchment. As the pregnancy became obvious, the Baroness of Ferjol heaped opprobrium on her poor daughter, and hoped for a miscarriage. Some months later, her grandson was actually stillborn, and she buried him in the garden. Lasthénie's disease was getting worse, and nobody could help her: she could never know why she had become pregnant. She died shortly thereafter, and her mother and Agathe found bloodstains on her blouse: a long time ago, Lasthénie had stuck eighteen needles into the region of her heart: "Lasthénie killed herselve, slowly killed herselve, every day a little more, with needles" (Barbey d'Aurevilly, 1990).

The term Lasthénie de Ferjol's syndrome, coined in 1967 by the French hematologist Jean Bernard and three co-authors, is defined as an "hypochromic anemia with microcythaemia and decreasing of serum iron, due to bleedings which are voluntarily provoked, repeated and hidden. It is observed in women with a particular psyche" (Garnier & Delamare, 2000). In this publication, the authors described 12 cases which had three things in common: all the patients were women (between 20 and 42 years old), they all practised a paramedical profession (nurses or laboratory assistants; only one of them was unemplyed but she wanted to become a nurse), and they all had a pathological personality (lack of affective adaptibility, most of them were either single, or divorced). The evolution of this psychiatric disease might be tragic: two patients of these twelve cases died before the age of 35 years, the one of cardiac failure, the other committed suicide. Women who are suffering from this strange mental disorder want to attract physician's attention by the way of a disease provoked by themselves. In that way, this syndrome belongs to the so-called pathomimia, which also include Munchausen's syndrome (Olry, 2001).

We tried in vain to find the term Lasthénie de Ferjol's syndrome in English psychiatric terminology: none of the dictionaries and handbooks we referred to mentioned this term (Dorland, 1994; Jablonski, 1991; Landau, 1986; Stedman, 2000; Wolman, 1983). But it was to be found in most French dictionaries and handbooks (Garnier & Delamare, 2000; Juillet, 2000; Porot, 1996). Coined by a French hematologist, referring to the novel of a French writer, this term of course emerged in French medical literature as the only one likely to be used. In 1973, Duke of Lévis-Mirepoix entitled one of his numerous history books *Grandeur et misère de l'individualisme français* (Greatness and miseries of French individualism). Lasthénie de Ferjol's syndrome might have formed one more chapter in his book ...

References

Barbey d'Aurevilly JA (1990): *Une Histoire sans nom*. Paris, Flammarion.

Bernard J, Najean Y, Alby N, Rain JD (1967): Les anémies hypochromes dues à des hémorragies volontairement provoguées. Syndrome de Lasthénie de Ferjol. *La Presse Méd 42*: 2087–2090.

Blavier A (1979): *René Magritte. Écrits Complets*. Paris, Flammarion, p. 525.

Dorland's Illustrated Medical Dictionary (1994) (28th ed.): Philadelphia: WB Saunders Company.

Garnier M, Delamare V (2000): *Dictionnaire des termes de médecine* (26e éd.). Paris, Maloine, p. 469.

Gould SC (1967): "Barbey d'Aurevilly, Jules Amédée", In: *Encyclopaedia Britannica* (Vol. 3). Chicago, London, Toronto, Geneva, Sydney, Tokyo, Manila, William Benton Publisher, p. 150.

Jablonski S (1991): *Dictionary of Syndromes & Eponymic Diseases* (2nd ed.). Malabar, Florida, Krieger Publishing Company.

Juillet P (2000): *Dictionnaire de psychiatrie*. Paris, Éditions CILF, p. 211.

Landau SI (1986): *International Dictionary of Medicine and Biology*. New York, Chichester, Brisbane, Toronto, Singapore, Wiley.

Lévis-Mirepoix, Duke of (1973): *Grandeur et misère de l'individualisme français à travers l'histoire*. Paris, Librairie Académigue Perrin.

Olry R (2001): Baron Münchhausen and the syndrome which bears his name: History of an endearing personage and of a *strange mental disorder* (submitted).

Porot A (1996): *Manuel alphabétique de psychiatrie clinique et thérapeutique* (7e éd.). Paris, Presses Universitaires de France, p. 395.

Stedman's Medical Dictionary (2000) (27th ed.): Philadelphia, Lippincott Williams & Wilkins.

Wolman BB (ed.) (1983): *International Encyclopedia of Psychiatry, Psychology, Psychonalysis & Neurology*. New York, Aesculapius Publishers.

Ansa Hypoglossi or Ansa Cervicalis?
That is the Question ...

The ansa cervicalis has two roots: the upper root leaves the hypoglossal nerve where it curves round the occipital artery, and contains only fibres from the first cervical spinal nerve. The lower root, or nervus descendens cervicalis, contains fibres from the second and third cervical spinal nerves. The two roots form the ansa cervicalis, from which branches supply the sternohyoid, sternothyroid and the inferior belly of the omohyoid (Williams et al., 1995). Aside from some German authors who met halfway and refered to it as "Plexus hypoglossocervicalis" (Rodrigues, 1929), most anatomists of the last centuries described this anastomosis between the cervical plexus and the hypoglossal nerve either as ansa hypoglossi, or as ansa cervicalis. In the first case, it was believed to arise from the hypoglossal nerve and join the cervical plexus, in the second case it was to be inferred that this ansa was formed only by fibres belonging to the cervical plexus.

The ansa cervicalis had been generally outlined by all anatomists who studied the nerve supply of the anterior cervical region (see Rodrigues, 1929, for review). However, until the early nineteenth century, most authors just mentioned an anastomosis between the cervical plexus and the hypoglossal nerve (Winslow, 1752; Verdier, 1752; Sabatier, 1792; Boyer, 1805). In 1825, the famous French anatomist Jules Cloquet refered to the upper and lower roots of the ansa as "branche cervicale descendante" (cervical descending branch) and "branche descendante interne" (internal descending branch), respectively (Cloquet, 1825), but the ansa itself remained unnamed.

The 1830s were a turning point in the history of the origin of the ansa cervicalis. On the one hand, Christophore Ernest Bach raised, for the very first time, the question of the origin of the fibres which form this anastomosis. He answered this question in his 1835 thesis in Zurich by noting that they are all supplied by the cervical plexus. On the other hand, the French anatomist Pierre Paul Broc claimed in the third volume of his textbook that this question didn't matter: "les nerfs naissent, se terminent, vont, viennent, partent, arrivent, de sorte que ces considérations sont tout-à-fait dépourvues de fondement" (nerves arise, end, come and go, leave, arrive, so that these considerations are totally unfounded: Broc, n.d.). Unfortunately, this third volume is undated (vols. 1 and 2 are dated 1833 and 1834, respectively). We cannot therefore assume that Broc's comments were directed to Bach's conclusions, but it seems likely since some copies of this third volume are dated 1836 (Index-Catalogue of the Library of the Surgeon-General's Office, 1881; General Catalogue of Printed Books in the British Museum, 1967). The following year, Cruveilhier seemed to elude this debate, and limited himself with describing the ansa as formed with a "Ramus descendens noni" (descending ramus of the ninth [cranial nerve]) and a "branche musculaire de la région sous-hyoïdienne" (muscular branch of the infrahyoid region) (Cruveilhier, 1837).

In the second half of the nineteenth century, the origin of the ansa cervicalis remained enigmatic. In 1876, the Austrian anatomist Moritz Holl supported Bach's description and was convinced that the hypoglossal nerve does not supply fibres to this ansa, whereas the Romanian neurologist Constantin Parhon and his collaborator claimed, twenty-three years later, that the central origins of this ansa lie in the medulla oblongata, and not in the cervical part of the spinal cord (Parhon and Goldstein, 1899).

In the late nineteenth and the early twentieth centuries, the real origin of the ansa was still controversial, but synonyms growed in number: "Ramus descendens hypoglossi" (descending ramus or branch of the hypoglossal [nerve]: Morel and Duval, 1883; Merkel, 1888; Debierre, 1890; Poirier and Charpy, 1901), "anse nerveuse de l'hypoglosse" (nervous ansa of the hypoglossal [nerve]: Fort, 1902; Testut, 1905) for the upper root; "branche descendante interne" (internal descending branch: Morel and Duval, 1883; Debierre, 1890; Poirier and Charpy, 1901; Fort, 1902; Testut, 1905) for the lower root. In 1894, the ansa was still believed to be formed by fibres belonging to the hypoglossal nerve: "On a voulu démontrer que la branche descendante de l'hypoglosse n'est autre chose que le filet anastomotique fourni par l'arcade des deux premiers nerfs cervicaux [...] mais ce fait nous semble loin d'être prouvé" (One wanted to demonstrate that the descending branch of the hypoglossus is nothing else but the anastomosis supplied by the arcade of the first two cervical nerves [.. .] but this fact seems to us far to be proved: Beaunis and Bouchard, 1894). That is why the 1895 Basel Nomina anatomica decided to coin the term ansa nervi hypoglossi (His, 1895), which was extended by the 1935 Iena Nomina anatomica (Kopsch, 1950). In 1955, the Paris Nomina anatomica deleted this term and replaced it by those of ansa cervicalis (Donath, 1960), which was maintained since that time (Terminologia anatomica, 1998).

As far back as in 1835, Christophore Ernest Bach claimed that the ansa cervicalis contained only fibres arising from the cervical plexus. It took one hundred and twenty years to acknowledge that he was right ...

References

Bach CE (1835): *Annotationes anatomicae de nervis hypoglosso et laryngeis.* Zurich: Orell, Füssli et Co., 32 pp.

Beaunis H, Bouchard A (1894): *Nouveaux éléments d'anatomie descriptive et d'embryologie.* Paris: Baillière et fils, 5th ed., pp. 659–660, and 668.

Boyer A (1805): *Traité complet d'anatomie, ou description de toutes les parties du corps humain.* Paris: Migneret, 2nd ed., Vol. 3, pp. 360, and 367–368.

Broc PP (n.d., 1836?): Traité complet d'anatomie descriptive et raisonnée. Paris: Just Rouvier, Vol. 3, pp. 771–772, and 776–777.

Cloquet J (1825): *Manuel d'anatomie descriptive du corps humain. Texte.* Paris: Béchet jeune, p. 344.

Cruveilhier J (1837): *Anatomie descriptive.* Bruxelles: Méline, Cans et Cie, Vol. 2, pp. 339–340, and 420.

Debierre C (1890): *Traité élémentaire d'anatomie de l'homme.* Paris: Félix Alcan, Vol. 1, pp. 798, and 920.

Donath T (1960): *Erläuterndes anatomisches Wörterbuch. Vergleichende Übersicht der Baseler, Jenaer und Pariser Nomenklaturen, gruppiert nach Organen.* Terra Budapest: Verlag Medicina Budapest, p. 233.

Fort JA (1902): *Anatomie descriptive et dissection*. Paris: Vigot Frères, 6th ed., Vol. 2, pp. 667, and 797–798.

General Catalogue of Printed Books in the British Museum to 1955, Compact Edition (1967): New York: Readex Microprint Corporation, Vol. 4, p. 204.

His W (1895): Die anatomische Nomenclatur. Nomia anatomica. Verzeichniss der von der Commission der anatomischen Gesellschaft festgestellten Namen, eingeleitet und im Einverständniss mit dem Redactionsausschuss erläutert. *Arch Anat Physiol (suppl)*: 90.

Holl M (1876): Beobachtungen über die Anastomosen des Nervus Hypoglossus. *Zeitschr Anat Entwick* 2: 82.

Index-Catalogue of the Library of the Surgeon-General's Office, United States Army (1881): Washington: Government Printing Office, Vol. 2, p. 465.

Kopsch F (1950): *Die Nomina anatomica des Jahres 1895 (B.N.A.) nach der Buchstabenreihe geordnet und gegenübergestellt den Nomina anatomica des Jahres 1935 (I.N.A.)*. Leipzig: Georg Thieme, 4th ed., p. 2.

Merkel F (1888): *J. Henle's Grundriss der Anatomie des Menschen. Text*. Braunschweig: Friedrich Vieweg und Sohn, pp. 404, and 407.

Morel C, Duval M (1883): *Manuel de l'anatomiste*. Paris: Asselin et Cie, pp. 825, and 833–834.

Parhon CI, Goldstein (1899): Sur l'origine de la branche descendante de l'hypoglosse. *Roumanie médicale: 1*.

Poirier P, Charpy A (1901): *Traité d'anatomie humaine*. Paris: Masson et Cie, 2nd ed., Vol. 3, pp. 784–785, 787–788, and 859–860.

Rodrigues AAP (1929): *Ansa hypoglossi. Novos subsidios para o seu estudo anatomico*. Pôrto: Tipografia Pôrto Médico, LTD., pp. 1–34.

Sabatier RB (1792): *Traité complet d'anatomie ou description de toutes les parties du corps humain*. Paris: Théophile Barrois, last ed., Vol. 4, pp. 227–228, 240, and 242.

Terminologia anatomica (1998): New York: Thieme.

Testut L (1905): *Traité d'anatomie humaine*. Paris: Octave Doin, 5th ed., Vol. 3, pp. 126–127.

Verdier C (1752): *Abrégé de l'anatomie du corps humain*. Bruxelles: Jean Léonard, new ed., Vol. 2, pp. 412–413, and 416–417.

Williams PL, Bannister LH, Berry MM, Collins P, Dyson M, Dussek JE, Ferguson MWJ (1995): *Gray's anatomy. The anatomical basis of medicine and surgery*. New York, Edinburgh, London, Tokyo, Madrid and Melbourne: Churchill Livingstone, 38th ed., pp. 1258, and 1265.

Winslow JB (1752): *Exposition anatomique de la structure du corps humain*. Amsterdam: E. Tourneisen, new ed., Vol. 3, pp. 176, and 180–184.

Reissner's Fibre: The Exception Which Proves the Rule, or the Devil According to Charles Baudelaire?

Since August 1997, we have been summarizing, with the collaboration of C. U. M. Smith and Edward G. Jones, the roots and history of some terms used in neurosciences, emphasizing their evolution and changes as the years or even centuries went by. Our previous columns might therefore lead the reader to consider the scientific, in this case neurological terminology as a neverending updating of terms that had been coined by previous researchers. This time we choose a counter-example, Reissner's fibre, which was discovered by Ernest Reissner in 1860, and surprisingly never received any other name since that time.

Reissner's fibre arises from the subcommissural organ and can be followed in the cerebral aqueduct, the fourth ventricle, and the central canal of spinal cord to its caudal end (Paturet, 1964; Leonhardt et al., 1987). It is probably formed by exocytosis of the secretory granules of the subcommissural organ into the ventricular lumen (Jarial, 2001).

The Dorpat professor of anatomy Ernest Reissner is remembered for the accurate description of the vestibular membrane of the cochlea he made in his 1851 thesis (Reissner, 1851). In the following years, he devoted his studies to human and mammal hair (Reissner, 1853, 1854). In 1860, he described in the central nervous system of the lamprey *Petromyzon fluvialis* a "circular string, which looks like a nervous fibre, from which it is however distinguished by its greater refringence" (Reissner, 1860). Shortly after that, this newly discovered formation was called Reissner's fibre by Kutschin (1863), and no synonym could be found in the literature since that time.

Let us now try to understand what may account for the unusual exclusivenes of this term coined almost hundred and fifty years ago.

First hypothesis: Reissner's fibre was described for the very first time by Ernest Reissner and was never observed after his initial description, leading therefore to a question of its actual existence. This does not prove to be right. On the one hand, Heinrich Friedrich Bidder and Karl Wilhelm von Kupffer in 1857, and then Benedict Stilling in 1859 had observed this formation, but they regarded it as excreted epithelial cells or coagulated albumins of the cerebrospinal fluid (Bidder & Kupffer, 1857; Stilling, 1859): Reissner's fibre had therefore well and truly been observed before 1860. On the other hand, and though its existence was either regarded as an artefact due to chromic acid (Stieda, 1870) or even denied (Orru, 1916; Pastori, 1929), many authors could find Reissner's fibre in various animal species after 1860 (see Legait, 1942, for review).

Second hypothesis: Reissner's fibre is to be found in many animal species, but not in human beings, accounting for the fact that researchers in human anatomy were not interested in this formation. Reissner's fibre was actually described in many animal species: birds and reptiles (Kölliker, 1902), monkeys (Horsley, 1908), ray and trout (Jordan, 1919, 1925), over two hundred vertebrate species (Agdhur, 1922), Mongolian gerbil (Jarial, 2001), and lizards (Ahboucha & Gamrani, 2001). Animal species lacking Reissner's fibre are not numerous: shrewmouse, hedgehog (Legait, 1942), bat, camel, and chimpanzee (Galarza, 2002). On the other hand, its existence in human beings was (and remains?) controversial. Etienne-Jules Legait pointed out in 1942 the fact that: "lorsque son existence est niée, ce fait doit être accepté avec prudence et discuté: on ne peut en tenir compte si la fixation est douteuse" [when its existence is denied, this fact should be carefully accepted and debated: one could not take it into account if fixation is uncertain]. It seems that human adults lack Reissner's fibre (Agdhur, 1922; Galarza, 2002), but its formation was observed in a 14-year teenager by Agduhr in the 1920s, and in 15 and 16-week human embryos by Keene and Hewer in 1935 (cited by Legait, 1942). More recently, "a successful immunoreaction against a proteinaceous compound of the fetal human subcommissural organ has been performed" (Galarza, 2002). In other words, Reissner's fibre might follow the involution of the subcommissural organ from which it arises. Our second hypothesis is therefore half one thing and half another.

Third hypothesis: our knowledge of Reissner's fibre is so accurate that there is no value in offering an alternative term or name. If its morphological description is far from being approved unanimously, its functions remain still much more debated: no function at all (Kappers, 1921), involvement in vision (Sargent, 1904) or olfaction (Houser, 1901), central sensory organ (Tretjakoff, 1913), elimination of cell metabolites and perception of body movements (Leonhardt et al., 1987). Recently, the involvement of the subcommissural organ in the correct development of the axial skeleton via the thread-like Reissner's fiber has been studied (Ahboucha & Gamrani, 2001), a question which had been previously raised by Nicholls in a series of publications in the 1910s (Nicholls, 1912, 1913, 1917). Obviously, our third hypothesis is far from being convincing.

Though Reissner's fibre has been observed in many animal species since 1860, its existence in human beings seems to be related to the age. Moreover, its functions remain hypothetic. In other words, our knowledge of this formation has not really improved during the last hundred and forty years. The French nineteenth century poet and critic Charles Baudelaire claimed that the Devil is the only one who does not need to exist to be respected (cited by Villeneuve, 1989). From time out of mind, the Devil was always called the Devil: now, we do not even know if it exists, and even less what it might be used as ...

References

Agdhur E (1922): Ueber ein zentrales Sinnesorgan (?) bei den Vertebraten. *Ztschr Anat Entwickelungsgesch 66*: 223–230.

Ahboucha S, Gamrani H (2001): Differences in protein expression in the subcommissural organ of normal and lordotic lizards (*Agama impalearis*). *Metab Brain Dis 16(3–4)*: 219–226.

Bidder HF, Kupffer C (1857): *Untersuchungen über die Textur des Rückenmarkes und die Entwickelung seiner Formelemente.* Leipzig, Breitkopf und Härtel.

Galarza M (2002): Evidence of the subcommissural organ in humans and its association with hydrocephalus. *Neurosurg Rev 25(4)*: 205–215.

Horsley V (1908): Note on the existence of Reissner's Fiber in Higher Vertebrates. *Brain 31*: 147–149.

Houser GL (1901): The neurons and supporting elements of the brain of a selachian. *J Comp Neurol 11*: 67–169.

Jarial MS (2001): Aspects of the ultrastructure and function of the subcommissural organ in the Mongolian gerbil (*Meriones unguiculatus*). *J Submicrosc Cytol Pathol 33(1–2)*: 73–82.

Jordan H (1919): Concerning Reissner's fiber in Teleosts. *J Comp Neurol 30*: 217–226.

Jordan H (1925): The structure and staining reactions of the Reissner fiber apparatus, particularly the subcommissural organ. *Am J Anat 34(3)*: 427–443.

Kappers NA (1921): *Die vergleichende Anatomie des Nervensystems der Wirbeltiere und des Menschen*. Haarlem, Bohn.

Kölliker A (1902): Über die oberflächlichen Nervenkerne im Marke der Vögel und Reptilien. *Ztschr Wiss Zool 72*: 126, 159 and 179.

Kutschin O (1863): *Über den Bau des Rückenmarks von Neunauges*. Kasan, thesis (reviewed by Ludwig Stieda in *Arch mikr Anat 2*: 525–530, 1866).

Legait G (1942): *Les organes épendymaires du troisième ventricule. L'organe sous-commissural. L'organe sub-fornical. L'organe para-ventriculaire*. Nancy, Georges Thomas, pp. 72–104.

Leonhardt H, Krisch B, Zilles K (1987): Graue und weisse Substanz des Zwischenhirns. In: *Rauber/Kopsch Anatomie des Menschen*. Stuttgart, New York, Georg Thieme, vol. 3, pp. 333–334.

Nicholls GE (1912): An experimental investigation on the function of Reissner's Fibre. *Anat Anz 40*: 409–432.

Nicholls GE (1913): The function of Reissner's Fibre and the Ependymal Groove. *Nature 82*: 217–218.

Nicholls GE (1917): Some experiments on the nature and function of Reissner's fiber. *J Comp Neurol 27*: 117–200.

Orru E (1916): *L'organo subcommesurale in Gongylus ocellatus*. Cagliari, Unione editrice sarda, p. 14.

Pastori G (1929): Morfologia comparata e struttura istologica dell'organo subcommesurale nei mammiferi in rapporto alle sue possibili funzioni. *Contrib Lab di Psicologia e Biologia dell' Univ Cattolica del S Cuore IV*: 39.

Paturet G (1964): *Traité d'anatomie humaine*. Paris, Masson, vol. IV, p. 589.

Reissner E (1851): *De auris internae formatione. Dissertatio inauguralis*. Dorpat, H. Laakmann.

Reissner E (1853): *Nonnulla de hominis mammaliumque pilis*. Dorpati Livonorum: typ. viduae J. C. Schünmanni et C. Mattieseni.

Reissner E (1854): *Beiträge zur Kenntnis der Haare des Menschen und der Säugethiere*. Breslau, Trewendt und Granier.

Reissner E (1860): Beiträge zur Kenntnis vom Bau des Rückenmarkes von Petromyzon fluvialis. *Arch Anat Physiol*: 545–588.

Sargent PE (1904): The optic reflex apparatus for short circuit transmission of motor reflexes through Reissner's fiber; its morphology, ontogeny, phylogeny and function. *Bull Mus Comp Zool Harvard 45*: 129–258.

Stieda L (1870): Studien über das centrale Nervensystem der Wirbeltiere. *Ztschr Wiss Zool 20*: 386–425.

Stilling B (1859): *Neue Untersuchungen über den Bau des Rückenmarkes*. Cassel, H. Hotop.

Tretjakoff D (1913): Die zentralen Sinnesorgane bei Petromyzon. *Arch mikr Anat 83*: 69–115.

Villeneuve R (1989): *Dictionnaire du Diable*. Paris, Pierre Bordas et fils, p. 7.

If There are "Deep" Cerebellar Nuclei, Where are the "Superficial" Ones?

Since its inception, this column has attempted to provide interesting vignettes on words: their origin, evolution, derivations, and current status or use. In some instances we have discussed words that may have been misused or improperly applied. In the current column we will consider the case of words, actually a term, that is commonly used but in reality was never officially recognized, and, when considered on its own merits, makes little sense. This is the interesting case of the "deep cerebellar nuclei".

Fifteen current textbooks of neuroanatomy or neuroscience were reviewed with a special interest in the cerebellar nuclei. These texts are used in teaching medical, graduate, and undergraduate students and are all published by well-recognized houses. Our survey revealed that eleven of these texts used the phrase "deep cerebellar nuclei" either in the text, illustrations, or in both, when describing the cerebellar nuclei. Three used only the term "cerebellar nuclei" and one used the term "central nuclei" when describing the grey masses in the cerebellum. It would appear from this brief overview, and when looking in the primary literature, that the phrase "deep cerebellar nuclei" is used by many authors. Recent variations on this theme include reference to "cerebellar deep nuclei", "basal cerebellar nuclei", and simply "deep nuclei".

Historically, it is not possible to pinpoint the origin of the most commonly used variant on these terms, "deep cerebellar nuclei". In 1890, Obersteiner described these cell groups as the "central nuclei"; Johnston, in 1906 as the "deep gray masses", while Barker, in 1899 appropriately enough refers to these cell groups by their correct names "... nucleus dentatus ... nuclei fastigi and adjacent masses of grey matter". Around the same period, the great German neuroanatomist Edinger (1900) and the man whom some have called one of the fathers of neurosurgery, Victor Horsely (see Clarke & Horsley, 1905), simply called these structures the "cerebellar nuclei". In the early twentieth, century the great American neuroanatomist C. J. Herrick described these as "deep nuclei" and as "deep gray centers" in his text (Herrick, 1918) and as "deep gray masses" in a neurology laboratory outline co-authored with his student E. C. Crosby (Herrick & Crosby, 1918). As the twentieth century progressed, the term "deep cerebellar nuclei", or one of its variants, became entrenched in the primary literature (Allen, 1924; Dow, 1936, 1938; Carpenter & Stevens, 1957; Earle & Matzke, 1974; Martin et al., 1974; Gould & Graybiel, 1976; Xu and Frazier, 2002) and appeared in some major textbooks (Krieg, 1942; Strong & Elwyn, 1943; Truex & Carpenter, 1969) but not in others (Larsell, 1951; Crosby et al., 1962). It appears that the term "deep cerebellar nuclei" is the descendent of earlier terms that were, in themselves, conceived in error; this is a term that has been propagated without consideration of its legitimacy.

The term "deep cerebellar nuclei" is somewhat nonsensical in that it does not follow the reasoning inherent in the creation of anatomical terms and, indeed, has never been recognized as an official anatomical term. Designating an anatomical part as "deep" (or medial, lateral, etc) requires that it have a "superficial" counterpart; otherwise, why call it "deep"? There are numerous examples of this part/counterpart in any standard textbook of neuroscience. For example, medial geniculate nucleus-lateral geniculate nucleus, medial lemniscus-lateral lemsiscus, anterior horn-posterior horn, medial longitudinal stria-lateral longitudinal stria, superior oliveinferior olive; many other examples abound. In addition, a review of earlier editions of the official international document establishing anatomical terminology (Nomina Anatomica [NA], 1956, 1968, 1983, 1989) and its successor (Terminologia Anatomica [TA], 1998) reveals that the words profundus, profunda or profundum have *never* appeared in relation to the cerebellar nuclei. This supports the view that the term "deep cerebellar nuclei" has never been officially established or recognized by the international body that oversees anatomical terminology.

It is true that the cerebellar nuclei are found deep within the white matter of the cerebellum. The phrase "... the cerebellar nuclei are located deep within the white matter of the cerebellar hemisphere ..." is true, correct, and perfectly acceptable. In this context 'deep' is an adverb that signifies position and does not modify either cerebellar or nuclei. However, in the phrase "deep cerebellar nuclei" deep becomes an adjective that modifies both cerebellar and nuclei and, consequently, becomes a part of the term. Along this same line of reasoning, position in itself does not justify a term. For example, there are numerous structures that are found "deep" within an overall larger entity. The globus pallidus is deep within the cerebral hemisphere, the decussation of the brachium conjunctivum is deep within the mesencephalon, and the centromedian nucleus is deep within the thalamus, yet these structures are never referred to as the 'deep globus pallidus', the 'deep decussation of the brachium conjunctivum', or the 'deep centromedian nucleus'.

A further crack in any defense of the term "deep cerebellar nuclei" is the total absence of any "superficial cerebellar nuclei". To the best of our knowledge, and in the opinion of others who have commented on this topic (Haines & Dietrichs, 2002), there has never been a description of "superficial" cerebellar nuclei either during development or in the adult. It is true that there is a superficial layer in the developing cerebellum called the "external germinal layer" (Altman & Bayer, 1997). However, this layer does not give rise to neurons of the cerebellar nuclei (only to cortical cells) and is a developmental structure only and not retained in the adult.

We return to the beginning and consider the question posed in the title of this column. There are actually four facets to the answer. First, since there are no superficial cerebellar nuclei, there can be no deep cerebellar nuclei; there are only *cerebellar nuclei*. In this respect, the term itself is fundamentally flawed since "deep" cerebellar do not exist. Second, even though this term/phrase has been used in its various incarnations for over 100 years, it has never been universally accepted or standardized. Third, position itself does not justify a direction within the term unless there is a corresponding counterpart; in this case there is not, and has never been, such a counterpart. Fourth, and perhaps most importantly, the international body of neuroanatomical scholars who have, collectively, labored to standardized anatomical terms for over 100 years (Basal Nomina Anatomica, the precursor to NA and now to TA appeared in 1895) have never endorsed this term.

References

Allen WF (1924): Distribution of the fibers originating from the different basal cerebellar nuclei. *J Comp Neurol 36*: 399–439.

Altman J, Bayer SA (1997): *Development of the Cerebellar System in Relation to its Evolution, Structure and Functions.* Boca Raton, CRC Press.

Barker LF (1899): *The Nervous System and its Constituent Neurones.* New York, D. Appleton and Co.

Carpenter MB, Stevens GH (1957): Structural and functional relationships between the deep cerebellar nuclei and the brachium conjunctivum in the rhesus monkey. *J Comp Neurol 107*: 109–163.

Clarke RH, Horsley V (1905): The intrinsic fibers of the cerebellum, its nuclei and its efferent tracts. *Brain 28*: 13–29.

Crosby EC, Humphrey T, Lauer EW (1962): *Correlative Anatomy of the Nervous System.* New York, The MacMillan Co.

Dow RS (1936): The fiber connections of the posterior parts of the cerebellum in the rat and cat. *J Comp Neurol 63*: 527–548.

Dow RS (1938): Efferent connections of the flocculonodular lobe in Macaca mulatta. *J Comp Neurol 68*: 297–305.

Earle AM, Matzke HA (1974): Efferent fibers of the deep cerebellar nuclei in hedgehogs. *J Comp Neurol 154*: 117–132.

Edinger L (1900): *The Anatomy of the Central Nervous System of Man and of Vertebrates in General.* Philadelphia, F.A. Davis Company.

Gould BB, Graybiel AM (1976): Afferents to the cerebellar cortex in the cat: Evidence for an intrinsic pathway leading from the deep nuclei to the cortex. *Brain Res 110*: 601–611.

Haines DE, Dietrichs E (2002): Letter to the editor, Cerebellar terminology. *The Cerebellum 1*: 163–164.

Herrick CJ (1918): *An Introduction to Neurology.* Philadelphia, WB Saunders Company.

Herrick CJ, Crosby EC (1918): *A Laboratory Guide of Neurology.* Philadelphia, W.B. Saunders Co.

Johnston JB (1906): *The Nervous System of Vertebrates.* Philadelphia, P. Blakiston's Son & Co.

Krieg WJS (1942): *Functional Neuroanatomy.* New York, The Blakiston Company.

Larsell O (1951): *Anatomy of the Nervous System.* New York, Appleton-Century-Crofts Inc.

Martin GF, King JS, Dom R (1974): The projections of the deep cerebellar nuclei of the opossum, Didelphis marsupialis virginiana. *J Hirnforsch 15*: 545–573.

Nomina Anatomica (1956): *Nomina Anatomica.* Baltimore, The Williams & Wilkins Co.

Nomina Anatomica (1968): *Nomina Anatomica.* Amsterdam, Excerpta Medica Foundation, 3rd edn.

Nomina Anatomica (1983): *Nomina Anatomica.* Baltimore, Williams & Wilkins, 5th edn.

Nomina Anatomica (1989): *Nomina Anatomica.* Edinburgh, Churchill Livingston, 6th edn.

Obersteiner H (1890): *The Anatomy of the Central Nervous Organs in Health and Disease.* P. Blakiston, Son & Company.

Strong OS, Elwyn A (1943): *Human Neuroanatomy.* Baltimore, The Williams & Wilkins Company.

Terminologia Anatomica (International Anatomical Terminology) (1998): *Terminologia Anatomica.* Stuttgart, Georg Thieme Verlag.

Truex RC, Carpenter MB (1969): *Strong and Elwyn's Human Neuroanatomy.* The Williams & Wilkins Company, 6th edn.

Xu F, Frazier DT (2002): Role of the cerebellar deep nuclei in respiratory modulation. *The Cerebellum 1*: 35–40.

"James Parkinson did not die of his own personal disease ... he died of a stroke" Eponyms: Possessive or Nonpossessive?

Eponyms are terms or phrases that associate the name of a person (or sometimes persons) with a structure, disease, syndrome, stain or other technique or method, space, sign, location such as a city or country (technically a toponym, see Anderson, 1996) or any of a number of other things. There are literally hundreds of eponyms that are commonly used in many different fields (for medicine see Firkin & Whitworth, 1987; Dorlands, 2000; Stedmans, 2000: for neurology see Koehler et al., 2000). This column will not argue for, or against, their use, but will consider the ongoing question of whether they are best expressed as possessive or nonpossessive. Naturally, we will focus on the nervous system.

When discussing eponyms and their use with colleagues, there are usually two views expressed representing opposite ends of a scale: those of the clinician and those of the basic scientist. On one hand, clinicians in general like and use eponyms with impunity. They are convenient, widely recognized by physicians, and in many instances collapse a long complicated scientific phrase into a single, usually short, name followed by a noun (disease, sign, or whatever). To the clinician, with his/her advanced and specialized educational standing, the eponym is perfectly clear. On the other hand, basic scientists use eponyms, but with much less enthusiasm. In some instances the use of eponyms may be discouraged in the basic science years of medical training. This is certainly not from a lack of a full appreciation for their usefulness, but because the eponym, in itself, is quite uninformative: it tells the reader absolutely nothing about the subject under consideration. This kind of eponym was called "éponymes confusionnants" (confusing eponyms) by Cavalerie in 1990. For example, to the nonspecialist which of the following is a neurological syndrome versus a developmental defect affecting the cranium and fingers versus a syndrome of obstruction of the branches of the aortic arch (Achenbach syndrome, Martorell syndrome, Avellis syndrome, Apert syndrome, Oglive syndrome, Kallermann syndrome, Seip syndrome, Thiemann syndrome)? The answers are, in order: the Avellis syndrome is the jugular foramen syndrome, the Apert syndrome is craniosynostosis with syndactyly, and the Martorell syndrome is the aortic arch syndrome. Only after the technical name of the disease, space, syndrome (etc) is learned and mastered does the use of the eponym flow easily.

The title of this column, a paraphrase of a comment made by one of our clinical colleagues, nicely illustrates the dilemma of the possessive versus nonpossessive forms of eponyms. Parkinson's disease (possessive) refers to the disease of Parkinson, as in a disease that was his own, a disease that he had (that he possessed). However, the historical record indicates that James Parkinson died two days after a sudden onset of aphasia and a right-sided hemiplegia (Rose, 2000), both characteristic of a stroke in the dominant (left) cerebral hemisphere. There is no evidence that Parkinson had "his" disease; he certainly did not die from it. Furthermore, if Parkinson did indeed have "his" disease, it is likely that mention of it would appear in the historical record since the mean age of onset is 55 (Rowland, 2000) and Parkinson was 69 at his death. It never was his own personal disease, rather a disease named after him (by Charcot, see Goetz et al., 1995; Rose, 2000) in recognition of his description

There are always exceptions, but they are few. For example, amyotropic lateral sclerosis is legitimately called Lou Gehrig's (possessive) disease in the United States. This famous baseball player actually had, and died of, this disease. In this respect it was his own personal disease. Having said this, it should be noted that some sources (Dorlands, 2000; Stedmans, 2000) use the nonpossessive form. Interestingly enough, amyotrophic lateral sclerosis is commonly known as Charcot's disease (Charcot disease) in Europe (Goetz et al., 1995).

The most ardent advocate of the nonpossessive form of eponyms over the last half century is almost certainly McKusick (1998a, 1998b) who has followed this style since the publication of his book '*Heritable Disorders of Connective Tissue*' (1956). In this early publication, McKusick (1956) used a combination of nonpossessive (Marfan syndrome, Hurler syndrome) and possessive (Paget's disease, Bruch's membrane) forms of the eponym clearly heralding the beginning of a fundamental change of style. A brief comment on the history of McKusicks conversion is noted in McKusick (1998b). Current editions of the American Medical Association Manual of Style (Iverson et al., 1998) and the Council of Biology Editors Style Manual (1994) endorse this approach. The AMA Manual states "...to promote clarity and consistency in scientific writing, we recommend that the possessive form be omitted in eponymous terms" (1998, p. 471). The CBE Manual is a shade more adamant: "It is recommended that the possessive form be eliminated altogether from eponymic terms so that they can be clearly differentiated from true possessives" (1994, p. 97).

In general, there are five rationale to be followed regarding use of the nonpossessive form of the eponym (the first four are summarized from Iverson et al., 1998; McKusick, 1998a). *First*, the possessive form should not be used when the word following the name begins with a 'c', 's', or 'z' as in Hortega cell, Babinski sign, or Zinn zonule. *Second*, the possessive form should not be used when the eponym itself ends in 'ce', 's' or 'z' as in Fordyce disease, Coats disease, or Lermoyez syndrome. McKusick (1998a) notes that this will avoid blatantly incorrect spellings such as 'Grave's disease' or 'Wilm's tumor', and one would never want to call these 'Graves's disease' or 'Wilms's tumor'. *Third*, the possessive form should not be used when two or more names are used in the eponym such as Kluver-Bucy syndrome or the Charcot-Weiss-Baker syndrome. *Fourth*, the possessive form should not be used when the article 'a', 'an' or 'the' appears before the name or full term. However, adding 'the' before the eponym, while not essential (see McKusick, 1998a), may ease the transition to a smoother sounding term; for example 'Weber's syndrome' to 'the Weber syndrome'. The *fifth* suggestion originates from the authors of this column and is a variation on point three above. The possessive form should not be used when the eponym is the name of one person but consists of two, or more, parts, hypenated or not hypenated. For example, the Brown-Sequard syndrome or the Cornelia de Lange syndrome should never be expressed as 'Brown-Sequard's syndrome' or 'Cornelia de Lange's syndrome' for all the same reasons discussed earlier.

Usage of the nonpossessive form of the eponym varies, but is becoming more widely seen in basic science and clinical books in the medical field and is common in dictionaries of eponyms (Firkin & Whitworth, 1987; Olry, 1995). It is certainly appropriate to move in this direction, and perhaps to move a bit more aggressively. McKusick, a scholar of significant note, has been a strong advocate of this approach for many decades, and anyone writing in the medical field (articles, textbooks, etc) should certainly be aware of the fact that the AMA Style Manual clearly recommends the nonpossessive form of eponyms.

In spite of the fact that several new editions of neuroscience books for graduate and/or medical students refer to "Huntington's" disease (or chorea), Huntington died of pneumonia (Bruyn & Bruyn, 2000); it never was his own personal disease!

References

Anderson JB (1996): The language of eponyms. *J Roy College Phys London 30:* 174–177.

Bruyn GW, Bruyn RP (2000): Huntington's chorea. In: Koehler PJ, Bruyn GW, Pearce JMS, eds., *Neurological Eponyms*. New York, Oxford University Press, pp. 330–334.

Cavalerie M (1990): *Analyse critique de la nouvelle terminologie anatomique*. Paris, Thesis.

Council of Biology Editors Style Manual Committee (1994): *Scientific Style and Format: The CBE Manual for Authors, Editors, and Publishers*. Cambridge, Cambridge University Press, pp. 96–97.

Dorland's Illustrated Medical Dictionary (2000): Philadelphia, W.B. Saunders Company, 29th edition.

Firkin BG, Whitworth JA (1987): *Dictionary of Medical Eponyms*. Park Ridge, New Jersey, The Parthenon Publishing Group Inc.

Goetz CG, Bonduelle M, Gelfand T (1995): *Charcot Constructing Neurology*. New York, Oxford University Press, pp. 99–126.

Iverson C, et al. (1998): *American Medical Association Manual of Style*. Philadelphia, Lippincott Williams & Wilkins, pp. 469–472.

Koehler PJ, Bruyn GW, Pearce JMS (2000): *Neurological Eponyms*. New York, Oxford University Press.

McKusick VA (1956): *Heritable Disorders of Connective Tissue*. St. Louis, The C.V. Mosby Company.

McKusick VA (1998a): *Mendelian Inheritance in Man*. Baltimore, The Johns Hopkins University Press, 12th edition, pp. xxvii–lii.

McKusick VA (1998b): On the naming of clinical disorders, with particular reference to eponyms. *Medicine 77*: 1–2.

Olry R (1995): *Dictionary of Anatomical Eponyms*. Stuttgart, Gustav Fischer Verlag.

Rose FC (2000): Parkinson's disease. In: Koehler PJ, Bruyn GW, Pearce JMS, eds., *Neurological Eponyms*. New York, Oxford University Press, pp. 335–342.

Rowland LP (2000): *Merrit's Neurology*. Philadelphia, Lippincott Williams & Wilkins, 10th edition.

Stedmans' Medical Dictionary (2000): Philadelphia, Lippincott Willaims & Wilkins, 27th edition.

Give a Kiss to a Frog and it Will Turn into ... A Neuropeptide: The Genealogy of the Bombesin-Like Family

Neurons have more than one trick up their sleeves. They have indeed many substances at their disposal to express themselves: neurotransmitters (acetylcholine, dopamine, serotonin, ...), neuropeptides (neurotensin, substance P, vasoactive intestinal polypeptide, ...) and even gazeous neuronal messengers (nitric oxide, carbon monoxid, ...). Among neuropeptides, the genealogy of the bombesin family, including bombesin, ranatensin, alytesin, litorin, and phyllolitorin, among others, is worth being summarized in this column. The bombesin family of peptides consists of several molecules which contain essentially homologous C-terminal decapeptides wherein the binding and biological activities reside (Fisher, 1987). Though discovered in the amphibian skin, bombesin and related peptides were subsequently observed in many areas of the central nervous system: hypothalamus, interpeduncular nucleus, tegmental central nucleus, parabrachial dorsal nucleus, solitary nucleus, periaqueductal grey matter, and, to a lesser extent, in the caudate nucleus, cingular gyrus and hippocampus (Panula, 1986; Leonhardt et al., 1987). Bombesin also occurs in paraganglia (Heym & Kummer, 1988).

In 1970, Nakajima and co-workers discovered, in the skin of the American frog *Rana pipiens*, an undecapeptide that displayed an essentially hypertensive action. It was therefore called ranatensin. This substance proved to have the same action on blood pressure in many animal species (dog, rabbit, rat, guinea pig), except in the cat (inactive) and in the monkey (hypertensive) (Geller et al., 1970). Nine years later, ranatensin-like substances were also isolated from the skin of two other frogs, *Rana rugosa* and *Rana catesbeiana*: they were called ranatensin-R and ranatensin-C, respectively (Yasuhara et al., 1979).

Also in 1970, two other peptides were discovered, again in the skin of the frog, but this time in European discoglossid frogs: the first one in *Bombina bombina*, called therefore bombesin, the second in *Alytes obstetricans*, called therefore alytesin (Erspamer et al., 1970). The occurrence of bombesin was not a prerogative of European frogs: three years later it was also isolated from the skin of the Korean frog *Bombina orientalis* (Yasuhara et al., 1973).

In the mid-1970s, Australian frogs join in: the skin of the genus *Litoria aurea* contains a new bombesin-like peptide which is, of course, called litorin (Anastasi et al., 1975, 1977). The same peptide would soon be found in the skin of the myobatrachid frog *Uperoleia rugosa* (Nakajima et al., 1980), and a similar substance, rohdeilitorin, in those of the South American phyllomedusid frog *Phyllomedusa rohdei* (Barra et al., 1985). In 1983, Yasuhara et al. isolated again a new litorin-like peptide;

they referred to it as phyllolitorin as it was isolated from the skin of the frog *Phyllomedusa sauvagei.*

In the last decades, there was a "dramatic explosion in the number of possible neurotransmitters" (Nieuwenhuys, 1985). Most neurotransmitters and neuropeptides were named after either their first and last aminoacids (galanin, owing to the presence of N-terminal glycine and C-terminal alanin amide: Tatemoto et al., 1983), or their function (somatostatin, discovered by virtue of its ability to inhibit growth hormone release from the rat pituitary in vitro: Krulich et al., 1973), or their molecular features (calcitonine gene-related-peptide, expressed in neural tissue by the calcitonin gene: Rosenfeld et al., 1983), or their structural similarities with previously known substances (neuropeptide Y, which shares considerable sequence homology with various pancreatic polypeptides and peptide YY: Tatemoto et al., 1982). The bombesin-like family acknowledges the involvement of frogs of all over the world: it was really worth giving them a kiss!

References

Anastasi A, Erspamer V, Endean R (1975): Aminoacid composition and sequence of litorin, a bombesinlike nonapeptide from the skin of the Australian frog *Litoria aurea. Experientia 31*: 510.

Anastasi A, Montecucchi P, Angelucci F, Erspamer V, Endean R (1977): Glu(Ome)^2-litorin, the second bombesin-like peptide occurring in a methanol extract of the skin of the Australian frog *Litoria aurea. Experientia 33*: 1289.

Barra D, Falconieri Erspamer G, Simmaco M, Bossa F, Melchiorri P, Erspamer V (1985): Rohdei-litorin: A new peptide from the skin of *Phyllomedusa rohdei. FEBS Lett 182*: 53–56.

Erspamer V, Falconieri Erspamer G, Inselvini M, Negri L (1970): Some pharmacological actions of alytesin and bombesin. *J Pharm Pharmacol 22*: 275–276.

Fisher LA (1987): Bombesin. In: Adelman G, ed., *Encyclopedia of Neuroscience.* Boston, Birkhaüser, Vol. 1, pp. 143–144.

Geller RG, Govier WC, Pisano JJ, Tanimura T, Van Clineschmidt B (1970): The action of ranatensin, a new peptide from amphibian skin, on the blood pressure of experimental animals. *Br J Pharmacol 40*: 605–616.

Heym C, Kummer W (1988): Regulatory peptides in paraganglia. *Progr Histochem Cytochem 18(2)*: 23–24.

Krulich L, Dhariwal APS, McCann SM (1973): Stimulatory and inhibitory effects of purified hypothalamic extracts on growth hormone release from rat pituitary in vitro. *Endocrin 83*: 783–790.

Leonhardt H, Krisch B, Zilles K (1987): Transmittersysteme im Zentralnervensystem. In: Leonhardt H, Töndury G, Zilles K, eds., *Rauber/Kopsch Anatomie des Menschen.* Stuttgart, New York, Georg Thieme, Vol. 3 (Nervensystem, Sinnesorgane), p. 493.

Nakajima T, Tanimura T, Pisano JJ (1970): Isolation and structure of a new vasoactive peptide. *Fed Proc 29*: 282.

Nakajima T, Yasuhara T, Erspamer V, Falconieri Erspamer G, Negri L, Endean R (1980): Physalaemin- and bombesin-like peptides in the skin of the Australian leptodactylid frog *Uperoleia rugosa. Chem Pharm Bull 28*: 680–685.

Nieuwenhuys R (1985): *Chemoarchitecture of the Brain.* Berlin, Heidelberg, New York, Tokyo, Springer-Verlag, p. 2.

Panula P (1986): Histochemistry and function of bombesin-like peptides. *Med Biol 64*: 177–192.

Rosenfeld MG, Mermod JJ, Amara SG, Swanson LW, Sawchenko JR, Rivier J, Vale WW, Evans RM (1983): Production of a novel neuropeptide encoded by the calcitonin gene via tissue-specific RNA processing. *Nature (Lond) 304*: 129–135.

Tatemoto K, Carlquist M, Mutt V (1982): Neuropeptide Y. A novel brain peptide with structural similarities to peptide YY and pancreatic polypeptide. *Nature (Lond) 296*: 659–660.

Tatemoto K, Ro"kaeus A, Jo"rnvall H, McDonald T, Mutt V (1983): Galanin. A novel biologically active peptide from procine intestine. *FEBS Lett 164*: 124–128.

Yasuhara T, Hira M, Nakajima T, Yanaihara N, Yanaihara C, Hashimoto T, Sakura N, Tachibana S, Araki K, Bessho M, Yamanaka T (1973): Active peptides on smooth muscle in the skin of *Bombina orientalis* Boulenger and characterization of a new bradykinin analogue. *Chem Pharm Bull 21*: 1388–1391.

Yasuhara T, Ishikawa O, Nakajima T (1979): The studies on the active peptides in the skin of *Rana rugosa*. II. The structure of ranatensin-R, the new ranatensin analogue, and granuliberin-R, the new mast cell degranulating peptide. *Chem Pharm Bull 27*: 492–498.

Yasuhara T, Nakajima T, Nokihara K, Yanaihara C, Yanaihara N, Erspamer V, Falconieri Erspamer G (1983): Two new frog skin peptides, phyllolitorins of the bombesin-ranatensin family from *Phyllomedusa sauvagei*. *Biomed Res 4*: 407–412.

Nomenclature of Persistent Carotid Vertebrobasilar Anastomoses

In the course of their development, the carotid and vertebrobasilar arterial systems are temporarily anastomosed with each other by small arteries which usually disappear from the stage 4 of development (12–14 mm embryos) (Padget, 1948). These vessels (hypoglossal, proatlantal, trigeminal, otic, and cervical intersegmental arteries) may persist in adult. They often coexist with other vascular abnormalities, and may sometimes be responsible for various neurological disorders (see Bracard, 1983, for review).

The *hypoglossal artery* arises from the posterior aspect of the internal carotid artery, usually at the level of the C1-C2 intervertebral space. It passes through the hypoglossal canal and joins the basilar artery (Bracard, 1983, pp. 292–310). It may give rise to the anterior spinal and anterior inferior cerebellar arteries (Resche, 1979; Resche et al., 1980). The first anatomical description of the hypoglossal artery was made in 1889 by Batujeff (who regarded it as a basilar artery arising from the internal carotid artery: Testut, 1905), and the first angiographical observation in 1953 by Dalle Ore and Galan (Resche, 1979). The term hypoglossal artery was coined in 1922 by Oertel (Bracard, 1983), pointing out the fact that this artery, whatever its course might be, always runs through the hypoglossal canal of occipital bone. Buntaro Adachi, the "pivotal figure of vascular anatomy" (Olry & Lellouch, 2003) and his Tokyo colleague Hirakô described this artery in 1928, but seemed not to know about the term coined six years earlier.

The *proatlantal artery* arises from the posterior aspect of the cervical part of the internal carotid artery, at the level of the C2-C3 intervertebral space. It inclines then backwards, passes over the lateral mass of the atlas (it should therefore have been called supra-atlantal artery), enters the cranial cavity by the foramen magnum, and joins the origin of the basilar artery (Bracard, 1983, pp. 311–320). It often gives rise to the occipital artery (Samra et al., 1969; Anderson & Sondheimer, 1976; Pinstein & Gerald, 1976; Legre et al., 1980; Obayashi & Furuse, 1980). The first anatomical description of a proatlantal artery was made by Gottschau in 1885. In 1960, on an angiography Luccarelli and de Ferrari could find a variant of proatlantal artery, that arose from the external carotid artery. This led Lie to acknowledge two types of proatlantal arteries: those arising from the internal carotid artery (which he called intersegmental proatlantal artery) and those arising from the external carotid artery (which he called primitive proatlantal artery) (Lie, 1968).

The first anatomical description of the *trigeminal artery* is to be found in Quain's *Anatomy of the arteries* (1844). It arises from the cavernous part of the internal carotid artery, at the junction of its C4-C5 segments, and passes between the petroclinoid ligament and the apex of the petrous part of the temporal bone. It then follows the medial aspect of the sensory root of the trigeminal nerve (Djindjian et al., 1965), and joins the basilar artery between the origin of the superior and middle cerebellar arteries (Bracard, 1983, pp. 262–285). The trigeminal artery often coexists in cases of hypoplasia of the posterior communicating, vertebral, basilar, and posterior cerebral (P1 segment) arteries. In 1959, Salzmann acknowledged three types of trigeminal arteries, according to the number of arteries injected by carotid angiography.

The *otic artery* is very rare (Altmann, 1947; Kempe & Smith, 1969; Dilenge & Heon, 1974; Wollschlaeger & Wollschlaeger, 1974; Karazawa et al., 1976; Huber, 1977; Tomsick et al., 1979; Reynolds et al., 1980). It arises from the intrapetrous part of the internal carotid artery, leaves the petrous part of the temporal bone via the internal acoustic meatus, and joins the caudal part of the basilar artery (Bracard, 1983, pp. 286–290). Altmann mistook this artery for a remnant of stapedian artery (Altmann, 1947), and Huber coined the term primitive otic artery (Huber, 1977).

Theoretically there might be up to five *cervical intersegmental arteries*. In fact, their persistence proved to be exceptional (Bracard, 1983, pp. 322–323). All the cervical intersegmental arteries were discovered from the late 1960s to the early 1980s: the first one in 1976 by Pinstein and Gerald, and by Murayama in 1981; the second one by Flynn in 1968; and the third one by Parkinson et al. in 1979, but this report remains questioned.

Persistent carotid vertebrobasilar anastomoses were all named after their anatomical or embryonal features: their course through the hypoglossal canal (hypoglossal artery) or through the internal acoustic meatus (otic artery), their relationship to the lateral mass of the atlas (proatlantal artery) or to the sensory root of the trigeminal nerve (trigeminal artery), or their embryonal features at the cervical level (cervical intersegmental arteries).

References

Adachi B (1928): *Das Arteriensystem der Japaner.* Kyoto, Verlag der Kaiserlich-Japanischen Universität zu Tokyo, Vol. 1, p. 119.

Altmann F (1947): Anomalies of the internal carotid artery and its branches. Their embryological and comparative anatomical significance. Report of a new case of persistent stapedial artery in man. *Laryngoscope 57*: 313–339.

Anderson RA, Sondheimer FV (1976): Rare carotid vertebrobasilar anastomoses with notes on the differentiation between proatlantal and hypoglossal arteries. *Neuroradiology 11*: 113–118.

Batujeff N (1889): Eine seltene Arterienanomalie (Ursprung der A. Basilaris aus der A. Carotis interna). *Anat Anz 4*: 282–285.

Bracard S (1983): *Variations des artères cérébrales du normal au pathologique.* Nancy, Thesis.

Dilenge D, Heon M (1974): The internal carotid artery. In: Newton TH, Potts DG, eds., Radiology of the Skull and Brain. Saint-Louis, CV Mosby Co., Vol. 2, pp. 1202–1295.

Djindjian R, Hurth M, Bories J, Brunet P (1965): L'artère trigéminale primitive. Aspects artériographiques et signification à propos de 12 cas. *Presse Méd 73*: 2905–2910.

Flynn RE (1968): External carotid origin of the dominant vertebral artery. Case report. *J Neurosurg 29*: 300–301.

Gottschau M (1885): Zwei seltene Varietäten der Stamme des Aortenbogens. *Arch Anat Entwick Gesch*, 245–252.

Huber G (1977): Die arteria primitiva otica, eine sehr seltene persistierende Primitivarterie. *Fortsch Röntgenst 127*: 350–353.

Karazawa J, Kikuchi H, Furuse S, Sakaki T, Yoshida Y, Ohnishi H (1976): Bilateral persistent carotid basilar anastomosis. *Am J Roentgenol 127*: 1053–1056.

Kempe LG, Smith DR (1969): Trigeminal neuralgia, facial spasm intermedius and glossopharyngeal neuralgia with persistent carotid basilar anastomosis. *J Neurosurg 31*: 445–451.

Legre J, Tapias PL, Nardin JY, Philip E, Perier E (1980): Anastomose intersegmentaire carotide externe-vertébrale d'origine embryonnaire. Problèmes nosologiques posés par l'artère proatlantale. *J Neuroradiology 7*: 97–104.

Lie TA (1968): *Congenital Anomalies of the Carotid Arteries*. Amsterdam, Excerpta Medica Foundation, 1968.

Lucarelli S, De Ferrari V (1960): Studio clinicoradiologico di un caso di origine anormala (dall'a carotide externa) dell'arteria vertebrale sinistra. *Radiol Med (Torino) 46*: 963–974.

Murayama K (1981): A case of persistent primitive first cervical intersegmental artery (proatlantal artery II). *Neuroradiology 22*: 47–56.

Obayashi T, Furuse M (1980): The proatlantal intersegmental artery. A case report and review of the literature. *Arch Neurol 37*: 387–389.

Olry R, Lellouch A (2003): Le Système artériel du Japonais de Buntaro Adachi: un sens nouveau à l'anatomie comparée. *Hist Sci Med 37* (1): 89–94.

Padget DH (1948): The development of the cranial arteries in the human embryo. *Contr Embryol Carneg Inst 32*: 205–261.

Parkinson D, Reddy V, Ross RT (1979): Congenital anastomosis between the vertebral artery and internal carotid artery in the neck. *J Neurosurg 51*: 697–699.

Pinstein ML, Gerald B (1976): Anomalous communication of the external carotid and vertebral arteries. Persistence of the proatlantal artery. *Radiology 118*: 626.

Quain R (1844): *The anatomy of the arteries of the human body and its application to pathology and operative surgery, with a series of lithographic drawings. The drawings from nature and on stone, by Joseph Maclise*. London, Taylor and Walton.

Resche I (1979): *L'artère hypoglosse*. Nantes, Thesis.

Resche I, Resche-Perrin I, Robert R, De Kersaint-Gilly A, Duveau D, Lajat Y (1980): L'artère hypoglosse. Rapport d'un nouveau cas. Revue de la littérature. *J Neuroradiol 7*: 27–43.

Reynolds AF, Stovring J, Turner PJ (1980): Persistent otic artery. *Surg Neurol 13*: 115–117.

Salzmann GF (1959): Patent trigeminal artery studied by cerebral angiography. *Acta Radiol (Stockholm) 51*: 329–336.

Samra K, Scoville WB, Yaghmai M (1969): Anastomosis of carotid and basilar arteries. Persistent primitive trigeminal artery and hypoglossal artery. Report of two cases. *J Neurosurg 30*: 622–625.

Testut L (1905): *Traité d'anatomie humaine*. Paris, Octave Doin, Vol. 2, 5th edition, p. 158.

Tomsick TA, Lukin RR, Chambers AA (1979): Persistent trigeminal artery: unusual associated abnormalities. *Neuroradiology 17*: 253–257.

Wollschlaeger G, Wollschlaeger PB (1974): The circle of Willis. In: Newton TH, Potts DG, eds., Radiology of the Skull and Brain. Saint-Louis, CV Mosby Co., Vol. 2, pp. 1171–1201.

Interthalamic Adhesion: Scruples About Calling a Spade a Spade?

The medial surface of the thalamus is usually connected to the opposite thalamus by a flat, grey interthalamic adhesion behind the interventricular foramen; its anteroposterior dimension is on average about 1cm and it is sometimes multiple, occasionally absent, and contains neurons, some of their axons crossing the midline, though many recurving back from this (Williams et al., 1995). It may be lamellar, arciform, prismatic, and even sometimes double, especially in women (see Viller [1887] for review). Its functional aspect has always been regarded as being of minor importance. As far back as in 1887, Viller concluded his study as follows: "[c'est un] vestige ancestral qui n'a aucune signification fonctionnelle" ([it is an] ancestral remnant which has no functional meaning" (p. 57). Exactly a century later, nothing has changed: "Funktionell scheint sie bedeutungslos zu zein" (it seems to be functionally meaningless) (Töndury & Kubik, 1987).

The interthalamic adhesion was discovered in 1719 by the famous Italian anatomist Giovanni Battista Morgagni, who called it *transversa lamina cinerea* (transverse ash-grey lamina [Morgagni, 1719]). Justus Gotffried Gunz contended with him for this discovery. We could actually find a publication of Gunz devoted to the anatomy of the brain, in which he described the *tubercula thalamorum* (thalamic tubercle), but this publication is dated 1750; Morgagni must therefore be regarded as the first anatomist to have described the interthalamic adhesion. Anatomists of the second half of the eighteenth century only went on pointing out this formation, like Jacques-Bénigne Winslow did when he wrote: "elles [les couches optiques] sont réellement unies . . .par la vraie continuation de la substance blanchâtre de leur convexité" (they [the thalami] are really united . . .by the true continuation of the whitish substance of their convexity) (Winslow, 1752). Until the mid-nineteenth century, this formation does not seem to have received any name (Bichat, 1819; Bayle, 1845).

The interthalamic adhesion was then described as, and called, a *mass*. In 1853, the French anatomist Alexandre Jamain refered to this formation as the "masse grise du troisième ventricule" (grey mass of the third ventricle) (Jamain, 1853). The term used later focused on its relationship to both thalami: *massa intermedia* (intermediate mass) (de Terra, 1913; Walker, 1938; Strong & Elwyn, 1943; Ranson, 1943), a term that has been kept by the first two international anatomical nomenclatures (Baseler and Jenaer Nomina Anatomica [Donath, 1960]). As it is very easily torn up during dissection, it was sometimes called *massa molis* (soft mass) (de Terra, 1913).

Meanwhile the term *commissure* appeared, which logically implies that nerve fibres cross the midline. In other words, this term should not have been coined before it became possible to prove nerve fibres' existence. According to Viller (1887, p. 34), Ludovic Hirschfeld, in the 1853 edition of his famous *Traité et iconographie du système nerveux*, is the very first to have assumed the presence of commissural fibres in the interthalamic adhesion. This commissure was called either *media* (Merkel, 1888; Obersteiner, 1893; de Terra, 1913), or *mollis* (Cruveilhier, 1871; Merkel, 1888; Obersteiner, 1893; Beaunis & Bouchard, 1894), or *interthalamic* (Walker, 1938), or *grey* (Cruveilhier, 1871; Féré, 1886; Beaunis & Bouchard, 1894; Poirier & Charpy, 1901; Testut, 1905; Cossa and Paillas, 1944).

In the 1880s, Marchi and Tenchini had made thorough studies on the interthalamic adhesion, and could conclude that it contains commissural fibres, but that it does not contain any nervous cell. This second assertion was recently proven wrong (Malobabic et al., 1990). In 1887, Viller denied their first assertion: "nous croyons que le terme de commissure est impropre" (we think that the term commissure is inappropriate). He therefore proposed the terms "soudure" (soldering), "coalescence" (coalescence), or "trabécule" (trabecula) (Viller, 1887, p. 56).

James Couper Brash did not want to settle on one of these earlier terms. He opted prudently for the term *interthalamic connexus,* which means "having a connection with something else" (Chatelain, 1962), and therefore did not restrict himself to any of these previous terms (Brash, 1951). The Terminologia Anatomica joined Brash in this approach, refused to commit itself, and ratified the term *Adhesio interthalamica* (1998), though commissural fibres have been proved to occur in it (Williams et al., 1995).

In 1889, the Portuguese anatomist Macedo presented to the *Congrès international d'anthropologie criminelle de Paris* the results of his research. He studied 215 brains and could observe the lack of interthalamic adhesion in 22.4% of men and 13.5% of women. Clinical correlations led him to conclude that "la caractéristique dominante des individus privés de commissure, c'est de relever dans leurs actes psychiques une singulière précipitation, accompagnée d'une certaine désharmonie entre les impressions internes et externes" (the prevailing feature of people deprived of commissure is to present in their psychical acts a remarkable precipitation, joined to a certain dysharmony between internal and external feelings) (Macedo, 1889). As usual in the history of science, a recently discovered formation received a name and was regarded as being involved in human behaviour, before being somewhat understood.

In the modern era, the terms *interthalamic adhesion* and *interthalamic mass* are commonly used, and frequently are considered interchangeable. In fact, these are two terms in the brain that are also frequently used in their Latin forms. The results of Macedo (1889) are still in vogue; in modern neurobiology/neuroscience courses it is taught that the interthalamic adhesion (or mass) is not present in about 20% of brains. But in contrast to the suggestion of Macedo, there is no known neurological deficit that is correlated with the absence of this structure in contemporary thinking. Then again, the future may modify this view.

References

Bayle ALJ (1845): *Traité élémentaire d'anatomie, ou description succincte des organes et des éléments organiques qui composent le corps humain.* Paris, Méquignon-Marvis Fils, p. 289.

Beaunis H, Bouchard A (1894) *Nouveaux éléments d'anatomie descriptive et d'embryologie*. Paris, J-B. Baillière et Fils, 5th edition, p. 591.

Bichat X (1819): *Traité d'anatomie descriptive*. Paris, J. A. Brosson, Gabon, new edition, vol. 3, p. 85.

Brash JC (1951): *Cunningham's text-book of anatomy*. London, Oxford University Press, 9th edition, p. 942.

Chatelain E (1962): *Dictionnaire Français-Latin*. Paris, Librairie Hachette, p. 294.

Cossa P, Paillas JE (1944): *Anatomie des centre nerveux*. Paris, Amédée Legrand & Jean Bertrand, p. 227.

Cruveilhier J (1871): *Traité d'anatomie descriptive*. Paris, P. Asselin, 4th edition, vol. 3, p. 430.

Donath T (1960): *Erlüterndes anatomisches Wörterbuch. Vergeleichende Übersicht der Baseler, Jenaer und Pariser Nomenklaturen, gruppiert nach Organen*. Terra Budapest, Verlag Medicina Budapest, p. 205.

Féré C (1886): *Traité élémentaire d'anatomie médicale du système nerveux*. Paris, A. Delahaye et Lecrosnier, p. 160.

Gunz JG (1750): *Prolusio observationes anatomicas de cerebro continens prima (-altera) exercitationibus splanchnologicis . . . in cadavere foeminae instituendis*. Lipsiae.

Jamain A (1853): *Nouveau traité élémentaire d'anatomie descriptive et de préparations anatomiques*. Paris, Germer Baillière, p. 700.

Macedo (1889): *De l'encéphale humain avec et sans commissure grise*. Congrès International d'Anthropologie criminelle, Paris, 1889.

Malobabic S, Puskas L, Vujaskovic G (1990): Golgi morphology of the neurons in frontal sections of human interthalamic adhesion. *Acta Anat (Basel) 139 (3)*: 234–238.

Merkel F (1888): *Henle's Grundriss der Anatomie des Menschen*. Braunschweig, Friedrich Vieweg und Sohn, 3rd edition, vol. 1 (Text), p. 372.

Morgagni GB (1719): *Adversaria anatomica Sexta*. Patavii: Excudebat Josephus Cominus.

Obersteiner H (1893): *Anatomie des centres nerveux. Guide pour l'étude de leur structure à l'état normal et pathologique*. Paris, Georges Carré, p. 425.

Poirier P, Charpy A (1901): *Traité d'anatomie humaine*. Paris, Masson et Cie, 2nd edition, vol. 3, p. 265.

Ranson SW (1943): *The anatomy of the nervous system from the standpoint of development and function*. Philadelphia and London, W.B. Saunders Company, 7th edition, p. 216.

Strong OS, Elwyn A (1943): *Human neuroanatomy*. Baltimore, The Wiliams & Wilkins Company, p. 278.

Terminologia Anatomica. International Anatomical Terminology (1998): Stuttgart & New York, Georg Thieme Verlag.

Terra P de (1913): *Vademecum anatomicum. Kritisch-etymologisches Wörterbuch der systematischen Anatomie. Mit besonderer Berücksichtigung der Synonymen*. Jena: Gustav Fischer, p. 265.

Testut L (1905): *Traité d'anatomie humaine*. Paris, Octave Doin, 5th edition, vol. 2, pp. 762–763.

Töndury G, Kubik St (1987): Gestalt und Gliederung des Gehirns. In: Leonhardt H, Töndury G, Zilles K, eds. *Rauber/Kopsch Anatomie des Menschen, vol. 3 (Nervensystem, Sinnesorgane)*. Stuttgart, New York, Georg Thieme, p. 157.

Viller R (1887): *Recherches anatomiques sur la commissure grise*. Nancy: Imprimerie Nancéenne.

Walker AE (1938): *The Primate Thalamus*. Chicago, Illinois, The University of Chicago Press, p. 29.

Williams PL, Bannister LH, Berry MM, Collins P, Dyson M, Dussek JE, Ferguson MWJ (1995): *Gray's anatomy. The anatomical basis of medicine and surgery*. New York, Edinburgh, London, Tokyo, Madrid, and Melbourne, Churchill Livingstone, 38th ed., p. 1082.

Winslow JB (1752): *Exposition anatomique de la structure du corps humain. Nouvelle édition*. Amsterdam, Emanuel Tourneisen, vol. 4, p. 158.

Herophilus' Press, Torcular and Confluens Sinuum: A Triple Mistake

The term confluence of sinuses, in modern parlance, "refers to the dilated posterior end of the superior sagittal sinus, to one side (usually right) of the internal occipital protuberance, where it turns to become a transverse sinus. It also connects with the occipital and contralateral transverse sinus" (Williams et al., 1995). Beginning in centuries past, and as time went by, the confluence of sinuses was called Herophilus' press, torcular, torcular herophili, sinus confluens, or fourth sinus.

Did Herophilus of Chalcedon (c.355–c.280 B.C.) actually describe the confluence of sinuses, and did he refer to it as a press? Unfortunately, "there are no surviving books by the chief Alexandrians who wrote on anatomy; the work of Herophilus…is known because Galen and others discussed and criticized it" (Roberts and Tomlinson, 1992). We must therefore rely on Galen when he ascribed the discovery of this formation to the most famous pupil of Praxagoras of Cos (Galen, 1576). The term actually coined by Herophilus was *lénos*, meaning *tank*, broadly speaking. Much later, the meaning of this word changed and it was credited as referring more specifically to a wine press. The fact that this transposition of meaning was made literally hundreds of years after Herophilus' death clearly indicates that he could not have coined this term during his lifetime (Longet, 1842). This mistake appeared early in the work of famous historians of medicine such as Lauth, and more recently in that of Bariéty and Coury, who wrote that Herophilus compared the confluence of sinuses with a wine press (Lauth, 1815; Bariéty and Coury, 1963).

The Latin term *torcular* means *wine press* or *press room* (Joubert, 1738; Chatelain, 1962). It is also appropriate to note that this relates to the word *torqueo* (from the French) which means *to twist*. It was used by many anatomists from the early seventeenth century (Dulaurens, 1605) to the mid-eighteenth century (Heister, 1719; Winslow, 1752). In the twelfth edition of his *Collected Works*, the celebrated French surgeon Ambroise Paré wrote that the confluence of sinuses was called torcular "parce que d'icelui est exprimé le sang qui nourrit le cerveau" ("for the blood supplying the brain is expressed out of it") (Paré, 1664). However, some anatomists did not even acknowledge the existence of this cavity (Verheyen, 1710; Morgagni, 1741; Sappey, 1869), while others reserved the word *press* to describe the superior sagittal sinus (Riolan, 1672) or the straight sinus (Verdier, 1752). In the 1830s, the term *torcular* gave rise to the adjectives *torcularian* and *atorcu-*

larian, depending on whether the sinuses open into the confluence (superior sagittal, inferior sagittal, straight, transverse, and occipital sinuses, which are called torcularian) or not (the other sinuses, which are called atorcularian) (Broc, n.d.). Fortunately, neither of these terms has survived in modern usage.

The current term *confluence of sinuses* was coined by Xavier Bichat in the early nineteenth century: "cet espace, de forme irrégulière, n'appartient proprement à aucun sinus...Je la nomme confluent des sinus...On sait que les anciens la nommaient pressoir d'Hérophile" ("this space, of irregular shape, does not really belong to any sinus...I call it confluence of sinuses...We know that the ancients referred to it as Herophilus' press") (Bichat, 1819).

The term *fourth sinus* was a synonym for what is currently called the straight sinus, the first one being the superior sagittal sinus, and the second and third ones being the transverse sinuses (Verheyen, 1710). From the late eighteenth century, the term *fourth sinus* seems to have faded into oblivion: we could not find it after 1752 (Winslow, 1752; Verdier, 1752).

To our knowledge, J. Aubry is the very first anatomist to have pointed out the unsuitability of both terms *press* and *confluence of sinuses*. In the article "Dure-mère" in the monumental *Dictionnaire Encyclopédique des Sciences Médicales*, directed by Dechambre and Lereboullet from 1864 to 1889, he wrote:

> La première dénomination est impropre, puisqu'il n'y a en ce point aucune pression des colonnes sanguines les unes sur les autres. Il en est de même de celle de Confluent des sinus qui tend à faire croire que dans tous les sinus le sang marche vers la protubérance occipitale interne, même dans les sinus latéraux, quand, au contraire, ceux-ci portent le liquide vers le trou déchiré postérieur. (The first name is incorrect, for there is at this point no pressure of the blood columns from one sinus onto another. It is the same for the term confluence of sinuses, which leads one to believe that in all sinuses the blood makes its way toward the internal occipital protuberance, even in transverse sinuses, whereas on the contrary, these bring the blood to the jugular foramen). (Aubry, cited in Dumont, 1894).

In the same time frame, the term *Sinus confluens* was also criticized by Joseph Hyrtl, who wrote: "Ein Sinus kann nicht zusammenlaufen (*confluere*), aber mehrere können es; deshalb ist *Sinus confluens* factisch unmöglich" ("a sinus cannot converge (*confluere*), but several sinuses can do it; that is why *Sinus confluens* actually is impossible). However, he regarded the term *confluence of sinuses* as accurate: "*Confluens sinuum* dagegen der Sache ganz entsprechend" ("when *Confluens sinuum* in comparison is an entirely suitable thing) (Hyrtl, 1880).

Since the first edition (Basler Nomina Anatomica in 1895) of the internationally ratified anatomical terminology document (currently Terminologia Anatomica, 1998), the term *Confluens sinuum* has been repeatedly reaffirmed, that is, the confluence of sinuses, a term that was coined by the French anatomist Xavier Bichat. The specific opinions of Aubry have largely faded into obscurity and are rarely noted by historians. However, his intriguing views, coupled with those of later investigators such as Hyrtl, gave rise to a more contemporary term that has withstood the test of the time.

References

Bariéty M, Coury C (1963): *Histoire de la médecine*. Paris: Fayard. 146.
Basler Nomina Anatomica (1895): Basel, Switzerland.

Bichat X (1819): *Traité d'anatomie descriptive*, Nouvelle edition, Vol. 4. Paris, J.A. Brosson et Gabon. 587–89.

Broc PP (n.d): *Traité complet d'anatomie descriptive et raisonnée*, Vol. 3. Paris: Just Rouvier. 424–30.

Chatelain E (1962): *Dictionnaire français-latin*. Paris, Hachette. 1103.

Dulaurens A (1605): *Historia anatomica humani corporis partes*. Lugduni, Apud Horatium Cardon. 765.

Dumont J (1894): *Les Sinus postérieurs de la Dure-Mère et le Pressoir d'Hérophile chez l'homme*. Nancy, A. Voirin et L. Kreis. 16–17.

Galen (1576): *Opera quae extant opera in Latinum sermonem conversa*, Cap. VI, Venetiis, Apud Juntas.

Heister L (1719): Compendium anatomicum totam rem anatomicam brevissime complectens. Edition altera. Altorfi & Norimbergae. In Bibliopolio Kohlesiano et Adolphiano. 109.

Hyrtl J (1880): *Onomatologia anatomica. Geschichte und Kritik der anatomischen Sprache der Gegenwart, mit besonderer Berücksichtigung ihrer Barbarismen, Widersinnigkeiten, Tropen, und grammatikalischen Fehler*. Wien: Wilhelm Braumüller. 144–45.

Joubert J (1738): *Dictionnaire françois et latin, tiré des auteurs originaux et classiques de l'une et l'autre langue*. Lyon: Declaustre. 916.

Lauth T (1815): *Histoire de l'anatomie*, Vol. 1. Strasbourg, F.G. Levrault . 133.

Longet FA (1842): *Anatomie et physiologie du système nerveux de l'homme et des animaux vertébrés contenant des observations pathologiques relatives au système nerveux et des expériences sur les animaux des classes supérieures*, Vol. 1. Paris, Fortin et Masson. 158–60.

Morgagni GB (1741): *Adversaria anatomica VI*. Lugduni-Batavorum, Apud Johannem Arnoldum Langerak.

Paré A (1664): *Les Oeuvres d'Ambroise Paré*. Lyon: Ian Grégoire. 108.

Riolan J (1672): *Manuel anatomique et pathologique, ou abrégé de toute l'anatomie, et des usages que l'on en peut tirer pour la connaissance, & pour la guérison des maladies. Nouvelle édition*. Lyon, Antoine Laurent. 383.

Roberts KB, Tomlinson JDW (1992): *The Fabric of the Body. European Traditions of Anatomical Illustration*. Oxford: Clarendon Press. 14.

Sappey PC (1869): *Traité d'anatomie descriptive*, Second edition, Vol. 1. Paris, Adrien Delahaye. 716.

Terminologia Anatomica (1998): Stuttgart and New York, Thieme.

Verdier C (1752): *Abrégé de l'anatomie du corps humain, où l'on donne une description courte et exacte des parties qui le composent, avec leurs usages. Nouvelle edition*, Vol. 2. Bruxelles, Jean Léonard. 269.

Verheyen P (1710): *Corporis humani anatomiae*, Vol. 1. Bruxellis, Apud Fratres t'Serstevens. 214.

Williams PL, Bannister LH, Berry MM, Collins P, Dyson M, Dussek JE, Ferguson MWJ (1995): *Gray's Anatomy. The anatomical basis of medicine and surgery*, 38th edition. New York, Churchill Livingstone.

Winslow JB (1752): *Exposition anatomique de la structure du corps humain. Nouvelle edition*, Vol. 4. Amsterdam, Emanuel Tourneisen. 140.

From Dante Alighieri's First Circle To Paul Donald MacLean's Limbic System

In 1314, at the age of forty-nine, the Italian poet and son of an exchange broker Dante Alighieri published his *Inferno*, which contains one of the most impressive descriptions in existence of limbo (Lewis, 2002). In 1952, at the age of thirty-nine, the American neuroscientist and son of a Presbyterian minister Paul Donald MacLean coined the term *limbic system* to refer to some components of the central nervous system. It took six hundred and thirty-eight years to provide a semantic link between the gates of hell and a part of the brain.

The term limbic system, sometimes regarded as synonymous with *rhinencephalon* (Olry and Haines, 1997) refers to different cortical and subcortical regions of the brain that are believed to have an unitary function related to emotion, memory, and identity (MacLean and Guyot, 1990). The anatomical definition of this system, though far from being univocal (Olry and Nicolay, 1994), usually includes the olfactory pathways (olfactory bulb, tract, and cortex) and the limbic lobe (hippocampal formation, cingulate gyrus, fornix, septum pellucidum, amygdaloid body, etc.) (Williams et al., 1995). We don't pretend to give an exhaustive list of limbic components for, at the present time, there are over one thousand terms refering to the differents parts of the limbic system.

Although the terms limbic system and rhinencephalon were historically equated, in modern terminology the term rhinencephalon has been abandoned (FICAT, 1998). This is due to the fact that many of the structures considered as part of the rhinencephalon (« *nose brain* » often used as « *smell brain* » - that part of the brain related to smell/olfaction) have no direct (or in some case even indirect) relation to olfactory function. In fact, these non-olfactory structures are now associated with regions of the brain with which they are functionally related. However, the terms limbic lobe and limbic system not only survive, but are quite appropriate in their modern usage.

Dante Alighieri subdivided his *Inferno* into nine circles descending to the center of the earth and gradually becoming smaller (Mazzoni, 1967). Limbo, the first circle, was described as a «valle d'abisso dolorosa che 'ntrono accoglie d'infiniti guai. Oscura e profonda era e nebulosa [painful valley of depth which receives a crash of eternal moans. Dark, deep, and misty] » (Dante, 1992). It was devoted to virtuous nonchristened spirits. The eight following concentric circles were concerned with various carnal sins and their punishment.

The Latin term *limbus* means border, edge, and, more specifically, *selvedge* (Joubert, 1738; Quicherat, 1962). It was so widely used in anatomy that there are at least sixteen limbus/limbi in human anatomy (de Terra, 1913), but its first apperance in neuroanatomy seems to go back to the second half of the seventeenth century. In 1677 the Danish anatomist Thomas Bartholin ascribed the term *Limbus* to a part of the lateral ventricles of the brain (Bartholin, 1677). Unfortunately, the plate depicting this region of the brain is uninterpretable, and it is not possible to determine what Bartholin meant, or was identifying, when he used this term in relation to the ventricular system. Exactly two centuries later, the French anatomist, neurologist, and anthropologist Paul Broca laid the foundation for the current limbic system when he called the ring formed by the cingulate and parahippocampal gyri the *great limbic lobe* (le grand lobe limbique) (Broca, 1877). From that time on, the meaning of the adjective *limbic* varied from author to author (Stefan, 1975). In 1881, Gustav Schwalbe enlarged the definition of great limbic lobe by including the hippocampus, the fornix, the septum pellucidum and the corpus callosum; his limbic lobe was then composed of two concentric rings, external and internal marginal gyri, respectively (Schwalbe, 1881). Emil Zuckerkandl also described this region as composed by two concentric rings, which he called *internal* and *external marginal arches* (Zuckerkandl, 1887). In 1923, Maurice Mutel classed his limbic convolution as *Broca's limbic lobe*, and described a secondary cortical limbus in its concavity, formed by the band of Giacomini (Giacomini, 1884), the dentate gyrus, the longitudinal striae or Lancisi's tracts (Lancisi, 1713), and the fasciola cinerea (Mutel, 1923). In 1928, Raoul Anthony restricted the adjective limbic to the posterior part (pars limbica) of the rhinencephalon, excluding therefore the olfactory apparatus (Anthony, 1928). Finally, Paul Donald MacLean coined the term *limbic system* in 1952 to refer to what he had called visceral brain barely three years before (MacLean, 1949; 1952). In this respect, MacLean ushered in a contemporary concept by introducing the idea of a system, and the implications of integrated function, rather than just a set of structures.

Whether it belongs to theology or to neuroanatomy, the term limbus always applies to a ring or a series of concentric rings (i.e., Dante Alighieri's first circle, Broca's limbic lobe, Schwalbe's external and internal marginal gyri, Zuckerkandl's external and internal marginal arches, and Mutel's limbic convolution and secondary limbic cortex). Etymologically, this ring should be the border of something. It remains to be seen the border of what....

The French neurobiologist Jean-Didier Vincent, within the limits of science and on the edge of spirituality, may have answered this question in his 1986 *Biologie des Passions*: « Comme les limbes de la mythologie chrétienne, le système limbique est l'intermédiaire entre le ciel néo-cortical et l'enfer reptilien [Like limbo of Christian mythology, the limbic system is the link between the neocortical sky and the reptilian hell] » (Vincent, 1986). Why not, but provided that the neocortex actually is the Holy Land on the one hand, and the striatum and reticular formation Hades on the other hand. A hypothesis far from being supported—but one that Paul Donald MacLean would most probably find very interesting.

References

Anthony R (1928): *Leçons sur le cerveau (cours d'anatomie comparée du Muséum)*. Paris: Octave Doin. 162–63.

Bartholin T (1677) : *Anatome quatrum renovata*. Lugduni: *Sumpt. Joan. Ant. Huguetan, & Soc*; 492 and Plate VII, 495.

Broca P (1877): Sur la circonvolution limbique et la scissure limbique. *Bull Soc Anthrop 12*: 646–57.

Dante (1992): *La divine comédie. L'Enfer*. [1314]. Paris: Flammarion, Song 4.

Federative International Committee on Anatomical Terminology (FICAT) (1998): *Terminologia Anatomica - International Anatomical Terminology*. Stuttgart, New York: Thieme. 124–32.

Giacomini C (1884): *Guida allo studio delle Circonvoluzioni Cerebrali dell'uomo*, 2nd edition. Torino: Ermanno Loescher. 142.

Joubert J (1738): *Dictionnaire françois et latin*. Lyon: Louis et Henry Declaustre. 163.

Lancisi GM (1713): *Dissertationes II. De physiognomia. De sede cogitantis animae*. In G.Fantoni, Observationes anatomico-medicae, Venetiis.

Lewis RWB (2002): *Dante*. Montréal: Fides.

MacLean PD (1949): Psychosomatic disease and the visceral brain. Recent developments bearing on the Papez theory of emotion. *Psychosom Med 11*: 338–353.

MacLean PD (1952): Some psychiatric implications of physiological studies on frontotemporal portion of limbic system (visceral brain). *Electroenceph Clin Neurophysiol 4*: 407–18.

MacLean PD, Guyot R (1990): *Les trois cerveaux de l'homme. Trois cerveaux hérités de l'évolution coexistent difficilement sous le crâne humain*. Paris: Robert Laffont. 65–66.

Mazzoni F (1967): *Dante*. In Encyclopaedia Britannica, Chicago, London, Toronto, Geneva, Sydney, Tokyo, Manila: William Benton, Publisher Vol. 7. 59–64.

Mutel M (1923): *Études morphologiques sur le rhinencéphale de l'homme et des mammifères*. Nancy: A. Humblot et Cie. 105–128.

Olry R, Haines DE (1997): Rhinencephalon: a brain for the nose?. *J Hist Neurosci 6(2)*: 217–18.

Olry R, Nicolay X (1994): De Paul Broca à la potentiation à long terme: les aléas de l'affrmation d'une identité limbique. *Hist Sci Med 28(3)*: 199–203.

Quicherat L (1962): *Dictionnaire français-latin*. Paris: Hachette. 176.

Schwalbe G (1881): *Lehrbuch der Neurologie*. Erlangen: E. Besold.

Stephan H (1975): *Allocortex.*, In Handbuch der mikroskopischen Anatomie de Menschen, Bargmann, W, ed., Vol. 4, Part 9. Berlin, Heidelberg, New York: Springer-Verlag. 868–70.

Terra P de (1913): *Vademedum anatomicum. Kritisch-etymologisches Wörterbuch der systematischen Anatomie. Mit besonderer Berücksichtigung der Synonymen*. Jena: Gustav Fischer. 247–48.

Vincent JD (1986): *Biologie des passions*. Paris: Odile Jacob. 134.

Williams PL, Bannister LH, Berry MM, Collins P, Dyson M, Dussek JE, Ferguson MWJ (1995): *Gray's Anatomy. The anatomical basis of medicine and surgery*, 38th edition. New York, Edinburgh, London, Tokyo, Madrid, and, Melbourne: Churchill Livingstone. 1115–41.

Zuckerkandl E (1887): *Über das Riechzentrum*. Stuttgart: F. Enke.

Elpenor's Syndrome: The Link Between One of Ulysses' Companions and the Tenth President of the Third French Republic

January 17, 1920, Paul Deschanel, at the age of sixty-four, was elected the tenth president of the third French Republic by 734 votes against 130, thus fulfilling the ambition of his life (Chastenet de Castaing, 1967). Unfortunately, this ambition will hang fire in less than one year, and the name of Paul Deschanel will be much more remembered by psychiatrists than by the majority of his constituents.

Four months after his election, on Sunday May 23, he left Paris on a train that went to Montbrison, where the President would dedicate a monument to the memory of the aviator Reymond who was killed during the first World War. Around midnight, about twelve kilometers before Montargis, Deschanel fell out of the window of his compartment. Only slightly hurt, he walked then along the track, wearing only his pajamas, and met André Radeau, the gatekeeper of the grade crossing number 79. Paul Deschanel, bloody face and haggard, introduced himself to the gatekeeper in these terms, "I am the President of the Republic and I fell off the train" (Lesueur, 1976). Of course, André Radeau found that hard to believe. He thought he was dealing with an alcoholic and brought him to Gustave Dariot, another gatekeeper, where the would-be president would receive first aid administrated by Dr Guillaumont. On May 24, around 7 am, Deschanel told subprefect Louis Lesueur who just arrived in a mad rush "I have a complete gap in memory between the moment I opened the door of my compartment and the moment I awoke here" (Lesueur, 1976). President Paul Deschanel, who had taken hypnotic drugs (50 centigrams of Trional) before travelling by night (Dérobert, 1974) had been just struck down by a strange and very rare syndrome, which was soon to be called Elpenor's syndrome (Bilikiewicz and Leszczynski, 1966).

Elpenor's syndrome belongs to parasomnias (Viot-Blanc, 2000). It is characterized by a "state of half-consciousness with disorientation in space and half-automatic movements occurring, on waking, in people who, shortly before, went to sleep in an unusual place after having drunk too much or having taken hypnotic drugs. This state may lead to a fall or to misdemeanours" (Garnier et al., 2000). The term was coined by the French psychiatrist Logre in the mid-twentieth century (Logre, 1961) and, surprisingly, we could not find any synonym in psychiatric literature since that time (Michaux, 1965; Marchais, 1970;

Porot, 1996; Kapsambelis, 1997; Juillet, 2000; Viot-Blanc, 2000; Garnier et al., 2000; Postel, 2003).

Like other medical terms (Empedocles' syndrome, hermaphroditism, Oedipus complex, and Proteus' syndrome, among others), Elpenor's syndrome refers to mythology. Homer's celebrated work, *The Odyssey*, relates the long and thrilling journey of Ulysses and his companions from Troy to Ithaca (Bérard, 1955). During this sea voyage, Ulysses visited the island of Circe, a famous sorceress who was able to change human beings into the forms of wolves, lions, or swines. He lived with her for a year, and when he decided to leave, Circe explained to him how to sail to the House of Hades in order to learn his fate from the prophet Teiresias. One of Ulysses's companions, the young Elpenor, was sleeping, dead drunk, on the roof of Circe's palace. When his companions were on the point of leaving, he hurriedly stood up. Disoriented by his state of drunkeness, he fell off the roof, fractured his cervical vertebral column and instantaneously died. Elpenor's misadventure was described as follows in a 1725 English translation of *The Odyssey* by Alexander Pope (1688–1744), William Broome (1689–1745), and Elijah Fenton (1683–1730):

> A youth there was, Elpenor was he nam'd,
> Nor much for sense, nor much for courage fam'd;
> The youngest of our band, a vulgar soul
> Born but to banquet, and to drain the bowl.
> He, hot and careless, on a turret's height
> With sleep repair'd the long debauch of night:
> The sudden tumult stirr'd him where he lay,
> And down he hasten'd, but forgot the way;
> Full endlong from the roof the sleeper fell,
> And snapt the spinal joint, and walk'd in hell.
> (Homer, 1967, p. 375)

Shortly after, Elpenor's ghost appeared to Ulysses and asked for the sepulchral honors he wanted:

> Soon as the morn restor'd the day, we pay'd
> Sepulchral honours to Elpenor's shade.
> (Homer, 1967, p. 430)

President Paul Deschanel, probably much more remembered as the most famous case report of Elpenor's syndrome than as a short-lived president of the French Republic, was not so fortunate. On September 21, 1920, neurotic trouble obliged him to resign. He died in Paris on April 28, 1922. Pending further information, his ghost appeared to nobody…

References

Bérard J (1955): Introduction and maps. In: Homer, *Iliade. Odyssée*. Paris, Gallimard, Bibliothèque de la Pléiade, pp. 539–558 and 1052–1053.

Bilikiewicz A, Leszczynski L (1966): Forensic-psychiatric expertise in a case of Elpenor syndrome (in Polish). *Neurol Neurochir Psychiatr Pol 16* (12): 1421–1423.

Chastenet de Castaing J (1967): Deschanel, Paul Eugène Louis. In: Encyclopedia Britannica. vol. 7, Chicago, London, Toronto, Geneva, Sydney, Tokyo, Manila: William Benton, publisher. p. 292.

Dérobert L (1974): *Médecine légale*. Paris: Flammarion Médecine Sciences. pp. 342–343.

Garnier M, Delamare V, Delamare J, Delamare T (2000): *Dictionnaire des termes de médecine*, 26 ème edition. Paris: Maloine. p. 259.

Homer (1967): *The Odyssey of Homer*. Maynard Mack, ed., London (New Haven): Methuen & Co Ltd (Yale University Press), vol. 1.

Juillet P (2000): *Dictionnaire de psychiatrie*. Paris: Éditions CILF. p. 132.

Kapsambelis V (1997): *Termes psychiatriques français d'origine grecque*. Paris: Masson. pp. 39–40.

Lesueur L (1976): Le Président tombé du train. *Historia 354*: 102–109.

Logre BJ (1961): *Psychiatrie clinique*. Paris: Presses Universitaires de France.

Marchais P (1970): *Glossaire de psychiatrie*. Paris: Masson et Cie. p. 69.

Michaux L (1965): *Psychiatrie*. Paris: Flammarion. pp. 95–96.

Porot A (1996): *Manuel alphabétique de psychiatrie clinique et thérapeutique* , 7ème edition. Paris: Presses Universitaires de France. p. 221.

Postel J (2003): *Dictionnaire de la psychiatrie*. Paris: Larousse. p. 172.

Viot-Blanc V (2000): Troubles du sommeil de l'adulte: hypersomnies, parasomnies et troubles circadiens. Encycl Méd Chir (Éditions Scientifiques et Médicales SAS, Paris), *Psychiatrie, 37-680-A-06*, p. 8.

Munchausen Syndrome By Proxy: Karl Friedrich Hieronymus, Baron von Münchhausen, Hasn't Got Anything To Do With It

We discussed in a previous paper the biography of Karl Friedrich Hieronymus, Baron von Münchhausen, and the origins of the strange mental disorder which bears his name (Olry, 2002). In short, Karl Friedrich Hieronymus, Baron von Münchhausen (1720–1797) became famous around Hanover as a raconteur of absurdly exaggerated anecdotes of his adventures and exploits as a soldier, hunter and sportsman. Twelve years before the Baron's death, Rudolph Erich Raspe (1737–1794) published anonymously the first edition of Baron von Münchhausen tales (Raspe, 1785), prefaced by the romantic poet and writer of ballads Gottfried August Bürger (1747–1794). The term *Munchausen syndrome—Münchhausen* has been corrupted to *Munchausen* (deletion of the umlaut and one h) in literature and medicine—was coined in 1951 by Richard Asher, a London physician to the Central Middlesex Hospital, and head of the Mental Observation Ward. *Munchausen syndrome* is characterized by "habitual presentation for hospital treatment of an apparent acute illness, the patient giving a plausible and dramatic history, all of which is false" (Dorland, 2000). Asher, in a paper including three cases of *Munchausen syndrome*, explained this eponym in these terms: "Here is described a common syndrome which most doctors have seen, but about which little has been written. Like the famous Baron von Münchhausen, the persons affected have always travelled widely; and their stories, like those attributed to him, are both dramatic and untruthful. Accordingly, the syndrome is respectfully dedicated to the baron, and named after him" (Asher, 1951).

Twenty–six years later, the name of the baron was associated with another syndrome, this time concerning children. *Munchausen syndrome by proxy*, a term coined by Roy Meadow in 1977, "includes situations in which one person produces symptoms in another, typically a parent creating symptoms in a child, for the purpose of indirectly assuming the sick role (by proxy)" (Kaplan and Sadock, 1995). The parents, most of the time the mothers (Fenelon, 1998; Epelbaum, 1999), of such children may have had nursing training as observed in the Lasthénie de Ferjol syndrome (Olry and Haines, 2002). Some of them may also have had a history of factitious illness themselves (Talbott et al., 1988). Similar observations had been made before Meadow's article. In 1964, Pickering published three observations of salicylate poisoning denied by the parents. In a subsequent paper, he refered to this syndrome as "a manifestation of the battered child syndrome" (Pickering, 1976). Rogers et al., reviewing six cases of non-accidental poisoning, coined the term "extended syndrome of child abuse" (Rogers et al., 1976). Since 1977, about two hundred case reports have been published in medical literature (Epelbaum, 1999), but it seems that many case reports of sudden infant death might be related to this syndrome. One of the most famous case reports of *Munchausen syndrome by proxy* took place in the United Kingdom in 1993: nurse Beverley Allitt was convicted of thirteen cases of murder or causing grievous bodily harm to children in her care at the Grantham and Kesteven General Hospital (Lane, 1995). In 2000, Eminson and Postlethwaite analyzed Beverley Allitt's personality in these terms: "an immature young woman with a personality disorder and a history of major somatization herself (i.e. severe handicapping somatic complaints without evidence or organic disease: probably Munchausen syndrome), she appears to have been attracted to the role of nursing (and harming) children as a way of resolving her own substantial interpersonal difficulties. It is surmised that this was partly for the attention the role gave her as a centre of rescue attempts after she had endangered the children, partly for the gratitude of the victims' families to whom she became close, and also for the sheer power over life and death her actions involved" (Eminson and Postlethwaite, 2000, p. 2).

From the mid-1980s, the term *Munchausen syndrome by proxy* was extended to similar psychopathological interactions between adults (Sigal, 1986; Krebs et al., 1996). In 1996, Bools cancelled the eponym and opted for the term "factitious illness by proxy".

Little is known about the private life of Baron von Münchhausen, so extravagant were his tales that his everyday life has been neglected by his contemporaries. But it seems that he got married at least twice, and that he had only one child, with his second wife Berhardine Brun. This child, a son named Polle, died unfortunately before the age of one. That is why *Munchausen syndrome by proxy* is sometimes called *Polle syndrome* (Juillet, 2000). However, the circumstances of Polle's death are not known, and nothing entitles us to believe that his father had anything to do with it.

Karl Friedrich Hieronymus, Baron von Münchhausen, was not only an endearing, but also a harmless personage. We could understand that "using a jokey title for the syndrome—the name of a hazy, foreign, fantastic tale-telling character, drawn to receit—Asher obscured the dreadful import of the situation" (Eminson and Postlethwaite, 2000, p. 3). However, we regret that Roy Meadow unfortunately associated Münchhausen's name with a maternal mental disorder leading to so many children suffering, and up to 10% of death rate (Rosenberg, 1987).

Baron von Münchhausen had harboured resentment against Raspe and Bürger who had cast a gloom over his old age in holding up to ridicule his name. Thank God! He will never know that this name was to become the eponym of two psychiatric diseases.

We owe you an apology, mister baron!

References

Asher R (1951) *Munchausen's syndrome.* Lancet 1: 339–341.

Dorland's Illustrated Medical Dictionary (2000) Philadelphia, London, Toronto, Montreal, Sydney, Tokyo: W.B. Saunders Company.

Eminson M, Postlethwaite RJ (2000) *Munchausen syndrome by proxy abuse. A practical approach.* Oxford: Butterworth Heinemann.

Epelbaum C (1999) Maltraitance et sévices à enfant (hors abus sexuel). *Encycl Méd Chir* (Elsevier, Paris), Psychiatrie, 37–204–H–15, 7 p.

Fenelon G (1998) *Le syndrome de Munchausen*. Paris: Presses Universitaires de France, p. 66.

Juillet P (2000) *Dictionnaire de psychiatrie*. Paris: Conseil international de la langue française, p. 277.

Kaplan HI, Sadock BJ (1995) *Comprehensive textbook of psychiatry*. Baltimore: Williams & Wilkins, 6th ed., vol. 1, p. 1271.

Krebs MO, Bouden A, Lô H, Olié JP (1996) *Le syndrome de Münchhausen par procuration entre deux adultes*. Presse méd Paris 25: 583–586.

Lane B (1995) *Chronicle of 20th century murder*. London: True Crime.

Meadow R (1977) *Munchausen syndrome by proxy. The hinterland of child abuse*. Lancet 2: 343–345.

Olry R (2002) Baron von Münchhausen and the Syndrome Which Bears His Name: History of an Endearing Personage and of a Strange Mental Disorder. *Vesalius* 8 (1): 53–57.

Olry R, Haines DE (2002) Lasthénie de Ferjol's Syndrome: A Tribute Paid by Jean Bernard to Jules Amédée Barbey d'Aurevilly. *J Hist Neurosci* 11 (2): 181–182.

Pickering D (1964) Salicylate poisoning: the diagnosis when its possibility is denied by the parents. *Acta Paediatr* 53: 501–504.

Pickering D (1976) Salicylate poisoning as a manifestation of the battered child syndrome. *Am J Dis Child* 130: 675–676.

Raspe RE (1785) *Baron von Munchausen's narrative of his marvellous travels and campaigns in Russia*. Oxford: Smith (anonymously published).

Rogers D, Tripp J, Bentovim A (1976) Non-accidental poisoning: an extended syndrome of child abuse. *Brit Med J* 1: 793–796.

Rosenberg DA (1987) Web of deceit: A literature review of Munchausen syndrome by proxy. *Child Abuse Negl* 11: 547–563.

Sigal M (1986) Münchhausen syndrome by adult proxy: a perpetrator abusing two adults. *J Nerv Ment Dis* 174: 696–698.

Talbott JA, Hales RE, Yudofsky SC (1988) *Textbook of psychiatry*. Washington: American Psychiatric Press, Inc., p. 551.

Oedipus Complex: A Confession to a Berlin Otorhinolaryngologist that Became a Cornerstone of Psychoanalysis

Medical terminology has often gleaned ideas from the imaginativeness of human beings. The literary word gave rise to Lasthénie de Ferjol's syndrome (Bernard, Najean, Alby, & Rain, 1967; Olry & Haines, 2002 for review), Munchausen's syndrome (Asher, 1951; Olry, 2002 for review), Munchausen syndrome by proxy (Meadow, 1977; Olry & Haines, 2006b for review), among others. Mythology also supplied medicine with many examples of mental pathologies or behavioral disorders, such as Elpenor's syndrome (Logre, 1961; Olry & Haines, 2006a for review), Jocasta's complex (Garnier & Delamare, 2000, p. 447), Empedocel's syndrome (Olry, 2006), Electra's complex (Manuila, Manuila, Nicole, & Lambert, 1981), and the Ondine curse (Garnier & Delamare, 2000, p. 585). However, the most celebrated involvement of mythology in medical terminology is undisputably the Oedipus complex (Davis, 1993; Gilman, 1997; Green, 1969).

Although sometimes debated (Astier, 1974), the legend of Oedipus could be briefly summarized as follows. Oedipus, the son of Laius, king of Thebes, and Jocasta was exposed by his father on Mt. Cithaeron, because Laius was warned by an oracle that his son would slay him. In order to ensure that no one would save the child, or perhaps to make it impossible for his ghost to walk, his father pinned the baby's ankles together. Oedipus (meaning "swell-foot") was then adopted by Polybus. Many years later, he unwillingly killed his father, solved the riddle of the sphinx and, in reward, received the throne of Thebes and the hand of the widowed queen, Jocasta, his mother. They had four children (Eteocles, Polynices, Antigone, and Ismene), but the whole truth came to light: Jocasta committed suicide, and Oedipus, after blinding himself, went into exile and met his end at Colonus near Athens, where he was swallowed into earth and became a guardian hero of the land (Homer, 1955; Vernant & Vidal-Naquet, 1988; Wormell, 1967).

Many tales were drawn from the legend of Oedipus: Sophocle's Oedipus Rex circa 430 BC (Voussaris, 2002), Hartmann von Aue's *Grégoire sur le rocher ou le Bon pêcheur* (Pérennec, 2002), and Hughes de Sainte-Marie's *Gesta Romanorum imperatum* (Rech, 2002) in the Middle Ages; Pierre Corneille's *Œdipe* in the seventeenth century (Corneille, 1950); Guy de Maupassant's *M. Jocaste* in the nineteenth century; Jean Cocteau's *Œdipe*

Roi and *La Machine infernale*, André Gide's *Œdipe*, Thomas Mann *Der Erwählte*, Alain Robbe-Grillet's *Les Gommes*, and Jean Anouilh's *Œdipe ou le Roi boiteux* in the twentieth century.

The term Oedipus complex was coined by the famous Vienna neurologist Sigmund Freud. Born in Freiberg (nowadays Pribor), Moravia, on May 6, 1856, Freud received his M.D. from the University of Vienna on March 31, 1881. He made numerous neurological studies under Ernst Wilhelm von Bruecke, Theodor Meynert, and Jean Charcot (Pagel, 1901). In 1878, he made, in a paper published as a medical student, a major contribution to evolutionary biology by showing that the spinal ganglion cells of Petromyzon represent a transition between the bipolar cells of lower and the unipolar cells of higher vertebrates (Freud, 1878; Norman, 1998, p. 339). In 1882, he studied the nerve cells of the river crayfish and was the first to demonstrate conclusively that the axes of nerve fibers are without exception fibrillary in structure, and that nerve cells and fibers were a single unit, thus paving the way to the neuron theory (Freud, 1882; Norman, 1998, p. 340). Two years later, he introduced a new method of staining nerve tissue with gold chloride (Freud, 1884; Norman, 1998, p. 341). From the mid-1880s Freud's career was changing direction. He was in Paris in October 1885 (Stone, 1973, p. 113) and was deeply impressed by Charcot's new way of looking at hysteria and hypnosis. Though remaining interested in clinical neurology — aphasia (Freud, 1891), childhood paralysis (Freud, 1893) — Freud then took a definitive direction towards psychoanalysis (Chasseguet-Smirgel & Grunberger, 1981; Hesnard, 1960; Jones, 1962; Robert, 1964; Stone, 1973).

In the early 1880s, he became friendly with the Berlin otorhinolaryngologist Wilhelm Fliess (1858–1928). Both men were drawn to each other immediately. Fliess, especially, was open-minded to the theories that Freud started to develop on the sexual roots of neurosis (Anzieu et al., 1977, p. 29). Moreover, Fliess was soon to be interested in the interactions between nasal mucosa and the genitals of women (Dupont, 1999; Fliess, 1897). Freud was then regularly in correspondence with his new friend, and his letters were more and more personal. Many authors consider that Fliess gradually became the substitute for Freud's father (Anzieu et al., 1977, p. 29).

The death of Freud's father, Jacob, on October 23, 1896, left a deep impression on him. In a letter to Wilhelm Fliess, he wrote: "The death of my father affected me greatly. I had a high opinion of him and I understood him very well" (Stone, 1973, p. 307). Almost one year later to the very day, on October 15, 1897, Freud put pen to paper and was on the point of becoming a legend. In a letter to Wilhelm Fliess, he expressed a sudden awareness that was soon to become the most celebrated complex of the history of psychoanalysis:

> I could find in myself (. . .) feelings of love towards my mother and of jealousy towards my father, feelings that are, I believe, common to all young children, even when their appearance is not so early than in children made hysterical . . . . The Greek legend perceived a compulsion that all recognized because all experienced it. Each hearer was one day in seeds, in imagination, an Oedipus, and takes fright of the accomplishment of his dream transposed into the reality. (Anzieu et al., 1977, p. 31)

The term Oedipus complex will remain, for 13 years, in Freud's mind before appearing in his first 1910 contribution à la psychologie de la vie amoureuse (cited by Anzieu et al., 1977, p. 34). In some lines further in this letter, Freud compared his feelings with those of Hamlet:

RHINENCEPHALON, TABES DORSALIS, ETC

But an idea crossed my mind: could not we find similar facts in the story of Hamlet? Without thinking of conscious intentions of Shakespeare, I suppose that a real event compelled the poet to write this drama, his own inconscious having allowed him to understand the inconscious of his hero . . . . Things are clearer when we think of the torment that creates in himself the vague recollection to have wished, by passion for his mother, to perpetrate towards his father the same heinous crime. (Anzieu et al., 1977, p. 32)

Freud had Oedipus complex in common with Hamlet, as confirmed by Gilbert Murray and Ernest Jones (cited in Shakespeare, 1959, p. XCI). Shakespeare lost his father, John, in 1601 (Payne, 1983), and registred his Hamlet in 1602 (Shakespeare, 1959, p. LXXXIX). Freud lost his father in 1896 and expressed his complex in 1897. One year that was rich in introspection for both celebrities!

References

Anzieu D, Chasseguet-Smirgel J, Deleuze G, Freud S, Guattari F, Grunberger B, Jones E, Klein M, Malinowski B, Muller J, Reich W, Roheim G (1977): *L'Œdipe. Un Complexe Universel*. N.p.: Laffont Canada Ltée.

Asher R (1951): Munchausen's syndrome. *Lancet 1*: 339–341.

Astier C (1974): *Le Mythe d'Œdipe*. Paris: Armand Colin.

Bernard J, Najean Y, Alby N, Rain JD (1967): Les anémies hypochromes dues à des hémorragies volontairement provoquées. Syndrome de Lasthénie de Ferjol. *La Presse Méd 42*: 2087–2090.

Chasseguet-Smirgel J, Grunberger B (1981): *Freud et ses Disciples*. N.p.: Laffont Canada Ltée.

Corneille P (1950): *Théâtre* (vol. 2). Paris: Bibliothèque de la Pléiade, Gallimard, pp. 531–610.

Davis DR (1993): Comple d'Œdipe. In: Gregory RL, ed., *Le Cerveau, un Inconnu*. Paris: Robert Laffont, pp. 210–211.

Dupont M (1999): *Dictionnaire Historique des Médecins dans et hors de la Médecine*. Paris: Larousse, p. 249.

Fliess W (1897): *Die Beziehungen Zwischen Nase und Weiblichen Geschlechtsorganen in Ihrer Biologischen Bedeutung Dargestellt*. Leipzig und Wien: F. Deuticke.

Freud S (1878): *Über Spinalganglien und Rückenmark des Petromyzon*. Vienna: K.k. Hof- und Staatsdruckerei (Offprint from: Stizb. Der k. Akad. Der Wissenschaften, 3. Abth., 78, 1878).

Freud S (1882): *Über den Bau der Nervenfasern und Nervenzellen beim Flusskrebs*. Vienna: K.k. Hof- und Staatsdruckerei (Offprint from: Sitzb. Der k. Akad. Der Wissenschaften, 3. Abth., 85, 1882).

Freud S (1884): *Eine neue Methode zum Studium des Faserverlaufs im Centralnervensystem*. Leipzig: Veit & Co. (Offprint from: Arch Anat Physiol, Anatomische Abth., 1884).

Freud S (1891): *Zur Auffassung der Aphasien. Eine kritische Studie*. Leipzig & Vienna: Franz Deuticke.

Freud S (1893): *Zur Kenntnis der cerebralen Diplegien des Kindesalters im Anschluss an die Little'sche Krankheit*. Leipzig & Vienna: Franz Deuticke.

Garnier M, Delamare V (2000): *Dictionnaire des Termes de Médecine*. Paris: Maloine, 26ème édition.

Gilman S (1997): Psychotherapy. In:Bynum WF, Porter R, eds., *Companion Encyclopedia of the History of Medicine*. London and New York: Routledge, vol. 2, pp. 1035–1036.

Green A (1969): *Un Œil de Trop, le Complexe d'Œdipe dans la Tragédie*. Paris: Éditions de Minuit.

Hesnard A (1960): L'Œuvre de Freud et Son Importance pour le Monde Moderne. Paris: Payot.

Homer (1955): *Iliade, Odyssée*. Paris: Bibliothèque de la Pléiade, Gallimard, Iliade XXIII: 697; Odyssée XI: 271–280.

Jones E (1962): *La Vie et l'Œuvre de Sigmund Freud*. Paris: Presses Universitaires de France, 3 vols.

Logre BJ (1961): *Psychiatrie clinique*. Paris: Presses Universitaires de France.

Manuila A, Manuila L, Nicole M, Lambert H (1981): *Dictionanire Français de Médecine et de Biologie*. Paris: Masson, vol. 4, p. 648.

Meadow R (1977): Munchausen syndrome by proxy. The hinterland of child abuse. *Lancet 2*: 343–345.

Norman HF (1998): *The Haskell F. Norman Library of Science and Medicine* (vol. 3). New York: Christie's.

Olry R (2002): Baron Münchhausen and the Syndrome Which Bears His Name: History of an Endearing Personage and of a Strange Mental Disorder. *Acta Intern Hist Med 8*: 53–57.

Olry (2006): Le suicide du philosophe grec Empédocle d'Agrigente. Conférences CFOU, Trois-Rivières.

Olry R, Haines DE (2002): Lasthénie de Ferjol's Syndrome: A Tribute Paid by Jean Bernard to Jules Amédée Barbey d'Aurevilly. *J Hist Neurosci 11*: 181–182.

Olry R, Haines DE (2006a): Elpenor's Syndrome: The Link Between One of Ulysses' Companions and the Tenth President of the Third French Republic. *J Hist Neurosci 15*: 159–161.

Olry R, Haines DE (2006b): Munchausen Syndrome By Proxy: Karl Friedrich Hieronymus, Baron Münchhausen, Hasn't Got Anything To Do With It. *J Hist Neurosci 15*: 276–278.

Pagel J (1901): *Biographisches Lexicon hervorragender Ärzte des neunzehnten Jahrhunderts. Mit einer historichen Einleitung*. Berlin & Wien: Urban & Schwarzenberg, p. 546.

Payne R (1983): *Shakespeare et l'Angleterre Élisabéthaine*. Paris: Librairie Académique Perrin, p. 343.

Pérennec R (2002): Hartmann von Aue. In: Gauvard C, de Libera A, Zink M, eds., *Dictionnaire du Moyen Âge*. Paris: Presses Universitaires de France, pp. 655–657.

Rech R (2002): Hugues de Sainte-Marie. In:Gauvard C, de Libera A, Zink M, eds., *Dictionnaire du Moyen Âge*. Paris: Presses Universitaires de France, pp. 695–696.

Robert M (1964): *La Révolution Psychanalytique. La Vie et l'Œuvre de Freud*. Paris: Payot.

Shakespeare W (1959): Œuvres Complètes (vol. 2). Paris: Bibliothèque de la Pléiade, Gallimard.

Stone I (1973): La Vie de Freud. Paris: Flammarion.

Vernant JP, Vidal-Naquet P (1988): Œdipe et ses Mythes. Bruxelles: Éditions Complexe.

Voussaris A (2002): Jocaste. In: Brunel P, ed., *Dictionanire des Mythes Féminins*. Paris: Éditions du Rocher, pp. 1059–1070.

Wormell DEW (1967): Oedipus. In: *Encyclopedia Britannica* (vol. 16). Chicago: William Benton, p. 868.

The Brain in its Birthday Suit: No More Reason to be Ashamed

We discussed in a previous paper the amazing etymology of the term fornix and its historical connection with sexual intercourse and prostitution at the time of ancient Rome (Olry & Haines, 1997). However odd it may seem, the anatomists of the last centuries also applied the terms vulva, penis, testicles, buttocks, and anus to some components of the central nervous system. In 1902, the French anatomist Joseph Auguste Aristide Fort wondered why "les anatomistes de ce siècle s'étaient plu à donner des noms indécents aux différentes parties qui entourent le troisième ventricule" (the anatomists of that century enjoyed giving indecent names to the different parts surrounding the third ventricle; Fort, 1902, p. 571). We shall attempt to show, in this paper, the grounds for these rather surprising terms.

The term vulva cerebri, or Schwalbe's triangular fossa (Olry, 1995), refers to a small recess between the anterior commissure and the division of both columns of the fornix. It is sometimes attributed to Vieussens (1684), but wrongly, for this term was to be found as early as seven years before (Bartholin, 1677, p. 494). It actually seems to have been coined by the Italian anatomist Matthaeo Realdo Colombo in the mid-sixteenth century (H. Cloquet, 1816, p. 57). We should not be surprised, if we remember that the tradition ascribes to Colombo the discovery of the clitoris (Colombo, 1559; for review, see Lauth, 1815; Laqueur, 1992; Andahazi, 1997; Mandressi, 2003). By the early seventeenth century, the term became a matter of controversy. In 1708, Philip Verheyen wrote in the German translation of his *Corporis humani anatomiae*: "eine Spalte [. . .] die man sehr unverschämet Vulvam nennet" (a groove [. . .] that we impudently call vulva; Verheyen, 1708). In 1752, the French anatomist and surgeon César Verdier criticized the term as follows: "[cette fente] que l'on a appelée vulva, mais que l'on appelle aujourd'hui avec plus de raison, ouverture commune antérieure" ([this groove] that we called vulva, but that we rightly call today, common anterior opening; Verdier, 1752, p. 280).

The term vulva remained however in use for a long time (Boyer, 1805, p. 46; H. Cloquet, 1816, p. 557; Debierre, 1890, p. 111; Féré, 1886, p. 56; Fort, 1902, p. 661; Morel & Duval, 1883, p. 713; Poirier & Charpy, 1901, p. 350; Sappey, 1872, p. 90; Testut, 1905, p. 759). Only some authors cautiously mentioned the term: "[créé] par les ancients anatomistes" ([coined] by the ancient anatomists; J. Cloquet, 1825, p. 302), "[créé] par les ancients" ([coined] by the ancients; Broc, n.d., p. 405), "[la] prétendue vulve" ([the]

so-called vulva; Debierre, 1907, p. 316). However, a question is still to be solved: unlike the opinion of most historians of neuroanatomy, the groove called vulva by Colombo might be something else: not the recess between the anterior commissure and the division of both columns of the fornix, but the groove, more posterior, between both habenulae, as stated by Diemerbroeck: "on voit la fente que Columbus appelle vulve, laquelle contient le trou de l'anus" (we can see the groove that Colombo calls vulva, which contains the hole of the anus; Diemerbroeck, 1695, p. 247). To our knowledge, only Paul de Terra pointed out this discrepancy (Terra, 1913).

The pineal gland was called penis cerebri by Thomas Bartholin and Isbrand van Diemerbroeck (Bartholin, 1677, p. 494; Diemerbroeck, 1695, p. 248). In the early twentieth century, some authors reminded the reader of the fact that the pineal gland "était appelée penis cerebri par les anciens" (was called penis cerebri by the ancients; Poirier & Charpy, 1901, p. 271) or was "appelée autrefois pénis, selon Portal" (called, in the past, penis, according to Portal; Fort, 1902, p. 659). This metaphor may have its roots in the position of the pineal gland above and between the colliculi, the inferior ones having been compared with testicles. Since that time, the metaphor sank into oblivion and was no more to be found in classical current textbooks.

From the sixteenth century, the superior and inferior colliculi of the tectum of the midbrain were called nates or eminentiae natiformes (buttocks) and testes or eminentiae testiformes (testicles), respectively (Bartholin, 1677, p. 493; Dulaurens, 1605; Tauvry, 1698, p. 232). In 1672, Jean Riolan explained these terms as follows: "ces noms leur ayant été donnés à cause qu'elles sont disposées d'une sorte qui répond à la situation de ces parties" (these terms having been coined because they are arranged as are these parts; Riolan, 1672, p. 386). Not convinced, Isbrand van Diemerbroeck wondered some years later why these terms had been coined: "à raison de quelle ressemblance" (on account of which resemblance; Diemerbroeck, 1695, p. 247).

In the mid-eighteenth century, Winslow considered that "les noms de Nates et Testes qu'on a donné à ces tubercules sont très impertinents, et ne marquent aucune ressemblance aux choses mêmes dont on les a tirés" (the Dames Nates and Testes that were given to these tubercles are very impertinent, and have no ressemblance with the things they were derived from; Winslow, 1752, p. 159). However, Nates and Testes were still to be found for a long lime (Boyer, 1805, p. 49; H. Cloquet, 1816, p. 537; J. Cloquet, 1825, p. 297; Heister, 1719, p. 113; Jamain, 1853; Marjolin, 1815; Sabatier, 1792; Santucci, 1739, p. 217; Verdier, 1752, p. 279; Verheyen, 1710, p. 223). In the late nineteenth century, Cruveilhier explained their roots in these terms: "Ces expressions sont une conséquence de la comparaison grossière qui a été faite par les anciens entre la moelle allongée et le corps d'un animal" (these expressions are derived from the comparison made by the ancients between the medulla oblongata and the body of an animal; Cruveilhier, 1871). Nates and Testes remained in use *for a long time* (Beaunis & Bouchard, 1894, pp. 562–563; Debierre, 1890, p. 68; Dejerine, 1895, p. 332; Féré, 1886, p. 193; Morel & Duval, 1883, pp. 715–716; Sappey, 1872, p. 128), even into the twentieth century (Debierre, 1907, p. 129; Poirier & Charpy, 1901, p. 259; Testut, 1905, p. 606).

The anus is the rostral opening of the aqueduct of the midbrain into the third ventricle. The term was used in the seventeenth century by Riolan (1672, p. 386), Bartholin "quod foramen quidam anus vocant" (1677, p. 493), Diemerbroeck (1695, p. 246), and Tauvry (1698, p. 231). In the eighteenth century, some authors, among whom were Verheyen (1710, p. 224), Heister (1719, p. 113), Santucci (1739, p. 217), and Verdier (1752, p. 280), refered to it without raising any objection. In contrast, Winslow sharply rejected the term: "Au lieu du nom ridicule de l'anus qu'on a donné à cette ouverture, on la peut appeler ouverture commune postérieure" (Instead of the ridiculous name anus which was given to this opening, we could refer to it as the common posterior opening; Winslow, 1752, p. 160). In the nineteenth century, the term anus was still to be found in many handbooks (Beaunis & Bouchard, 1894, p. 597; Boyer, 1805, p. 47; H. Cloquet, 1816, p. 558; Debierre, 1890, p. 86; Fort, 1902, p. 660; Morel & Duval, 1883, p. 714; Poirier & Charpy, 1901, p. 270; Sappey, 1872, p. 90; Testut, 1905, p. 758). Only some authors pointed out that the anus was an obsolete word (Broc, n.d., p. 405; J. Cloquet, 1825, p. 302; Debierre, 1907, p. 316; Féré, 1886, p. 58).

All these terms have now been struck off the neuroanatomical indexes, and the brain is no more in its birthday suit. The *nervus pudendus* should therefore have no more reason to be called ashamed.

REFERENCES

Andahazi F (1997): *El anatomista*. Buenos Aires, Planeta.

Bartholin T (1677): *Anatome quartum renovata*. Lugduni, Joan. Ant. Huguetan.

Beaunis H, Bouchard A (1894): *Nouveaux éléments d'anatomie descriptive et d'embryologie*. Paris, J.-B. Baillière et Fils, 5ème édition.

Boyer A (1805): *Traité complet d'anatomie, ou description de toutes les parties du corps humain*. Paris, Migneret, vol. 4.

Broc PP (n.d.): *Traité complet d'anatomie descriptive et raisonnée*. Paris, Just Rouvier, vol. 3.

Cloquet H (1816): *Traité d'anatomie descriptive*. Paris, Crochard, vol. 2.

Cloquet J (1825): *Manuel d'anatomie descriptive du corps humain*. Paris, Béchet jeune, vol. 1 (Texte).

Colombo MR (1559): *De re anatomica libri XV*. Venetiis, 1559, ex typographia Nicolai Bevilacquae, p. 243.

Cruveilhier J (1871): *Traité d'anatomie descriptive*. Paris, P. Asselin, 4ème édition, vol. 3, p. 423.

Debierre C (1890): *Traité élémentaire d'anatomie de l'homme*. Paris, Félix Alcan, vol. 2.

Debierre C (1907): *Le cerveau et la moelle épinière*. Paris, Félix Alcan.

Dejerine J (1895): *Anatomie des centres nerveux*. Paris, Rueff et Cie, vol. 2, p. 332.

Diemerbroeck I van (1695): *L'anatomie du corps humain*. Lyon, Anisson & Posuel, vol. 2.

Dulaurens A (1605): *Historia anatomica, humani corporis partes*. Lugduni, Apud Horatium Cardon, p. 775.

Féré C (1886): *Traité élémentaire d'anatomie médicale du système nerveux*. Paris, A. Delahaye et Lecrosnier.

Fort JA (1902): *Anatomie descriptive et dissection*. Paris, Vigot Frères, vol. 1.

Heister L (1719): *Compendium anatomicum, totam rem anatomicam brevissime complectens, Editio altera prima longe auctior atque emendatior*. Altorfi et Norimbergae: in Bibliopolio Kohlesiano et Adolphiano.

Jamain A (1853): *Nouveau traité élémentaire d'anatomie descriptive et de préparations anatomiques*. Paris, Germer Baillière, p. 679.

Laqueur T (1992): Amor veneris, vel dulcedo appeletur. In: M. Feher, ed., *Fragmentos para una historia del cuerpo humano*. Madrid, Taurus, pp. 90–131.

Lauth T (1815): *Histoire de l'anatomie*. Strasbourg, F. G. Levrault, volume 1 [All published], p. 512.

Marjolin JN (1815): *Manuel d'anatomie*. Paris, Méquignon-Marvis, vol. 2, p. 137.

Mandressi R (2003): *Le regard de l'anatomiste*. Paris, Éditions du Seuil, pp. 7–11.

Morel C, Duval M (1883): *Manuel de l'anatomiste* (Anatomie descriptive et dissection). Paris, Asselin et Cie.

Olry R (1995): *Dictionary of Anatomical Eponyms*. Stuttgart, New York, Gustav Fischer Verlag, p. 138.

Olry R, Haines DE (1997): Fornix and Gyrus Fornicatus: Carnal Sins? *J Hist Neurosci* 6: 338–339.

Poirier P, Charpy A (1901): *Traité d'anatomie humaine*. Paris, Masson et Cie, 2èmeédition, vol. 3, fasc. 1.

Riolan J (1672): *Manuel anatomique et pathologique.* Lyon, Antoine Laurens.

Sabatier RB (1792): *Traité complet d'anatomie, ou description de toutes les parties du corps humain.* Paris, Théophile Barrois, dernière édition, vol. 4, p. 415.

Santucci B (1739): *Anatomia do corpo humano.* Lisboa Occidental, Na Officina de Antonio Pedrozo Galram.

Sappey PC (1872): *Traité d'anatomie descriptive.* Paris, Adrien Delahaye, vol. 3.

Tauvry D (1698): *Nouvelle anatomie raisonnée, ou l'on explique les usages de la structure du corps humain, et de quelques autres animaux, suivant les loix des mécaniques.* Paris, Barthelemy Girin.

Terra P de (1913): *Vademecum anatomicum. Kritisch-etymologisches Worterbuch der systematischen Anatomie. Mit besonderer Berücksichtigung der Synonymen. Nebst einem Anhang: Die anatomischen Schriftsteller des Altertums bis zur Neuzeit.* Jena, Gustav Fischer, p. 598.

Testut L (1905): *Traité d'anatomie humaine.* Paris, Octave Doin, 5ème édition, vol. 2.

Verdier C (1752): *Abrégé de l'anatomie du corps humain.* Bruxelles, Jean Léonard, vol. 2.

Verheyen P (1708): *Anatomie oder Zerlegung des menschlichen Leibes.* Leipzig, Thomas Fritschen, p. 371.

Verheyen P (1710): *Corporis humani anatomiae.* Bruxellis, Apud Fratres T'Serstevens, Bibliopolas, vol. 1.

Vieussens R (1684): *Nevrographia universalis.* Lugduni, J. Celte.

Winslow JB (1752): *Exposition anatomique de la structure du corps humain.* Amsterdam, Emanuel Tourneisen, nouvelle édition, vol. 4.

The Pen Nib and the Bolt: The Rhomboid Fossa of the Fourth Ventricle or the Symbol of the Censorship of the Press?

The walls and roof of the fourth ventricle are formed in their rostral part by the superior cerebellar peduncles and the superior medullary velum, and in their caudal part, interrupted by the median aperture, by the ventricular ependyma and the pia mater of the tela choroidea. The floor of the fourth ventricle, or rhomboid fossa, is divided into three areas. The superior area, limited laterally by the superior cerebellar peduncles and caudally by an arbitrary line through the rostral ends of both superior foveae, is continuous rostrally with the cerebral aqueduct's wall. The intermediate area is characterized by the striae medullares. The inferior area, showing mainly the hypoglossal and vagal triangles, is continuous below with the wall of the central medullary canal (Williams et al., 1989). The floor is divided vertically by a median sulcus that seems to have been described by Herophilus, who coined the term *calamus scriptorius* (pen nib). The question is to know what he exactly meant with this term *(calamus),* which is known to be at the root of about 45 terms in different languages (Delaveau, 1995).

Herophilus of Chalcedon (c. 355–c. 280 BC), a pupil of Praxagoras of Cos, carried out extensive investigations of human anatomy (Bynum & Porter, 1997), but unfortunately his anatomical studies have been lost (Kemper, 1905; Lauth, 1815). We must therefore rely on Galen to understand Herophilus' descriptions. The famous historian of medical terminology, Joseph Hyrtl, could find the description in Galen's 1531 *De anatomicis administrationibus* and concluded therefore that the term *calamus scriptorius* referred not to a whole pen nib but only to its point (Hyrtl, 1880). In that way, the *calamus scriptorius* should only be the caudal end of the rhomboid fossa (Ranson, 1943; Strong & Elwyn, 1943).

Unfortunately, many authors misunderstood or modified the real meaning of the term. In the first edition of the *Nomina anatomica,* Wilhelm His called *calamus scriptorius* the caudal part of the fourth ventricle's cavity; namely the part located underneath the striae medullares, without distinguishing between the roof and the rhomboid fossa of the ependymal cavity (His, 1895). Achille-Louis Foville reserved the term for the caudal end of the median sulcus of the fourth ventricle (Foville, 1844). Jules Cloquet and Ludwig

Edinger classified the *calamus scriptorius* as the whole median sulcus of the fourth ventricle (Cloquet, 1825; Edinger, 1893). The *calamus scriptorius* was sometimes divided into a caudal end or *bec du calamus* (calamus' bill) and a rostral part or *tige du calamus* (calamus' scape; Dejerine, 1901, pp. 496–503; Mineff, 1907; Paturet, 1964, pp. 594–608; Rouvière, 1979). The term *calamus scriptorius* was also translated either to *Federnhöhle* (feather cavity), *Federspalte* (feather split), or *Schreibfeder* (pen nib; Hyrtl, 1884).

A bird feather has a scape, but also some barbs; a term that was used to refer to the striae medullares of the fourth ventricle. The striae medullares (or striae acusticae, or chordae acusticae: de Terra, 1913), sometimes called *barbes du calamus* (calamus' barbs: Paturet, 1964, p. 595) belong to the intermediate area of the rhomboid fossa. They vary in number (0 to 12: Mineff, 1907, p. 11) and may be "slender or large, parallel, converging or divergent, transversal, oblique, or longitudinal" (Dejerine, 1901, p. 499). One of them, running almost vertically along the rhomboid fossa, was discovered by Gottlob Heinrich Bergmann and called *conductor sonorus* (Bergmann, 1857). Although the terms striae acusticae, chordae acusticae, and conductor sonorus should imply a link with the auditory system, the striae medullares are an aberrant cerebropontocerebellar connection from the arcuate nuclei to the opposite flocculus.

The hypoglossal triangle of the rhomboid fossa is sometimes divided by a vertical sulcus into a large medial area, facing the hypoglossal nucleus, and a small lateral area, facing Staderini's intercalated nucleus. This lateral area, covered by corrugated ependyma, was compared with a bird feather by Gustav Retzius, who coined the term area plumiformis (Retzius, 1896).

Whatever the misunderstandings may be, all anatomists described a vertical pen nib in the fourth ventricle. We may have therefore expected its point to be dipped in an ink pot. Surprisingly, the point of the pen nib is dipped in a bolt (see Figure 1). The obex (bolt) is a small triangular plate located at the rostral end of the posterior median sulcus of

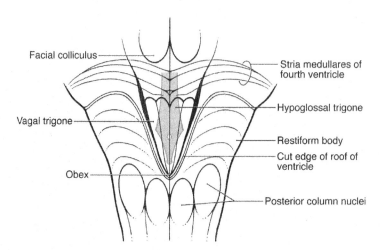

Figure 1. A representation of the superior surface of the caudal medulla showing the roof of the fourth ventricle removed to expose the caudal floor of the ventricle. By superimposing the shadow of the nib of a pen it is easy to see how the shape of the caudal portions of the fourth ventricle caused early anatomists to refer to this area as the calamus scriptorius. This is the portion of the caudal end of the fourth ventricle that is continuous with the central canal of the medulla and cervical spinal cord.

the medulla oblongata. It is formed by the fusion of both taeniae, which overlaps the ventricle's inferior angle (Williams et al., 1989). Many authors studied the origin and the morphology of the obex (Blake, 1900; Staderini, 1906a, 1906b; Streeter, 1903). In the early 1900s, Wilson observed two types of obex: the "real obex", formed by a medullary thickening on the one hand, and the "membranous obex", formed only by the ependyma and the pia mater on the other hand (Wilson, 1906a, 1906b).

It may look paradoxical to see a pen nib fixed in a bolt and not dipped in an ink pot. The floor of the fourth ventricle may therefore have been used as a symbol of the censorship of the press. In that way, it may even have been found on the armorial bearings of so many writers who were put in prison for having published their opinions.

References

Bergmann GH (1857): Notiz über ein Strukturverhältniss des Cerebellum und Rückenmarks. *Ztschr Rat Med*, 8: 300.

Blake JA (1900): The roof and lateral recessus of the fourth ventricle. *J Comp Neurol*, *10* (1): 79–108.

Bynum WF, Porter R (1997): *Companion Encyclopedia of the History of Medicine*. London and New York, Routledge, vol. 1.

Cloquet J (1825): *Manuel d'anatomie descriptive du corps humain. Texte*. Paris, Béchet jeune.

Dejerine J (1901): *Anatomie des centres nerveux*. Paris, J. Rueff, vol. 2.

Delaveau P (1995): *La Mémoire des Mots en médecine, pharmacie et sciences*. Paris, Louis Pariente.

de Terra P (1913): *Vademecum anatomicum. Kritisch-etymologisches Wörterbuch der systematischen Anatomie. Mit besonderer Berücksichtigung der Synonymen*. Jena, Gustav Fischer Verlag.

Edinger L (1893): *Anatomie des centres nerveux. Guide pour l'étude de leur structure à l'état normal et pathologique*. Paris, Georges Carré.

Foville AL (1844): *Traité complet de l'anatomie, de la physiologie et de la pathologie du système nerveux cérébrospinal. Première partie. Atlas*. Paris, Fortin, Masson et Cie.

Galen (1531): *De anatomicis administrationibus libri novem, Joanne Guinterio Andernaco Medico interprete*. Paris, S. Colinaeus.

His W (1895): Die anatomische Nomenklatur. Nomina anatomica. Verzeichnis der von der Commission der anatomischen Gesellschaft festgestellten Namen, eingeleitet und im Einverständniss mit dem Redactionausschuss erläutert. *Arch Anat Physiol* (Suppl.): 164.

Hyrtl J (1880): *Onomatologia anatomica. Geschichte und Kritik der anatomischen Sprache der Gegenwart, mit besonderer Berücksichtigung ihrer Barbarismen, Widersinnigkeiten, Tropen, und grammatikalischen Fehler*. Wien, Wilhelm Braumüller.

Hyrtl J (1884): *Die alten deutschen Kunstworte der Anatomie*. Wien, Wilhelm Braumüller.

Kemper GWH (1905): *The World's Anatomists*. Philadelphia, P. Blakiston's Son & Co.

Lauth T (1815): *Histoire de l'anatomie*. Strasbourg, F. G. Levrault, vol. 1.

Mineff M (1907): *Le plancher du quatrième ventricule chez l'homme (étude morphologique)*. Louvain, Imprimerie des Trois Rois.

Paturet G (1964): *Traité d'anatomie humaine*. Paris, Masson & Cie, vol. 4.

Ranson SW (1943): *The Anatomy of the Nervous System from the Standpoint of Development and Function*. Philadelphia and London, W.B. Saunders Company, 7th edition.

Retzius G (1896): *Das Menschenhirn. Studien in der makroskopischen Morphologie*. Stockholm, P.A. Norstedt & Söner.

Rouvière H (1979): *Anatomie humaine. Descriptive, topographique, fonctionnelle*. Paris, Masson, 11ème édition, vol. 3.

Staderini R (1906a): Nucleo intercalato. Pars inferior fossae rhomboideae. A proposito della nuova edizione del Van Gehuchten. *Anat Anz*, *29* (13/14): 329–334.

Staderini R (1906b): Sopra alcune particolarita anatomiche della midolla allungata. Risponsa al Signor A. van Gehuchten. *Anat Anz*, *30* (11/12): 363–368.

Streeter G (1903): Anatomy of the floor of the fourth ventricle. *Am J Anat*, 2 (3): 299–313.

Strong OS, Elwyn A (1943): *Human Neuroanatomy*. Baltimore, The Williams & Wilkins Company.

Williams PL, Warwick R, Dyson M, Bannister LH (1989): *Gray's Anatomy*. Edinburgh, London, Melbourne, New York, Churchill Livingstone.

Wilson TJ (1906a): On the anatomy of the calamus region in the human bulb; With an account of a hitherto undescribed "Nucleus postremus." *J Anat Physiol*, *1*(3): 210–241 and part IV: 357–386.

Wilson TJ (1906b): On the anatomy of the calamus region in the human bulb; With an account of a hitherto undescribed "Nucleus postremus." *J Anat Physiol*, *1*(4): 357–386.

A Concert Hall for Stringed Musical Instruments Under the Splenium of the Corpus Callosum

Some medical terms originate from their resemblance to musical instruments (Bossy, 1999). The tympanic membrane refers to the Latin *tympanum*, meaning drum. The syrinx, song organ in birds, is derived from the Greek *syrinx, syringos*, meaning flute, and gave rise to the term syringomyelia (Olivier d'Angers, 1824), the anatomical lesions of the spinal cord having been compared with the pipe of a flute. In the sixteenth century, Bartolomeo Eustachi and Gabriele Fallopio described horns, *tuba* in Latin, in the human body: the Eustachian or pharyngotympanic tube on the one hand, the Falloppian or uterine tubes on the other hand (Eustachi, 1564; Falloppio, 1569). The neurosciences were not an exception to this trend: in the last centuries — the hippocampal commissure was compared with a lyre or a psaltery.

The hippocampal commissure, or commissure of the fornix (*Commissura fornicis*), is a thin triangular sheet of transverse fibers that interconnect the two crura of the fornix under the splenium of the corpus callosum. In the second half of the nineteenth century, the French anatomist Philibert Constant Sappey made a mistake when he ascribed the term *Lyra* to Félix Vicq d'Azyr (Sappey, 1872): this term was mentioned almost 150 years earlier by Jacques-Bénigne Winslow who told us that it had been coined by the ancients (Winslow, 1752). In the same way, the term *psalterium* seems to date back to the early first millennium (Hyrtl, 1880). The term *lyra* was then completed in *Lyra Davidis* (David's lyre), and the *psalterium* was subdivided into a ventral (rostral) and a dorsal (caudal) psalterium (Stephan, 1975). Which grounds may account for these metaphors? What do a lyre and a psaltery look like? And who was David?

The lyre (Latin: *lyra*) is one of the most ancient stringed musical instruments. It was formed by a sound box, originally made of tortoise shell (like the kissar, a current Ethiopian lyre), from which project two arms joined by a yoke. The strings run from the sound box over a bridge to the yoke, where they are tuned by means of twisted thongs or pegs (Winnington-Ingram, 1967). The number of strings, initially 3, was increased to 8 by Simonides of Ceos (c. 556–467 BC), a Greek lyric poet and epigrammatist who wrote an elegy on the Battle of Marathon, and then to 12 by the Greek poet and musician Thimotheus (447–357 BC), a disciple of Phrynis. According to the Greeks, at least four mythological figures may have invented the lyre: Orpheus, Apollo, Linus, or Amphion. Orpheus, known to have had a particular gift of superhuman skill in music and song, was the son of the Muse Calliope and the Thracian river-god Oeagrus; he was depicted by the French painter Alexandre Séon, lying on a beach and holding a lyre in his hands. Appolo appeared on a painting by Martaen de Vos, sitting with Muses and playing his lyre. Linus was, in the Thebian version, the son of Urania and Amphimarus and put to death by Appolo or Hercules, to whom he taught music. Amphion, one of the twin sons of Zeus and Antiope, became a great singer and musician but killed himself after the loss of his wife and children.

The psaltery (Latin: *psalterion*), probably introduced in the West after the Crusades, is a stringed musical instrument related to the dulcimers and the zithers. It has gut or metal strings stretched over a flat sound box, which may be trapezoid, triangular, or square (Baines, 1967).

David, the youngest son of Jesse, was the founder and first ruler of the united kingdom of Israel and Judah (Rylaarsdam, 1967). He could be regarded as a pioneer in musicotherapy for he succeeded in quietening the rage, sadness, and jealousy of King Saul by playing his musical instrument.

But which musical instrument did David play? In 1970, Friedrich Ellermeier wrote: "Die Musikgeschichte Altisraels ist weithin noch in undurchdringliches Dunkel gehüllt" ("History of music of old Israel is still covered with unfathomable abstruseness"; Ellermeier, 1970). This accounts for the difficulty to know precisely which instrument David played. It could have been a harp (Bricout, 1925; Augé, 1929), a zither (Dhorme, 1956; Mourre, 1986), or a lyre (Gérard, 1989).

The hippocampal commissure was sometimes called *corpus psalloides* (from the Greek *psallo*, to pluck the strings of an instrument; Dejerine, 1895), or *fornix transversus* (Forel, as cited by Ludwig & Klingler, 1956). According to Gottlieb Heinrich Bergmann, the terms *psalterium* and *lyra,* however, referred to other regions of the central nervous system, the folds on the walls of the cerebral aqueduct and the ependymal folds on the medial surface of the thalamus, respectively (Bergmann, 1831).

In conclusion, does the hippocampal commissure more closely resemble a lyre or a psaltery? Though it is difficult to settle this question once and for all, let us explain why we should favor the psaltery. A lyre, with its arms, yoke, and sound box, is more or less rectangular and the strings run parallel to the arms. The two crura of the fornix having been compared with these arms, the interconnecting fibers should run parallel to them, whereas they are directed transversally that is to say perpendicular to the arms. In this regard, the term *psalterium* seems more appropriate, and all the more because it does not involve King David, whose musical instrument remains much debated.

References

Augé P (1929): *Larousse du XXe siècle*. Paris, Librairie Larousse, volume 2.

Baines AC (1967): "Psaltery." In: *Encyclopedia Britannica*. Chicago, London, Toronto, Geneva, Sydney, Tokyo, Manila, William Benton, volume 18.

Bergmann GH (1831): *Neue Untersuchungen über die innere Organisation des Gehirns*. Hannover, Helwing.

Bossy J (1999) : *La grande aventure du terme médical. Filiations et valeurs actuelles*. Montpellier, Sauramps Médical.

Bricout J (1925) : *Dictionnaire pratique des connaissances religieuses*. Paris, Librairie Letouzey et Ané, volume 2.

Dejerine J (1895): *Anatomie des centres nerveux*. Paris, Rueff et Cie, volume 1.

Dhorme E (1956): *La Bible. Ancien Testament*. Paris, Gallimard, Bibliothèque de la Pléiade, volume 1.

Ellermeier F (1970): Beiträge zur Fruhgeschichte altorientalischer Saiteninstrumente. In: Kuschke A, Kutsch E, ed., *Archäologie und Altes Testament. Festschrift für Kurt Galling zum 8. Januar 1970.* Tübingen, J.C.B. Mohr.

Eustachi B (1564): Epistola in auditus organo. In: *Opuscula anatomica.* Venetiis, Vincentius Luchinus, pp. 148–164.

Falloppio G (1569): *Observationes anatomicae.* Venetiis, apud Marcum Antonium Ulmum, p. 197.

Gérard AM (1989): *Dictionnaire de la Bible.* Paris, Robert Laffont.

Hyrtl J (1880): *Onomatologia anatomica. Geschichte unf Kritik der anatomischen Sprache der Gegenwart, mit besonderer Berücksichtigung ihrer Barbarismen, Widersinnigkeiten, Tropen, und grammatikalischen Fehler.* Wien, Wilhelm Braumüller.

Ludwig E, Klingler J (1956): *Atlas cerebri humani. Der innere Bau des Gehirns, dargestellt auf Grund makroskopischer Präparate.* Basel, New York, Karger.

Mourre M (1986): *Dictionnaire encyclopédique d'histoire.* Paris, Bordas, volume 3.

Olivier d'Angers CP (1824): *De la moelle épinière et de ses maladies.* Paris, Crevot.

Rylaarsdam JC (1967): "David." In: *Encyclopedia Britannica.* Chicago, London, Toronto, Geneva, Sydney, Tokyo, Manila, William Benton, volume 7.

Sappey PC (1872) : *Traité d'anatomie descriptive.* Paris, Adrien Delahaye, 2ème édition, vol. 3.

Stephan H (1975): *Allocortex (Handbuch der mikroskopischen Anatomie des Menschen).* Berlin, Heidelberg; New York, Springer-Verlag, volume 4, part 9.

Winnington-Ingram RP (1967): "Lyre. In: *Encyclopedia Britannica.* Chicago, London, Toronto, Geneva, Sydney, Tokyo, Manila, William Benton, volume 14.

Winslow JB (1752): *Exposition anatomique de la structure du corps humain.* Amsterdam, Emanuel Tourneisen, nouvelle édition, vol. 4.

The Cerebellum, the Earthworm and the Freshwater Crayfish: An Unpublished Fable of Jean de La Fontaine?

We discussed in previous columns the presence of seahorses, silkworms, hippos, rams, shells, and spiders in the head (Olry, 1991; Olry and Martinoli, 1995, Olry & Haines, 2001a, 2001b). However odd it may seem, some ancient anatomists also described an earthworm and a freshwater crayfish in the central nervous system.

The Latin term *vermis*, meaning worm, is at the root of at least 40 French words (Augé, 1933), many of them belonging to medical terminology (Gladstone, 1990): vermetoid, vermicidal, vermicide, vermicular, vermiculation, vermiculous, vermiform (appendix), vermifugal, vermifuge, vermin, verminal, verminous, vermiphobia, vermography, etc. The first cerebral formations to have been compared with worms were the current choroid plexus of the lateral ventricles, which Mondino dei Luzzi called *vermis* in 1478, and Walther Hermenius Ryff *Hirnwurm* (brain worm) in 1541. In the early first millenary, Rufus of Ephesus had already applied the Greek term *koroeides* (choroid) to the cerebellum, in what could be regarded as the very first attempt to establish an outline of anatomical terminology (Olry, 1989). The choroid plexus passing from one ventricle to another, the term *vermis* was applied to the communication between the anterior (*Sensus communis, Phantasia, Imaginativa*) and the middle (*Cogitativa, Aestimativa*) cerebral cells, a communication called *Via perforata* by Constantinus Africanus (Hyrtl, 1880). We could therefore find the term *vermis* on plates in Gregor Reisch's *Margarita philosophica* (1503), Guillaume Le Lièvre's *Ars memorativa* (1523) published by Mondete Guimbaude, Hieronymus Brunschwig's *Surgery* (1525), Johann Host von Romberch's *Congestorium artificiose memorie* (1533), Cosimo Rosselli's *Thesaurus artificiose memoriae* (1579) edited by Damiano Rosselli, Lodovico Dolce's *Dialogo* (1586), Bernard de Lavinheta's edition of Ramon Lull's *Opera omnia* (1612), and Robert Fludd's *Utriusque cosmi majoris* (1617–1621). One of the last authors to have used the term *vermis* in this meaning seems to be John Elliotson in the 1840 fifth edition of his *Human physiology*.

Currently, the term *vermis* describes the midline part of the cerebellum, between both hemispheres. The reason why this part of the cerebellum was compared with a worm is clearly explained by Ernest Belzung, who wrote that the vermis is *"divisé transversalement par de nombreux plis parallèles rappelant eux d'un ver"* (crosswise divided by numerous parallel folds reminding us of those of a worm: Belzung, 1891); a comparison that had been previously outlined André Dulaurens (*"vermium figuram exprimentes"*: Dulaurens, 1605) and Isbrand van Diemerbroeck, who noted that it looks like *"des vers qu'on trouve dans les bois pourris"* (worms which are to be found in rotten wood: Diemerbroeck, 1695). With the passing centuries, the vermis went through many synonyms, all of them referring to a worm: *Wurmgewächs* (worm vegetation or neoplasm) by Mathaeus Dressler (1581), *processus vermiformis* (vermiform process) by Thomas Bartholin (1677), Philip Verheyen (1710), and the Cloquet brothers (1816, 1825), *productions vermiculaires* (vermicular productions) by Isbrand van Diemerbroeck (1695), *appendices vermiformes* (vermiform appendices) by Jacques-Bénigne Winslow (1752), *eminence vermiculaire* (vermicular eminence) by Alexis Boyer (1805) and Pierre-Paul Broc (n.d.), and purely and simply *Wurm* (worm) by Friedrich Sigmund Merkel (1888).

To the best of our knowledge, Jacques-Bénigne Winslow was the only one to apply the adjective *vermiformis* not only to the midline part of the cerebellum, but also to its hemispheres (*Appendices vermiformis lateralis*: lateral vermiform appendices), explaining that *"[ils] ressemblent à un gros bout de vers de terre"* (they look like a big piece of earthworms: Winslow, 1752).

After the earthworm, it is the turn of the freshwater crayfish to appear on the scene. This amazing metaphor is due to the French anatomist and polemicist Jean Riolan, who compared the cerebellar vermis with *"une queue d'une écrevisse de rivière écorchée"* (a tail of a flayed freshwater crayfish: Riolan, 1672). He also coined the term *conduit scalicoïde* (scalicoid duct). The origin of the adjective *scalicoïde* is quite obscure. First, it may derive from the Greek *skalis* (weeding hoe), though it seems difficult to understand the comparison of the cerebellar vermis with a tool used to clear weeds. Second, and we favor this hypothesis, it might be a typing error in Riolan's treatise: *scalicoïde* could have read *scolécoïde*, from the Greek *skolex* (worm), an adjective that had been previously used by Galen to describe the lateral choroid plexuses (*Apophyses scolecoideae*: Galen, 1528).

It is now time to answer the question raised in the title of this paper. The famous Jean de La Fontaine actually involved a freshwater crayfish in one of his numerous fables, *The Freshwater Crayfish and its Daughter* (La Fontaine, 2000), but neither earthworm nor — of course — cerebellum.

References

Augé P (1933): *Larousse du XXe siècle*. Paris, Librairie Larousse, vol. 6.

Bartholin T (1677): *Anatome quartum renovata*. Lugduni, sumpt. Joan. Ant. Huguetan, & Soc.

Belzung E (1891): *Anatomie et physiologie animales*. Paris, Félix Alcan, 2nd edition.

Boyer A (1805): *Traité complet d'anatomie ou description de toutes les parties du corps humain*. Paris, Migneret, vol. 4.

Broc PP (n.d., ca. 1834): *Traité complet d'anatomie raisonnée et descriptive*. Paris, Just Rouvier, vol. 3.

Brunschwig H (1525): *The noble experyence of the vertuous handy warke of surgeri, practysyd & compyled by the moost experte mayster Jherome of Bruynswyke*. London, Petrus Treveris.

Cloquet H (1816): *Traité d'anatomie descriptive*. Paris, Crochard, vol. 2.

Cloquet J (1825): *Manuel d'anatomie descriptive du corps humain*. Paris, Béchet Jeune, Texte.

Diemerbroeck I van (1695): *L'anatomie du corps humain*. Lyon, Anisson & Posuel, vol. 2.

Dolce L (1586): *Dialogo nel quale si ragiona del modo di accrescere et conservar la memoria*. Venetia, Giovanbattista Sessa.

Dressler M (1581): *De partibus corporis humani, et de anima ejusque potentiis, libri duo*. Wittebergae, excud. Haeredes J. Cratonis.

Dulaurens A (1605): *Historia anatomica humani corporis partes*. Lugduni, Apud Horatium Cardon.

Elliotson J (1840): *Human physiology*. With which is incorporated much of the elementary part of the *Institutiones physiologicae* of J.F. Blumenbach. London, Longmans, 5th edition.

Fludd R (1617–1621): *Utriusque cosmi majoris scilicet et minoris metaphysica, physica atque technical historia in duo volumina secundum cosmic differentiam divisa.* Oppenheimii, Aere Johan-Theodori de Bry, typis Hieronymi Galleri.

Galen (1528): *De usu partium corporis humani . . . ad exemplaris Greaci veritatem castigatum . . . Nicolao Regio interprete.* Paris, ex officina Simonis Colinaei, Lib. VIII, Cap. 12.

Gladstone WJ (1990): *English-French dictionary of medical and paramedical sciences.* Paris, Maloine, 3rd edition.

Host von Romberch J (1533): *Congestiorum artificiose memorie . . . Omnium de memoria preceptiones aggregatim complectens; opus omnibus theologis; predicatoribus & confessoribus . . . medicis: philosophis, atrium liberalium professoribus, insuper mercatoribus nuntiis & tabellariis pernecessarium.* Venetiis, Per Melchiorem Sessam.

Hyrtl J (1880): *Onomatologia anatomica. Geschichte und Kritik der anatomischen Sprache der Gegenwart, mit besonderer Berücksichtigung ihrer Barbarismen, Widersinnigkeiten, Tropen, und grammatikalischen Fehler.* Wien, Wilhelm Braumüller.

La Fontaine J de (2000): *Fables. Texte intégral. Illustré par Born.* Paris, Gründ.

Lavinheta B de (1612): Opera omnia quibus tradidit artis Raymundi Lullii compendiosam explicationem. Coloniae, Sumptibus Lazari Zetzneri.

Le Lièvre G (1523): *Ars memorativa.* Tolosae: Veneunt in calchographia Joannis Fabri, cujus anima in pace requiescit. Mondete Guimbaude.

Merkel F (1888): *J. Henle's Grundriss der Anatomie des Menschen.* Braunschweig, Friedrich Vieweg und Sohn, dritte Auflage, Text.

Mondino dei Luzzi (1478): *Anothomia.* Papie, per Antonium de Carcano, leave 37.

Olry R (1989): Histoire des nomenclatures anatomiques. *Doc Hist Voc Sci CNRS 9*: 91–98.

Olry R (1991): Métaphores zoologiques au sein des ventricules latéraux du cerveau, ou l'imagination au service de la linguistique. *Hist Sci Med 25*: 221–224.

Olry R, Haines DE (2001a): Arachnophobia: Spiders and spider's webs in the head. *J Hist Neurosci 10*: 198–200.

Olry R, Haines DE (2001b): Claustrum: A sea wall between the island and the shell. *J Hist Neurosci 10*: 321–322.

Olry R, Martinoli MG (1995): Hippocampal genealogy: Analysis of a prolific semantic lineage. *Soc Neurosci Abstr 21*: 246.

Reisch G (1503): *Margarita philosophica.* Friburgi, J. Schotti.

Riolan J (1672): *Manuel anatomique et pathologique.* Lyon, Antoine Laurens.

Rosselli C (1579): *Thesaurus artificiose memoriae, concionatoribus, philosophicis, medicis, juristis, oratoribus, procuratoribus, caeterisque bonarum litterarum amatoribus.* Venetiis, Apud Antonium Paduanium, bibliopolam Florentinum.

Ryff WH (1541): *Wahrhafftige Beschreibung oder Anatomi, seines wunderbarlichen Ursprungs, Entpfängknisz, Schöpffung inn Mutterleib, und sorglicher Geburt.* Strazburg, Balthassar Beck.

Verheyen P (1710): *Corporis humani anatomiae liber primus.* Bruxellis, Apud t'Serstevens, Bibliopolas.

Winslow JB (1752): *Exposition anatomique de la structure du corps humain.* Amsterdam, Emanuel Tourneisen, nouvelle édition, vol. 4.

Korbinian Brodmann: The Victor Hugo of Cytoarchitectonic Brain Maps

In 1946, Karl Spencer Lashley and G. Clark wrote: "Unless the criteria are clearly stated and objectively verifiable . . . architectonic charts of the cortex represent little more than the whim of the individual student" (cited by Bailey & von Bonin, 1951, p. 189). Five years later, Percival Bailey and Gerhardt von Bonin added: "After long and careful study of the human isocortex, the main impression we have retained is that vast areas are so closely similar in structure as to make any attempt at subdivision unprofitable, if not impossible" (Bailey & von Bonin, 1951, p. 189). A whim? Unprofitable? Impossible?

The fact remains that numerous studies on the cerebral cortex, cyto- and/or myeloarchitecture, have resulted in architectonic brain maps springing up like mushrooms since the late nineteenth century: the whole cortex (Brodmann, 1909; Campbell, 1905; Economo & Koskinas, 1925; Exner, 1881; Sarkissov et al., 1955; Vogt, 1903), the temporal cortex (Blinkow, 1935; Kakeshita, 1925), the cortex of Broca's area (Knauer, 1909; Kreht, 1936; Riegele, 1931), the frontal cortex (Hof, Mufson, & Morison, 1995; Kononova, 1935; Ngowyang, 1934; Öngür, Ferry, & Price, 2003), the parietal cortex (Gerhardt, 1940; Gurewitsch & Khatchaturian, 1938; Stankewitsch & Schewchenko, 1935), the insular cortex (Brockhaus, 1940), among many others.

The best remembered name of this nonexhaustive list is without doubt that of Brodmann. Korbinian Brodmann, the son of the farmer Joseph Brodmann, was born at Liggersdorf, Hohenzollern, on November 17, 1868. He studied medicine in Munich, Würzburg, Berlin, and Freiburg im Breisgau and received his MD on February 21, 1895. He then planned to work as a general practitioner in Schwarzwald, but after having caught diphtheria he changed his mind and opted for research. He died of sepsis on August 22, 1918 (Vogt, 1959; Winckelmann, 1985, pp. 325–332).

As a researcher at the Berlin Institute of Neurology from 1901 to 1910, Brodmann published many contributions to the structure of cerebral cortex, including a series of seven papers (1903a, 1903b, 1905, 1906, 1908) that paved the way to his 1909 masterpiece *Vergleichende Lokalisationslehre der Grosshirnrinde in ihren Prinzipien dargestellt auf Grund des Zellbaues*. Page 131 of this book, which first appeared in a 1907 paper, is rightly regarded as a cornerstone of neurosciences, being probably one of the most often reproduced illustrations of that kind (Figure 1). In fact, almost every single text on the anatomy of the brain published in the modern era has reproduced this figure.

Brodmann subdivided the cerebral cortex into areas indicated by a simple Arabic number, from area 1, or *area postcentralis intermedia* (intermediate part of postcentral gyrus) to area 52, or *area parainsularis* (transitional cortex between insula and superior temporal gyrus). However, Brodmann's areas actually are not 52 in number, but only 44 because areas 13–16 and 48–51 do not exist!

Why did Brodmann's brain map survive all its competitors in common vocabulary? In 1987, Edward G. Jones accounted for this question as follows: "Among these names, that

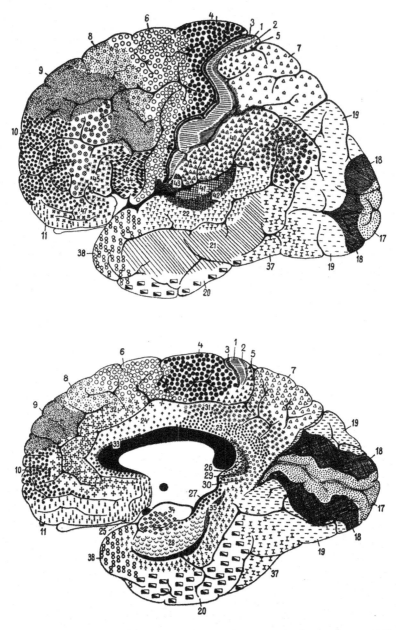

Figure 1. Brodmann's areas on lateral and medial aspects of human brain (Brodmann, 1909, p. 131).

of Brodmann is perhaps the best remembered since the numbers he assigned to the cortical fields he identified have entered into the common vocabulary of cortical anatomy and physiology" (Jones, 1987, pp.180–181). To explain that Brodmann is the best remembered because his nomenclature entered into common usage cannot be the entire explanation. The explanation, or more exactly the explanations, lay elsewhere, but not in chronology since, as mentioned above, Brodmann's brain map was neither the first one nor the last one.

A comparison of different terminologies used on some brain maps may lead us to find the answer to the riddle. On the lateral cerebral cortex, Brodmann's area 4 may be considered as overlapping Economo and Koskinas' 4 areas FAγ, FA, FBA, and Faop (1925), Ngowyang's 8 areas 42d, 42e, 42f, 42k, 42l, 42h, 39c, and 40β (1934), and Exner's 13 areas 23, 24, 29, 41, 47, 53, 59, 66, 72, 78, 85, 92, and 99 (1881). In Brockhaus' terminology, some insular areas are labelled *moipd* or *i5aa* (1940), and Gerhardt's map some tens of parietal areas, such as $90a_{ip}$, $90t_10$, and $89p_m$ (1940). Obviously, most authors coined a terminology that proved to be unusable because it was excessively complicated and difficult to recall.

Brodmann's cytoarchitectonic brain map is far and away the most practical, having a relatively low number of subdivisions, on the one hand, and the extreme simplicity of the names, on the other hand. And that is probably a major reason why his cytoarchitectonics is described as "the most comprehensive account of the subject" (Norman, 1991, pp. 227–228).

On December 2, 1852, Victor Hugo concluded his *Ultima verba* (My Last Word; Hugo, 1968, pp. 767–768) with this stanza:

> *Si l'on n'est plus que mille, eh bien, j'en suis! Si même*
> *Ils ne sont plus que cent, je brave encore Sylla;*
> *S'il en demeure dix, je serai le dixième;*
> *Et s'il n'en reste qu'un, je serai celui-là.*
>
> *(If a thousand are left to meet that [...] challenge, among those brave names*
> * will also be mine [...]*
> *And if to one hundred their number decline, I will be with them all [...]*
> *And if the hundred should dwindle to ten [...] I will be found among those*
> * ten men.*
> *And should fate this honor to one man decree [...] the last I will be!)*

And should fate the honor of being remembered as the pivotal figure of cytoarchitectonics to one man decree, the last Korbinian Brodmann will be.

References

Bailey P, von Bonin G (1951): *The Isocortex of Man.* Urbana, University of Illinois.

Blinkow SM (1935): Some questions relating to the cytoarchitecture of the cortex of the temporal lobe. *Sov Neuropath Psychiat Psych Hygiene 4*: 23–44.

Brockhaus H (1940): Die Cyto- und Myeloarchitektonik des Cortex claustralis und des Claustrum beim Menschen. *J Psychol Neurol 49*: 249–348.

Brodmann K (1903a): Der Regio rolandica. *J Psychol Neurol 2*: 79–107.

Brodmann K (1903b): Der Calcarina typus. *J Psychol Neurol 2*: 133–159.

Brodmann K (1905): Die Rindenfelder der niederen Affen. *J Psychol Neurol 4*: 177–226.

Brodmann K (1906): Über den allgemeinen Bauplan des Cortex pallii bei den Mammaliern und zwei homologe Rindenfelder im besonderen. Zugleich ein Beitrag zur Furchenlehre. *J Psychol Neurol* 6: 275–400.

Brodmann K (1908): Cortexgliederung des Menschen. *J Psychol Neurol 10*: 231–246.

Brodmann K (1909): *Vergleichende Lokalisationslehre der Grosshirnrinde in ihren Prinzipien dargestellt auf Grund des Zellbaues.* Leipzig, Johann Ambrosius Barth.

Campbell AW (1905): *Histological Studies on the Localization of Cerebral Functions.* Cambridge, University Press.

Economo C von, Koskinas GN (1925): *Die Cytoarchitektonik der Hirnrinde des erwachsenen Menschen.* Wien und Berlin, J. Springer.

Exner S (1881): *Untersuchungen über Localisation der Functionen in der Grosshirnrinde.* Wien, Wilhelm Braumüller.

Gerhardt E (1940): Die Cytoarchitektonik des Isocortex parietalis beim Menschen. *J Psychol Neurol* 49: 367–419.

Gurewitsch M, Khatchaturian A (1938): The variability of the structure of the cerebral cortex. The superior parietal region of man. *Publ Brain Inst Moscow 3*: 275–310.

Hof PR, Mufson EJ, Morison JH (1995): Human orbitofrontal cortex: Cytoarchitecture and quantitative immunohistochemical parcellation. *J Comp Neurol 359*: 48–68.

Hugo V (1968): Châtiments, XIV: Ultima Verba. In: Massin J, ed., *Victor Hugo. Oeuvres complètes.* Paris, Club français du livre, Vol. 8, pp. 767–768. (English translation by Manuel A. Tellechea).

Jones EG (1987): Brodmann's Areas. In: Adelman G, ed., *Encyclopedia of Neurosciences.* Boston Basel Stuttgart, Birkhäuser, Vol. 1.

Kakeshita T (1925): Zur Anatomie der operkularen Temporal Region. *Arb Neurol Inst Wiener Univ* 27: 292–326.

Knauer A (1909): Die Myeloarchitektonik der Broca's Schen Region. *Neurol Centralbl 28*: 1240–1243.

Kononova EP (1935): Variability of structure of the cerebral cortex. Lower frontal convolution of an adult. *Brain Res Inst Publ Moscow 1*: 49–116.

Kreht H (1936): Cytoarchitektonik und motorisches Sprachcentrum. *Ztschr mikr-anat Forschg 39*: 331–354.

Ngowyang G (1934): Die Cytoarchitektonik des menschlichen Stirnhirns. I. Teil. Cytoarchitektonische Felderung der Regio granularis und Regio dysgranularis. Monogr 7. *Nat Res Inst Psychol Acad Sinica*: 1–54.

Norman JM, ed. (1991): *Morton's Medical Bibliography* (fifth edition). Aldershot, Scholar Press.

Öngür D, Ferry AT, Price JL (2003): Architectonic subdivision of the human orbital and medial prefrontal cortex. *J Comp Neurol 460*: 425–449.

Riegele L (1931): Die Cytoarchitektonik der Felder der Broca'schen Region. *J Psychol Neurol 42*: 496–515.

Sarkissov SA, Filimonoff IN, Kononova EP, Preobraschenskaja IS, Kukuew LA (1955): *Atlas of the Cytoarchitectonics of the Human Cerebral Cortex.* Moscow, Medgiz.

Stankewitsch IA, Schewchenko JG (1935): Variability of structure of the cerebral cortex. Inferior parietal lobule of the adult. *Contr Brain Inst Moscow 1*: 119–172.

Vogt O (1903): Zur anatomischen Gliederung des Cortex cerebri. *J Psychol Neurol 2*: 160–180.

Vogt O (1959): Korbinian Brodmann, Lebenslauf. In: Kolle K, ed., *Grosse Nervenärzte*, Vol. 2, pp. 40–44.

Winckelmann E (1985): Postface. In: *Vergleichende Lokalisationslehre der Grosshirnrinde in ihren Prinzipien dargestellt auf Grund des Zellbaues.* Leipzig, Ambrosius Barth, pp. 325–335. (Original work published in 1909).

Brain Heraldic Tinctures and Evolution Theory: A Sensational Turn of Events That Should Have Been Kept Secret

Colors are often used in medical terminology: white in albinism (Latin *albus*) and leukocyte (Greek *leukos*), yellow in flavobacterium (Latin *flavos*) and icterus (Greek *ikteros*), blue in ceruloplasmin (Latin *caeruleus*) and cyanosis (Greek *kyanos*), green in chloroma (Greek *chloron*), red in rubedo (Latin *ruber*) and erythrocyte (Greek *erythron*), purple in purpura (Latin *purpureus*) and porphyrine (Greek *porphyreos*), pink in roseola (Latin *roseus*) and rhodopsin (Greek *rodeos*), brown in fuchsin (Latin *fuscus*) and pheochromocytoma (Greek *phaios*), black in nigrosin (Latin *niger*) and melanoma (Greek *melas*), grey in canities (Latin *canus*) and tephrosis (Greek *tephros*), silver in argentaffin (Latin *argenteus*) and argyrophil (Greek *argyreos*), and gold in aurotherapy (Latin *aureus*) and chrysotherapy (Greek *chrysos*), among many others (Bossy, 1999, pp. 39–41). To the best of our knowledge, the forerunners in neuroanatomical terminology had recourse to five colors: red (for the red nucleus), blue (for the locus coeruleus), black (for the substantia nigra), and white and grey (for the white and grey matters).

The red nucleus, or "olive supérieure" (superior olive) (Luys, 1865), is located in the mesencephalic tegmentum, dorsomedial to the substantia nigra. Its pink tinge, sometimes attributed to the richness of its vascularization (Bossy, 1990, p. 138)" appears only in fresh material and is caused by a ferric iron pigment in its multipolar neurons" (Standring, 2008, p. 290). Though previously outlined by Giovanni Domenico Santorini, Félix Vicq d'Azyr, Johann Christian Reil, and Karl Friedrich Burdach (Dejerine, 1895, p. 526), the first accurate description of the red nucleus is usually ascribed to the German anatomist and surgeon Benedikt Stilling, probably in his 1846 *Disquisitiones de structura et functionibus cerebri*. Some historians also involved the French anatomist Marie Philibert Constant Sappey in the discovery of the red nucleus (Terra, 1913, p. 368). Sappey's treatise of descriptive anatomy went through four editions. Having found a description of the red nucleus in the 1875 edition of Joseph Auguste Fort's *Anatomy* (Fort, 1875 p. 710), this would imply that Sappey pointed out this formation in one of the earlier editions of his treatise; we therefore consulted both first and second editions (Sappey, 1852–1857, 1867–1874). Unfortunately, we could not find the slightest allusion to the red nucleus. Pending further investigation, it seems that Sappey was therefore not involved in the discovery of this structure.

The locus coeruleus, which should actually read caeruleus (Donath, 1960, p. 356), or cell group A6 (Dahlström & Fuxe, 1964), is a noradrenergic nucleus located in the lateral corner of the rostral pole of the fourth ventricle (Nieuwenhuys, Voogd, & van Huijzen, 2008, p. 204). It was discovered by Félix Vicq d'Azyr in 1786 (Roberts & Tomlinson, 1992, p. 532), but the name locus coeruleus was coined 65 years later by Friedrich Arnold (1851). It seems, however, that Arnold did not actually apply this term to the current locus coeruleus but to an area of the superior fovea of the fourth ventricle's floor characterized by "la présence presque constante d'une ou plusieurs veines superficielles" (the almost constant presence of one or many superficial veins; Dejerine, 1895, p. 498). Moreover, Arnold also coined the term *Substantia ferruginea* (ferruginous substance), for this formation could appear either bluish — the adjective *coeruleus* meaning sky-blue — or brownish — the adjective *ferruginea* meaning to look like iron-rust. The term *Substantia ferruginea* was still in use in some treatises of the early twentieth century (Charpy, 1901, p. 382).

The substantia nigra (black substance) was discovered by Félix Vicq d'Azyr who coined the term *Locus niger crurum cerebri* (Vicq d'Azyr, 1786, p. 82) and depicted this formation on Plate XXVII of his masterpiece, engraved by Angélique Briceau. It was called *Nucleus niger* in the 1935 Jena Nomina Anatomica (Kopsch, 1950, p. 96) but became *Substantia nigra* again from the 1955 Paris revision.

The distinction between white and grey matters is usually (Clarke & Dewhurst, 1984, p. 76) ascribed to the 1586 *Anatomicae praelectiones* of Roman Professor of Anatomy Arcangelo Piccolomini (Lauth, 1815, pp. 557–559). Albrecht von Haller, who did not like him and called him a peripatetic, however acknowledged that he "cineream cerebri partem distinxit" (distinguished the ash-grey part of the brain) (Haller, 1774, p. 260). Actually, the difference between grey and white matter was observed earlier. As far back as in 1539, his book being published only in 1545 because of proceedings, Charles Estienne pointed out the fact that the brain has more white color inside than outside, and Andreas Vesalius' plates clearly depicted the limit between grey and white matter on horizontal brain sections (Huard & Imbault-Huart, 1980, pp. 180–185).

What would these colors mean in heraldry? Heraldic tinctures are divided into metals (argent for white, or for gold), colors (azure for blue, gules for red, sable for black, vert for green, purpure for purple), and furs (essentially ermine and vair) (Galbreath & Jéquier, 1977, pp. 91–95; Neubecker, 1977, pp. 86–87; Pautet du Parois, 1854/1979, art. 70–92, pp. 100–102). The red color is associated with "charité, magnanimité, vaillance & hardiesse" (charity, magnanimity, bravery, and boldness), the blue color with "justice, loyauté, louange, beauté, clarté, pureté, science, gentillesse & renommée" (justice, honesty, praise, beauty, clearness, purity, science, kindness, and renown), the black color with "prudence, patience, douleur, tristesse et fermeté" (carefulness, patience, pain, sadness, and firmness), and the white color with "espérance, pureté, innocence, humilité, beauté, victoire et félicité" (hope, purity, innocence, humbleness, beauty, victory, and felicity) (Bara, 1581, pp. 16–18). The red nucleus, the locus coeruleus, the substantia nigra, and the white matter should therefore rightly be proud of their coat of arms.

But what about the grey color? Hiérosme de Bara does not mention it because it belongs to heraldic tincture that "sont de création récente" (are of recent creation) (Morin, 1919, p. 42). As for its meaning, here comes the sensational turn of events announced in our title: the grey color is regarded "plutôt comme une déchéance" (rather as a downfall) (Morin, 1919, p. 42), as though the amount of grey matter was in inverse ratio to the intellectual faculties.

References

Arnold F (1851): *Handbuch der Anatomie*. Freiburg in Breisgau, Herder.

Bara H de (1581): *Le blason des armoieries, Auquel est monstree la maniere de laquelle les Anciens & Modernes ont vsé en icelles*. Lyon, Barthelemi Vincent.

Bossy J (ed.) (1990): *Anatomie clinique: Neuroanatomie*. Paris, Springer-Verlag.

Bossy J (1999): *La grande aventure du terme médical: Filiation et valeurs actuelles*. Montpellier, Sauramps Médical.

Charpy A (1901): Système nerveux. In Poirier P, Charpy A, eds., *Traité d'anatomie humaine*. Paris, Masson et Cie, 2nd edition, vol. 3.

Clarke E, Dewhurst K (1984): *Histoire illustrée de la fonction cérébrale*. Paris, Roger Dacosta.

Dahlström A, Fuxe K (1964): Evidence for the Existence of Monoamine-Containing Neurons in the Central Nervous System: 1. Demonstration of Monoamines in the Cell Bodies of Brain Stem Neurons. *Acta Physiol Scand 62*(Suppl. 232): 1–55.

Dejerine J (1895): *Anatomie des centres nerveux*. Paris, J. Rueff, vol. 2.

Donath T (1960): *Erläuterndes anatomisches Wörterbuch. Vergleichende Übersicht der Baseler, Jenaer und Pariser Nomenklaturen, gruppiert nach Organen*. Budapest, Verlag Medicina Budapest.

Estienne C (1545): *De dissectione partium corporis humani libri tres*. Paris, Apud Simonem Colinaeum, liber II, c. 48.

Fort JA (1875): *Anatomie descriptive et dissection*. Paris, Adrien Delahaye, 13th edition, vol. 2.

Galbreath DL, Jéquier L (1977): *Manuel du blason*. Lausanne, Spes.

Haller A von (1774): *Bibliotheca anatomica, qua scripta ad anatomen et physiologiam facientia a rerum initiis recensentur*. Tiguri, apud Orell, Gessner, Fuessli, et Socc., vol. 1.

Huard P, Imbault-Huart MJ (1980): *André Vésale. Iconographie anatomique (Fabrica, Epitome, Tabulae sex)*. Paris, Roger Dacosta.

Kopsch F (1950): *Die Nomina anatomica des Jahres 1895 (B.N.A.) nach der Buchstabenreihe geordnet und gegenübergestellt den Nomina anatomica des Jahres 1935 (I.N.A.)*. Leipzig, Georg Thieme.

Lauth T (1815): *Histoire de l'anatomie*. Strasbourg, F. G. Levrault, vol. 1 (all published).

Luys JB (1865): *Recherches sur le système nerveux cérébrospinal, sa structure, ses fonctions et ses maladies*. Paris, J. B. Baillière et fils, 2 vols.

Morin V (1919): *Traité d'art héraldique*. Montréal, Beauchemin.

Neubecker O (1977): *Le grand livre de l'héraldique*. Bruxelles, Elsevier Séquoia.

Nieuwenhuys R, Voogd J, van Huijzen C (2008): *The Human Central Nervous System*. Berlin Heidelberg, Springer, 4th edition.

Pautet du Parois JF (1979): *Nouveau manuel complet du blason ou code héraldique*. Paris, Leonce Laget. (Original work published in 1854)

Piccolomini A (1586): *Anatomicae praelectiones . . . explicantes mirificam corporis humani fabricam; et quae animas vires, quibus corporis partibus, tanquam instrumentis, ad suas obeundas actiones, utantur; sciutu tota anima, toto corpore*. Romae, Ex typographia Bartholomaei Bonfadini.

Roberts KB, Tomlinson JDW (1992): *The Fabric of the Body: European Traditions of Anatomical Illustration*. Oxford, Clarendon Press.

Sappey PC (1852–1857): *Traité d'anatomie descriptive*. Paris, Victor Masson, 3 vols.

Sappey PC (1867–1874): *Traité d'anatomie descriptive*. Paris, Adrien Delahaye, 12th edition, 4 vols.

Standring S (ed.) (2008): *Gray's Anatomy: The Anatomical Basis of Clinical Practice*. Churchill Livingstone Elsevier, 40th edition.

Stilling B (1846): *Disquisitiones de structura et functionibus cerebri: I. De structura protuberantiae annularis, sive pontis varolii*. Jena, Friedrich Mauke.

Terra P de (1913): *Vademecum anatomicum: Kritisch-etymologisches Wörterbuch der systematischen Anatomie: Mit besonderer Berücksichtigung der Synonymen*. Jena, Verlag von Gustav Fischer.

Vicq d'Azyr F (1786): *Traité d'anatomie et de physiologie, avec des planches coloriées représentant au naturel les divers organes de l'homme et des animaux*. Paris, François Ambroise Didot l'Aîné.

Renfield's Syndrome: A Psychiatric Illness Drawn from Bram Stoker's *Dracula*

The myth of vampirism is in the best of health, witness the many films (Karg, Spaite, & Sutherland, 2009; Ross, 1990), studies (Barber, 1988; Finné, 2010; Gaston, 2009; Ponnau, 1997; Pozzuoli, 2010; Stiles, Finger, & Bulevich, 2010; Stiles, Finger, & Petrain, 2010) and bestsellers devoted to the descendants of Bram Stoker's 1897 *Dracula*. This never-ending success shows that "the image [of vampire] is omnipotent, and this has been a reality since the most early times of history" (Markale, 2010, p. 9). Indeed, as pointed out by Robert Ambelain (1977), some of King David's Psalms already made an allusion to creatures we refer today to as vampires: *"et de viris sanguinum salva me. Quia ecce ceperunt animam meam [. . .] Convertentur ad vesperam: et famem patientur ut canes [. . .] et gladius in labiis eorum"* ("and save me from these blood men. Because they took possession of my live [. . .] They will be back in the evening: and they will be starving like dogs [. . .] and they have a sword on their lips": Psalm 58: 3, 4, 7, 8; D'Allioli, 1884). We must, however, point out the fact that these psalms are not always so explicit: We could find some discrepancies between more ancient translations and comments (for example, see Mege, 1675).

The etiology of Renfield's syndrome — as that of other mental disorders we described previously (Olry & Haines, 2002, 2006a, 2006b, 2007) — remains unknown. However, its symptomatology obviously leads us to include it in psychiatrical and/or neurological diseases. But who is Renfield?

Renfield is a background character of Bram Stoker's 1897 *Dracula*. He is mentally ill, is confined and keeps up a telepathic correspondence with his master, Count Dracula, who has just left Transylvania to settle in the suburbs of London. Stoker introduces the personage of Renfield in three steps. Firstly, he makes the reader observe that a clinic of psychiatry is to be found close by Carfax estate, the house recently bought by Count Dracula: "There are but few houses close at hand, one being a very large house only recently added to and formed into a private lunatic asylum" (Stoker, 1897, p. 25). Secondly, he takes advantage of a letter from Lucy Westenra to Mina Murray to reveal the name of the psychiatrist: "Dr. John Seward, the lunatic-asylum man" (Stoker, 1897, p. 61). The name of Renfield, a patient Dr. Seward described in his diary, finally appears: "R. M. Renfield, aetat 59.- Sanguine temperament; great physical strength; morbidly excitable; periods of gloom, ending in some fixed idea which I cannot make out. I presume that the sanguine temperament itself and the disturbing influence end in a mentally-accomplished finish; a possibly dangerous man, probably dangerous if unselfish" (Stoker, 1897, p. 66). Over the following pages, Dr. Seward becomes more and more puzzled about his patient: "His moods change so rapidly that I find it difficult to keep touch of them, and as they always mean something more than his own well-being, they form a more than interesting study" (Stoker, 1897, p. 292). Finally, the death of Renfield is ascribed to Dracula by Quincey Morris who "saw a bat rise from Renfield's window, and flap westward" (Stoker, 1897, p. 311).

In the 1980s, Herschel Prins developed the idea of vampirism as a clinical condition (Prins, 1985), and the term Renfield's syndrome was coined in 1992 by the Philadelphia psychologist Richard Noll (1992) who gives its diagnostic:

1. A pivotal event often leads to the development of vampirism (blood drinking). This usually occurs in childhood, and the experience of bleeding or the taste of blood is found to be exciting. After puberty, the excitement associated with blood is experienced as sexual arousal.

2. The progression of Renfield's syndrome follows a typical course in many cases:

   Autovampirism is generally developed first, usually in childhood, by initially self-inducing scrapes or cuts in the skin to produce blood, which is then ingested, to later learning how to open major blood vessels (veins, arteries) in order to drink a steady stream of warm blood more directly. The blood may then be ingested at the time of the opening, or may be saved in jars or other containers for later imbibing or for other reasons. Masturbation often accompanies autovampiristic practices.

   Zoophagia (literally the eating of living creatures, but more specifically the drinking of their blood) may develop prior to autovampirism in some cases, but usually is next to develop. Persons with Renfield's syndrome may themselves catch and eat or drink the blood of living creatures such as insects, cats, dogs, or birds. The blood of other species may be obtained at places such as slaughter houses and then ingested. Sexual activity may or may not accompany these functions.

   Vampirism in its true form is the next stage to develop — procuring and drinking the blood of living human beings. This may be done by stealing blood from hospitals, laboratories, and so forth, or by attempting to drink the blood directly from others. Usually this involves some sort of consensual sexual activity, but in lust-murder type cases and in other nonlethal violent crimes, the sexual activity and vampirism may not be consensual.

3. The compulsion to drink blood almost always has a strong sexual component associated with it.

4. Blood will sometimes take on an almost mystical significance as a sexualized symbol of life or power, and, as such, an experience of well-being or empowerment will be reported by those with Renfield's syndrome following such activities.

5. Persons with Renfield's syndrome are primarily male.

6. The defining characteristic of Renfield's syndrome is the blood-drinking compulsion. Other related activities such as necrophilia and necrophagia that do not have as their goal the drinking of blood are not to be considered aspects of this disorder.

True case reports of Renfield's syndrome seem to be of the utmost rarity (Benezech et al., 1981; Bergh & Kelly, 1964; Bourguignon, 1977; Halevy et al., 1989; Hemphill & Zabow, 1983; Jaffe & Di Cataldo, 1994; Jensen & Poulsen, 2002; McCully, 1964) but, as concluded by Richard L. vanden Bergh and John F. Kelly, "The syndrome and fantasies of vampirism are more frequent and important than their relative absence in the literature would suggest" (Bergh & Kelly, 1964, p. 547).

Twentieth-century criminology has applied the metaphor of vampirism to some serial killers, on the basis of their alleged dealings with animal or human blood: Fritz Haarman, the *Hannover Vampire* (born in 1879, beheaded on April 15, 1925); Peter Kürten, the *Düsseldorf Vampire* (born in 1883, beheaded on July 2, 1931); John George Haigh, the *London Vampire* (born in 1909, hanged on August 10, 1949); and Richard Trenton Chase, the *Sacramento Vampire* (born in 1950, suicide on December 26, 1980). Who, among them, was really affected by Renfield's syndrome?

Neither Fritz Haarman — who was in fact necrophagous and a salesman of human flesh (Monestier, 2000) — nor John George Haigh, who claimed vampirism was nothing more than a ruse to establish a defense of insanity, fit the definition (Lane, 1995). Peter Kürten might be a case of Renfield's syndrome: He indeed revealed that in some instances he drank the blood of his victims (Everitt, 1993). But it is beyond question that Richard Trenton Chase long fulfilled the diagnosis criteria of Renfield's syndrome (Bourgoin, 1993), as confirmed by the forensic psychiatrist Ronald Markman who was in charge of his psychiatric expert's report: "While in prison, he repeatedly asked for fresh blood, human or otherwise, to drink for sustenance" (Markman & Bosco, 1993, p. 191).

Contemporary popularization of the types of behavior exemplified by Renfield, such as programs/movies portraying vampires or werewolves, may actually serve a positive scientific purpose. While they do not get to the root of the clinical condition, and rarely or never offer a "treatment," the observer is treated to a vivid impression (and hopefully some degree of understanding) of the personal and societal torment that individuals with actual clinical conditions of similar types actually experience. Renfield would probably feel somewhat vindicated.

References

Ambelain R (1977): *Le vampirisme*. Paris, Robert Laffont.

Barber P (1988): *Vampires, Burial, and Death: Folklore and Reality*. New Haven and London, Yale University Press.

Benezech M, Bourgeois M, Boukhabza D, Yesavage J (1981): Cannibalism and vampirism in paranoid schizophrenia. *J. Clin Psychiat 42*: 7.

Bergh RL vanden, Kelly JF (1964): Vampirism: A review with new observations. *Arch Gen Psychiat 11*: 543–547.

Bourgoin S (1993): *Serial Killers: Enquête sur les tueurs en série*. Paris, Grasset.

Bourguignon A (1977): Status of vampirism and of auto-vampirism. *Ann Méd-Psychol 1*: 191–196.

D'Allioli JF (1884): *Nouveau commentaire littéral, critique et théologique avec rapport aux textes primitifs sur tous les livres des divines écritures*. Paris, Louis Vivès, vol. 3.

Everitt D (1993): *Human Monsters: An Illustrated Encyclopedia of the World's Most Vicious Murderers*. Chicago, Contemporary Books.

Finné J (2010): Dracula. In: Delestré S, Desanti H, eds., *Dictionnaire des personnages populaires de la littérature XIXe et XXe siècles*. Paris, Éditions du Seuil.

Gaston D (2009): *Les vampires de A à Z. Histoire, mythes et légendes de l'univers des vampires*. N.p., City Editions.

Halevy A, Levy Y, Shnaker A, Orda R (1989): Auto-vampirism: An unusual cause of anaemia. *J. R. Soc Med 82*: 630–631.

Hemphill RE, Zabow T (1983): Clinical vampirism: A presentation of 3 cases and a reevaluation of Haigh, the "acid-bath murderer." *S Afr Med J 63*: 278–281.

Jaffe PD, Di Cataldo F (1994): Clinical vampirism: Blending myth and reality. *Bull Am Acad Psychiatry Law 22*: 533–544.

Jensen HM, Poulsen HD (2002): Auto-vampirism in schizophrenia. *Nord J Psychiatry 56*: 47–48.

Karg B, Spaite A, Sutherland R (2009): *Tout sur les vampires*. Varennes, Éditions AdA Inc.

Lane B (1995): *Chronicle of 20th Century Murder*. London, Virgin Publishing Ltd.

Markale J (2010): *L'énigme des vampires*. Paris, Pygmalion.

Markman R, Bosco D (1993): *Alone with the Devil: Psychopathic Killings that Shocked the World*. London, BCA.

McCully RS (1964): Vampirism: Historical perspective and underlying process in relation to a case of auto-vampirism. *J. Nerv Ment Dis 139*: 440–452.

Mege J (1675): *Explication des pseaumes de David, tirée des saints pères et des interprètes*. Paris, Louïs Billaine.

Monestier M (2000): *Cannibales: Histoire et bizarreries de l'anthropophagie hier et aujourd'hui*. Paris, le cherche midi éditeur.

Noll R (1992): *Vampires, Werewolves, and Demons: Twentieth Century Reports in the Psychiatric Literature*. New York, Brunner/Mazel, Publishers.

Olry R, Haines DE (2002): Lasthénie de Ferjol's Syndrome: A tribute paid by Jean Bernard to Jules Amédée Barbey D'Aurevilly. *J. Hist Neurosci 11*: 181–182.

Olry R, Haines DE (2006a): Munchausen Syndrome by proxy: Karl Friedrich Hieronymus, Baron von Münchhausen, hasn't got anything to do with it. *J. Hist Neurosci 15*: 276–278.

Olry R, Haines DE (2006b): Elpenor's Syndrome: The link between one of Ulysses' companions and the tenth president of the third French republic. *J. Hist Neurosci 15*: 159–161.

Olry R, Haines DE (2007): Oedipus Complex: A confession to a Berlin otorhinolaryngologist that became a cornerstone of psychoanalysis. *J. Hist Neurosci 16*: 337–340.

Ponnau G (1997): *La folie dans la literature fantastique*. Paris, Presses Universitaires de France.

Pozzuoli A (2010): *La Bible Dracula: Dictionnaire du vampire*. N.p., Le Pré aux Clercs.

Prins H (1985): Vampirism: A Clinical Condition. *Br J. Psychiat 146*: 666–668.

Stiles A, Finger S, Bulevich J (2010): Somnambulism and trance states in the works of Dr. John Polidori, author of *The Vampyre*. *Eur Romantic Rev 21*: 789–807.

Stiles A, Finger S, Petrain DE (2010): A new look at Polidori. *Eur Romantic Rev 21*: 771–773.

Stoker B (1897): *Dracula*. London, Archibald Constable and Company.

"Matthew Effect" in Neurosciences

Some years ago, we devoted a column to possessive/nonpossessive eponyms in neuroscience (Haines & Olry, 2003). The world of eponyms, of course, provides an inexhaustible supply of linguistic material for historians to scrutinize (Anonymous, 1986; Cooper, 1983; Burchell, 1985; Endtz, 1989; Dervaud, 1990; Olry, 1995). Let's give two typical examples. Firstly, Ganser's commissure, described in 1882 by Dresden neuropsychiatrist Sigbert Joseph Maria Ganser (1882). This commissure actually was discovered by Franz Schnopfhagen five years earlier (Schnopfhagen, 1877), and "par suite d'une confusion regrettable" ("by an unfortunate mistake"; Dejerine, 1901) L. O. Darkschewitsch and G. I. Pribytkov called it Forel's commissure in 1891. Secondly, Bronislaw Onuf-Onufrowicz (1899) coined the term "Nucleus X" to refer to a parasympathetic subpopulation of sacral spinal cord neurons at the very end of the nineteenth century. His name was kept in anatomical literature but only in the form of "Onuf's nucleus X" (Paturet, 1964).

In the present column, we would like to explore another facet of eponyms: their involvement in the so-called "Matthew effect."

Robert King Merton (1910–2003), an American sociologist and Giddings Professor at Columbia University, coined the term "Matthew effect" to refer to the act of a priori ascribing an important scientific discovery to the head of the laboratory, even when the real discoverer had been one of his/her students (Merton, 1973; for review, see Rigney, 2010). In other words, history is more inclined to memorize the names of generals than those of lesser soldiers. The Matthew effect has its roots in the Gospel of Matthew, probably written in Syria in the late first century AD: "For unto every one that hath shall be given, and he shall have abundance: but from him that hath not, even that which he hath shall be taken away" (Matthew 25:29; American Standard Version). One of the most famous examples of the Matthew effect, and one that became a media event, occurred in 1974, when British radio astronomer Anthony Hewish (b. 1924) won the Nobel Prize for Physics (together with Martin Ryle) for the discovery of pulsars. In reality, the first person to notice the stellar radio source was not him but his student Jocelyn Bell (b. 1943) (Wade, 1975; Broad & Wade, 1987; Greenstein, 1987).

What about the Matthew effect in neurosciences? Let us look at two well-known eponyms (Gasser's ganglion and Lasègue's sign) and two less classical ones (Schacher's ganglion and Davidoff-Schechter's artery).

Gasser's ganglion, or the trigeminal ganglion (*Ganglion trigeminale*), lies on the trigeminal impression of the anterior surface of the petrous part of temporal bone. Johann Lorenz Gasser (1723–1765) taught anatomy at the Vienna University as a substitute for the titular professor Franz Joseph Jaus (1696–1771), who hated teaching. Gasser was so successful in his lectures that he received an MD degree without an examination on Gerard van Swieten's (1700–1772) and Anton de Haën's (1704–1776) advice (Hirsch, 1884–1888, vol. 6, pp. 813–814; Dupont, 1999, p. 270). Gasser's ganglion was, however, not described by Gasser, but by his pupil, Anton Balthasar Raymund Hirsch (1743–?), who coined the term semilunar ganglion in his 1765 dissertation (Hirsch, 1765; reprinted in Sandifort, 1778, and Ludwig, 1791–1795).

Lasègue's sign is a pain caused by the flexion of the hip when the knee is extended, whereas this movement is painless when the knee is flexed; it is suggestive of ischiatic neuralgia (Leiber & Olbert, 1968; Cohen, 1979). Paris neurologist Ernest Charles Lasègue (1816–1883) was appointed Professor of Clinical Medicine at the Necker Hospital in 1869 and a member of the *Académie de médecine* in 1876 (Hirsch, 1884–1888, vol. 3, pp. 616–617; Dupont, 1999, p. 382). When a factory inspector named Dujardin-Baumetz asked him to expose a shirker feigning an ischiatic neuralgia, Lasègue entrusted some of his students with this question. The first one P. A. Lagrelette did not mention the future Lasègue's sign in his 348-page dissertation (Lagrelette, 1869). But 12 years later, another student J. J. Forst finally described and accurately depicted on a drawing the sign that was to become the cornerstone for the diagnosis of ischiatic neuralgia (Forst, 1881; Leca, 1984).

The ciliary ganglion (*Ganglion ciliare*), sometimes known as Schacher's ganglion, is a parasympathetic ganglion located near the apex of the orbit, between the optic nerve and lateral rectus (Devos, Rénier, & Marcelle, 1939). Polycarp Gottlieb Schacher (1674–1737) was appointed professor of anatomy and surgery at Leipzig University in 1701 and served as dean of the medical faculty from 1724 until his death (Hirsch, 1884–1888, vol. 5, p. 200; Albert, Norton, & Hurtes, 1995, p. 300; Dupont, 1999, p. 517). Many of his medical contributions were actually dissertations of his numerous students (Haller, 1774–1777, vol. 1, p. 786; Index-Catalogue, 1880–1895, vol. 12, pp. 623–624). Among these students we find Georg Friedrich Jäschke, who in 1701 submitted a 32-page dissertation on cataract, which included the description of the ciliary ganglion (Jäschke, 1701).

In the mid-1960s, P. M. Wollschlaeger and G. Wollschlaeger, using dissected brains, described a hitherto unknown thin branch of the posterior cerebral artery supplying the medial aspect of the tentorium cerebelli and the posterior portion of the falx cerebri (Wollschlaeger & Wollschlaeger, 1965). This branch was called Davidoff-Schechter's artery, the name of their former mentors.

Should we go so far as to say that Hirsch, Forst, Jäschke, and both Wollschlaegers were victims of the Matthew effect? Should, for example, Gasser's ganglion have been more rightfully remembered as Hirsch's ganglion, or at least as Hirsch-Gasser's ganglion? This question merits some reflection, and for historians, it has some history.

As far back as 1895, the founder of official anatomical terminology already raised the question of the upholding of eponyms but could not succeed in reaching a decision: "Die Frage, ob man persönliche Namen beibehalten soll oder nicht, konnte nicht Gegenstand einer Abstimmung sein" ["the question whether eponyms should be kept or not could not be unanimously decided"] (His, 1895, p. 19). That is why the most classical anatomical eponyms remained mentioned, though in brackets. In 1935, they were totally eliminated by the so-called *Iena Nomina Anatomica* (Kopsch, 1950) and never officially reappeared since that time. In neuroanatomy, the Matthew effect should therefore be just a memory now.

But another question should be clarified case by case: how to differentiate a true Matthew effect from an intentional decision of the student to honor his/her mentor? Gratitude of students seems to have been at the root of the terms Gasser's ganglion and Davidoff-Schechter's artery. In other cases, it is less obvious, but the protagonists are unfortunately no longer here to explain themselves, and so some wonderment about certain terms may endure.

References

Albert DM, Norton EWD, Hurtes E (1995): *Source Book of Ophthalmology*. Cambridge, MA, Blackwell Science.

Anonymous (1986): Eponyms in oncology. *European Journal of Surgical Oncology* 12(2):199.

Broad W, Wade N (1987): *La souris truquée. Enquête sur la fraude scientifique*. Paris, Éditions du Seuil.

Burchell BH (1985): Thoughts on eponyms. *International Journal of Cardiology* 8: 229–234.

Cohen A (1979): *Dictionnaire médical illustré de sémiologie patronymique*. Paris, Maloine S. A.

Cooper R (1983): Expanded eponyms: An aid to medical education. *Journal of the American Osteopathic Association* 82(10): 788–792.

Darkschewitsch LO, Pribytkov G (1891): Ueber die Fasersysteme am Boden des dritten Hirnventrikels. *Neurologisches Centralblatt* 10: 417.

Dejerine J (1901): *Anatomie des centres nerveux, vol. 2*. Paris, J. Rueff.

Dervaud G (1990): *Des éponymes en médecine*. Lille, thèse médecine.

Devos L, Rénier M, Marcelle R (1939): *Contribution à l'étude du système végétatif de l'œil*. Lille, Félix Planquart.

Dupont M (1999): *Dictionnaire historique des médecins dans et hors de la médecine*. Sans lieu., Larousse.

Endtz LJ (1989): Défense et illustration des éponymes. *La Presse médicale* 18(13): 653.

Forst JJ (1881): *Contribution à l'étude clinique de la sciatique*. Paris, thèse médecine no. 33.

Ganser SJM (1882): Vergleichend-anatomische Studien über das Gehirn des Maulwurfs. *Morphologisches Jahrbuch* 7: 591–725.

Greenstein G (1987): *Le destin des étoiles. Pulsars et trous noirs*. Paris, Éditions du Seuil.

Haines DE, Olry R (2003): "James Parkinson did not die of his own personal disease . . . he died of a stroke" eponyms: Possessive or nonpossessive? *Journal of the History of the Neuroscience* 12: 305–307.

Haller A von (1774–1777): *Bibliotheca anatomica. Qua scripta ad anatomen et physiologiam facientia a rerum initiis recensentur*. Zurich, apud Orell, Gessner, Fuessli, et Socc., 2 vols.

Hirsch ABR (1765): *Pars quinti nervorum encephali: disquisitio anatomica, in quantum ad ganglion sibi proprium semilunare et ad originem nervi intercostalis pertinet*. Vienna.

Hirsch A (1884–1888): *Biographisches Lexikon der hervorragenden Aerzte aller Zeiten und Völker*. Wien und Leipzig, Urban & Schwarzenberg, 6 vols.

His W (1895): Die anatomische Nomenclatur. Nomina anatomica, Verzeichniss der von der Commission der anatomischen Gesellschaft festgestellten Namen, eingeleitet und im Einverständniss mit dem Redasctionsausschuss erläutert. *Archiv für Anatomie und Physiologie (Supplement-Band)*: 1–183.

Index-Catalogue (1880–1895): *Index-Catalogue of the Library of the Surgeon-General's Office, United States Army*. Washington, DC, Government Printing Office, 16 vols.

Jäschke GF (1701): *Disputationem medico-chirurgicam. De cataracta. Submittit Polycarpus Gottlieb Schacher, respondente Georg Friedrich Jäschke*. Lipsiae, Typis Jo. Chr. Brandenburgeri.

Kopsch F (1950): *Die Nomina anatomica des Jahres 1895 (B.N.A.) nach der Buchstabenreihe geordnet und gegenübergestellt den Nomina anatomica des Jahres 1935 (I.N.A.)*. Leipzig, Georg Thieme.

RHINENCEPHALON, TABES DORSALIS, ETC

Lagrelette PA (1869): *Étude historique, séméiologique et thérapeutique de la sciatique.* Paris, thèse médecine no. 216.

Leca AP (1984): *Histoire illustrée de la rhumatologie. Goutte, rhumatismes et rhumatisants.* Paris, Roger Dacosta.

Leiber B, Olbert T (1968): *Die klinischen Eponyme. Medizinische Eigennamenbegriffe in Klinik und Praxis.* München Berlin Wien, Urban & Schwarzenberg.

Ludwig CF (1791–1795): *Scriptores neurologici minores selecti sive opera minora ad anatomiam physiologiam et pathologiam nervorum spectantia, vol. 1.* Lipsiae, J. F. Junius, J. G. Feind.

Merton RK (1973): *The Sociology of Science: Theoretical and Empirical Investigations.* Chicago, University of Chicago Press.

Olry R (1995): *Dictionnaire critique des éponymes en anatomie.* Stuttgart New York, Gustav Fischer.

Onuf-Onufrowicz B (1899): Notes on the arrangement and function of the cell groups in the sacral region of the spinal cord. *Journal of Nervous and Mental Disease* 26: 498–504.

Paturet G (1964): *Traité d'anatomie humaine. Tome IV. Système nerveux.* Paris, Masson & Cie.

Rigney D (2010): *The Matthew Effect: How Advantage Begets Further Advantage.* New York, Columbia University Press.

Sandifort E (1778): *Thesaurus dissertationum, programmatum, aliorumque opusculorum selectissimorum, ad omnem medicinae ambitum pertinentium, vol. 3.* Lugduni Batavorum, S. et J. Luchtmans.

Schnopfhagen F (1877): Beiträge zur Anatomie des Sehhügels und dessen nächster Umgehung. *Sitzungsberichte der Preussischen Akademie der Wissenschaften zu Wien* 76: 315.

Wade N (1975): Discovery of pulsars: A graduate student's story. *Science* 189: 358–364.

Wollschlaeger PM, Wollschlaeger G (1965): Eine infratentorielle meningeale Arterie. *Radiologie* 5: 451–452.

Is Poetry a Disease of the Brain, as Alfred de Vigny Said?

Except for the ode titled *Des beautez qu'il voudroit en S'Amie* printed on the verso of page 79 of Jacques Peletier's (1517–1582) *Oeuvres poetiques* (Peletier, 1547), the very first book published by French poet Pierre de Ronsard (1524–1585) was an epithalam (Ronsard, 1549). Forty-six years later, the first printing of Edmund Spenser's (1552–1599) *Epithalamion* appeared (Spenser, 1595), and it was rightly regarded as a landmark in Elizabethan literature.

What do these books have in common? Firstly, and by a strange coincidence, these two bibliographical treasures are exactly of the same and utmost rarity: only fives copies of each one are known to be extant (Maggs and Maggs, 1926, p. 298; O'More, 1989, no. 71, respectively). Secondly, they both include the term "epithalam" in their title (in French and in Greek, respectively), a term which of course reminds all neuroscientists of epithalamus. But the latter won't be the subject of this column.

The word "epithalam" was coined in 1536 to describe a poem or a song written to celebrate a marriage (Bloch and Wartburg, 2002, p. 229). Let's get back to our two examples mentioned in the preceding paragraph. Ronsard's epithalam was addressed to Antoine de Bourbon (1518–1562) and Jeanne d'Albret (1528–1572) who got married on October 20, 1548 and were soon to be parents of future King Henri IV. As for Spencer's epithalam, it seems to have been written in celebration of his own marriage to Elizabeth Boyle in 1594 (Drabble, 1996, p. 327). It is therefore about poetry that we are about to write.

Versification was quite usual in scientific literature of the past centuries (Schmidt, 1938), especially in morphological sciences (Vallant, n.d.; Gerberon, 1629; Quarré, 1638; Bimet, 1664; Brion, 1668; Spon, 1685; Abeille, 1685, 1689; Artance, 1846) and in the popular medical encyclopedias known as *Regimen sanitatis Salernitanum* (Le Long, 1637; Du Four de la Crespelière, 1671; Pougens, 1825; Meaux Saint Marc, 1861). Neurosciences, of course, did not escape this trend. In 1776, the surgeon and lexicographer Allouel gave an example of a poem (though its alexandrines should not be described as a masterpiece!) aimed at helping students to memorize the ten cranial nerves that were acknowledged at that time (Allouel, 1776, p. 94) :

Le plaisir des Parfums nous vient de la première;
(Pleasure of perfumes arises from the first one; *Olfactory*)
La seconde nous fait jouir de la lumière;
(The second one makes us enjoy light; *Optic*)
La troisième à nos yeux donne les mouvements;
(The third one to our eyes gives movements; *Oculomotor*)
La quatrième instruit du secret des Amans;
(The fourth one informs of the lover's secret; *Trochlear*)
La cinquième parcourt l'une et l'autre mâchoire;
(The fifth one travels through both jaws; *Trigeminal*)
La sixième nous peint le mépris & la gloire;
(The sixth one gives us an account of scorn & glory; *Abducens*)
La septième connait les sons & les accords;
(The seventh one knows sounds & chords; *Vestibulocochlear*)
La huitième au-dedans fait jouer les ressors;
(The eighth one works the springs inside; *Vagus*)
La neuvième au discours tient notre langue prête;
(The ninth one keeps our tongue ready for speech; *Hypoglossal*)
La dixième enfin meut & le col & la tête.
(The tenth one, finally, moves and the neck and the head; *Suboccipital*.)[1]

Why did some scientists decide to write their books in verse? French historian Antoine-Augustin Bruzen de la Martinière (1683–1746), the translator of the aphorisms of the Salerno Medical School, gave the following explanation : "Les verse ont l'avantage d'être retenus plus facilement que la prose" ("verse have the advantage of being memorized more easily than prose"; Bruzen de la Martinière, in : Hippocrate, 1934, p. 168). He had therefore already answered the question Harvard mathematician Robert Kaplan had recently asked himself: "les Indiens, comme les Grecs, avaient-ils tendance à associer la sagesse, le savoir et la mémoire, si bien qu'on écrivait les sujets importants comme les mathématiques en vers, plus faciles à apprendre?" ("Were Indians, like Greeks, inclined to unite wisdom, knowledge and memory, so that one wrote important subjects like mathematics in verse, more easy to learn?"; Kaplan, 2004, p. 46). Poetry was then considered as one of the numerous branches of mnemonics. Science and poetry got on well together, as illustrated by the nickname "anatomist poet" attributed without ulterior motive or touch of irony to the Lyons physician and anatomist Claude Bimet (Bouchet, 1958).

What about the relationship between scientific language and poetry nowadays? French astrophysicist (and poet!) Jean-Pierre Luminet deplores that, "Tout au long de l'histoire, cette façon de conter la science a connu des succès, mais aussi des critiques virulentes. Certains esprits se croyant puristes ont estimé que nulle expression littéraire ne pouvait rendre compte de la subtilité et de la complexité de la pensée scientifique" ("All along history, this way to relate science achieved success, but also violent criticisms. Some great minds which thought they were purist considered that no literary expression may account for subtlety and complexity of scientific view"; Luminet, 2005, p. 15). Verses have indeed totally disappeared from scientific literature; any attempt to reintroduce them would probably look "outmoded". Even mnemotechnic acrostics, though so appreciated by students, have unfortunately deserted textbooks. It is a pity, for it is true that "le poème est une grappe

---

[1] The italized terms in the poem are the contemporary versions of the cranial nerves known in 1776.

d'images" ("the poem is a cluster of pictures") and that "c'est par le poème que le langage atteint l'ordre le plus élevé" ("It is with the poem that language reaches the most elevated order") (from philosopher Gaston Bachelard and writer and poet Georges-Emmanuel Clancier, cited in Duhamel, 2003, pp. 413 and 421, respectively).

Having stated this, there is one phrase regarding cranial nerves that has been used for many years as a memory/learning tool. That phrase is "**O**n **O**ld **O**lympus **T**owering **T**ops **A F**inn **A**nd **G**erman [or Greek] **V**iewed **S**ome **H**ops" (the bold letters indicating the 12 cranial nerves from rostral —Olfactory— to caudal— Hypoglossal). Even within this comparatively simple mnemomic, there are some misnomers. For example, the so-called acoustic nerve (of the **A**nd) is more correctly called the vestibulocohlear nerve, and the spinal accessory nerve (of the **S**ome) is actually only the accessory nerve; it does not have spinal and bulbar parts.

To come back to the title of this column, Alfred de Vigny's (1797–1863) quotation is taken from his drama *Chatterton* (part of his 1832 *Stello*), acted for the first time at the *Théâtre Français* on February 12, 1835 with his own mistress Marie Dorval as Kitty Bell. The main character, a 18-year old man named Thomas Chatterton, was made to say (in Act 3, Scene 5) that, "la poésie est une maladie du cerveau" ("poetry is a disease of the brain" (Vigny, 1968, p. 93), a sentence summarizing the general theme of the piece — namely, the misfortune of poets in the society of that time (La Salle, 1963, pp. 123–158). Far from being a disease of the brain, poetry proved to be a catalyst of cerebral activity, in literature of course, but also in its flair for coining meaningful, and more easily memorized, scientific terms and descriptions.

References

Abeille S (1685): *Nouvelle histoire des os selon les anciens et les modernes, enrichie de vers*. Paris, R. Chevillion.

Abeille S (1689): *Chapitre singulier tiré de Guidon . . . en deux parties, et enrichie de vers*. (Part 2 of *L'anatomie de la tête et de ses parties*). Paris, Laurent d'Houry.

Allouel M (1776): *Explication des mots d'usage en anatomie et en chirurgie*. Paris, Rémont.

Artance F (1846): *Abrégé d'anatomie descriptive, en vers français. Première partie, renfermant l'ostéologie, la syndesmologie, la description des dents et des cinq organes des sens*. Paris, Chez les libraires de médecine.

Bimet C (1664): *Quatrains anatomiques des os et des muscles du corps humain. Ensemble un discours de la circulation du sang*. Lyon, Marc Antoine Gaudet.

Bloch O, Wartburg W von (2002): *Dictionnaire étymologique de la langue française*. Paris, PUF/QUADRIGE.

Bouchet A (1958): Un poète anatomiste au XVIIe siècle Claude Bimet, Chirurgien de l'Hôtel-Dieu de Lyon. *Cahiers d'Histoire de la Médecine* 3(2): 3–35.

Brion R (1668): *L'anatomie en vers français, contenant l'ostéologie, myologie & angiologie*. Chinon, F. d'Aryrem.

Drabble M (1996): The Oxford Companion to English Literature. Oxford New York, Oxford University Press, 5th and revised edition.

Du Four de la Crespelière CD (1671): *Commentaire en vers françois, sur l'École de Salerne . . . ou sont adjoustez. La sanguification, circulation et transfusion du sang, la poudre . . . de sympathie, le thé, le caphé, le chocolate et le grand secret de la pierre philosophale . . . aussi en vers françois, et l'ouromantie, scatomancie, et hydromantie en prose. Par Monsieur D.F.C. docteur en la Faculté de Médecine*. Paris, G. Clouzier.

Duhamel J (2003): *La passion des livres. Quand les écrivains parlent de la littérature, de l'art d'écrire et de la lecture*. Paris, Albin Michel.

Gerberon G (1629): *Le bouquet anatomique, où sont dénommées toutes les parties du corps humain et le lieu de leur situation, soient os, veines, muscles, tendons, artères, nerfs : parties nobles, parties génitales mesme le coït de l'homme et de la femme.* Paris.

Hippocrate (1934): *Les aphorismes d'Hippocrate suivis des aphorismes de l'École de Salerne.* Paris, Antiqua.

Kaplan R (2004): *À propos de rien. Une histoire du zéro.* Paris, Dunod.

La Salle B de (1963): *Alfred de Vigny.* S.l., Fayard.

Le Long M (1637): *Le régime de santé de l'Ecole de Salerne traduit et commenté par Michel Le Long avec l'esprit de Diodi Carystène touchant le présage des maladies et le serment d'Hippocrate, mis de prose en vers français.* Paris, Costi.

Luminet JP (2005): *L'Univers chiffonné.* S.l., Gallimard.

Maggs BD, Maggs EU (1926): *Books printed in France and French books printed in other countries from 1470 to 1700 A.D. (catalogue No. 484).* London, Maggs Bross.

Meaux Saint Marc C (1861): *L'école de Salerne, traduite en vers français avec le texte latin en regard, précédée par une introduction par le Dr Daremberg de la Sobriété, conseils pour vivre longtemps . . .* Paris, Baillière.

O'More H (1989): *The Collection of The Garden Ltd. Magnificent Books and Manuscripts.* New York, Sotheby's.

Peletier J (1547): *Les Oeuvres poetiques de Jacques Peletier du Mans.* Paris, de l'imprimerie de Michel de Vascosan pour luy et Gilles Corrozet.

Pougens MJFA (1825): *L'art de conserver la santé avec une traduction en vers français des vers latins de l'Ecole de Salerne.* Montpellier Paris, Pougens Bechet Gabon.

Quarré G (1638): *Myographia Heroico versu explicata.* Lutetiae Parisiorum, Impressis Authoris.

Ronsard P de (1549): *Epithalame d'Antoine de Bourbon, et Ianne de Navarre, par Pierre de Ronsart Vandomois.* Paris, de l'Imprimerie de Vascosan.

Schmidt AM (1938) *La poésie scientifique au XVIᵉ siècle.* Paris, Albin Michel.

Spenser E (1595): *Amoretti and Epithalamion. Written no long since by Edmunde Spenser.* [London], P[eter] S[hort] for William Ponsonby.

Spon C (1685): *Myologia heroico carmine expressa.* In: Le Clerc D, Manget JJ, eds., *Bibliotheca anatomica.* Geneva, Joannis Anthonii Chovet, vol. 2, pp. 584–597.

Vallant N (n.d.) : *La miologie ou méthodique description des muscles du corps humain.* (Bibliothèque nationale, Manuscrits français, no. 17057).

Vigny A de (1832): *Stello.* Paris, Ch. Gosselin et E. Renduel.

Vigny A de (1968): *Chatterton.* Paris, Garnier-Flammarion.

Between André Du Laurens' Horse Tail and William Cadogan's Pony Tail

The Genevan physician Théodore Colladon, the Dresden bibliographer Ludwig Choulant, and the Berlin historian of medicine Julius Leopold Pagel had at least one thing in common: All three were harsh critics of André Du Laurens' *Historia anatomica humani corporis*. In the early-seventeenth century, Théodore Colladon (d. ca. 1636), a student of Girolamo Fabrici (ca. 1533–1619), simply considered it as being not worth much (Colladon, 1615, Vol. 1, p. 1). In his mid-1800s famous study on anatomical iconography, Ludwig Choulant (1791–1861) wrote that its illustrations were *"ohne besonderen anatomischen oder künstlerischen Werth"* ["without special anatomical or artistic value"] (Choulant, 1852, p. 75). In the late nineteenth century, Julius Leopold Pagel (1851–1912) considered it as a *"Gewebe von Aberglauben, halbverdauten, unrecht verstandenen und schief vorgetragenen Grundsätzen, ohne dass dabei die grossen Entdeckungen seiner Vorgänger und Zeitverwandten gehörig benutz worden wären"* ["tissue of superstition, indigestible, misunderstood and wrongly presented principles, without any reference to the great discoveries made by his predecessors and contemporaries"] (Pagel, cited in Wolf-Heidegger & Cetto, 1967, p. 231).

Objection your honor! Every day, thousands of anatomists, neurologists, neuroradiologists, and neurosurgeons around the world pay homage—wittingly or not—to the memory of André Du Laurens, whose 1600 *Historia anatomica* included the roots of the term *"cauda equine,"* and an explicit engraved plate accounting for this metaphor (Figure 1). Let's recall that the term *"cauda equina"* (meaning horse's tail) refers to "the bundle of lumbar, sacral and coccygeal roots surrounding the *filum terminale*, caudal to the cord" (Nieuwenhuys, Voogd, & van Huijzen, 2008, p. 177), and that it is also used in comparative anatomy (Leyh, 1871, p. 525).

Who was André Du Laurens and what about the book in question? André Du Laurens (often wrongly spelled Dulaurens), the son of a physician, was born at Arles, South of France, in 1558. He studied medicine at the University of Montpellier from which he received his MD in 1583. In 1586, he succeeded Laurent Joubert (1529–1583) as Professor of Medicine, in 1600 joined the court of the King of France, three years later was appointed chancellor of the Montpellier University, and in 1606 replaced Roch Baillif de la Rivière

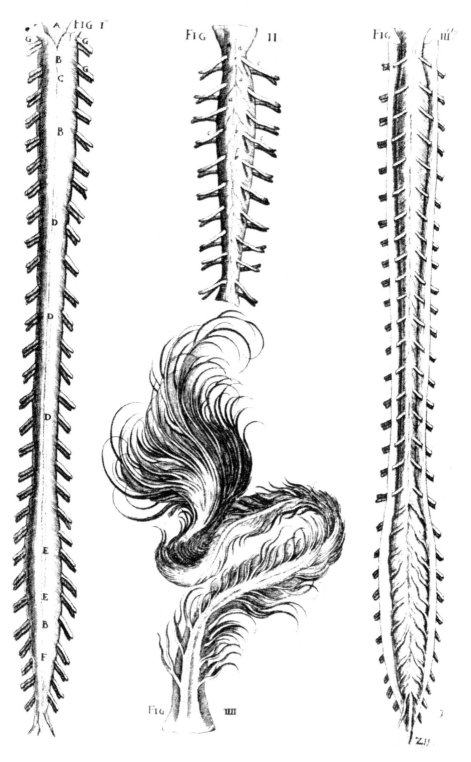

Figure 1. The famous plate of Dulaurens' 1600 *Historia anatomica* depicting the lower spinal nerves as a horse's tail or *cauda equina* (author's [R.O.] private collection).

(d. 1605) as personal physician to Queen Marie de Médicis and King Henry IV. André Du Laurens died on August 16, 1609 (Lauth, 1815, pp. 584–585; Rodrigues, 1842; Turner, 1880; Hirsch, 1884–1888, Vol. 3, p. 626; Dupont, 1999, pp. 210–211).

André Du Laurens wrote many publications on various medical subjects: preservation of the sight (Dunn, 1916), goiter, therapeutics, melancholy, catarrh. However, his masterpiece undeniably was his treatise of anatomy, "the most popular anatomical text of its time" (Albert, Norton, & Hurtes, 1995, pp. 91–92) that, with different titles, went through about 20 editions and translations from the Lyons 1593[1] to the Paris 1781 edition.

Du Laurens coined the term "*cauda equina*" because "*medulla spinalis dispersio caudae equinae similis*" ["the spinal cord breaks up in the same way that a horse's tail"] (Du Laurens, 1605, p. 274). According to the Jewish physician Benjamin Wolf Ginzburger (b. 1713), this metaphor has its roots in the Talmud (Ginzburger, 1743, p. 10), an assumption taken up by many historians of medicine (Haller, 1774–1777, Vol. 1, p. 126; Hyrtl, 1880, pp. 97–98; Hagelin, 1989, p. 53). We couldn't find the name of the engraver of the unnumbered plate depicting the *cauda equina*. The engraved title of the book is signed "C. D. Malleri," that is, Karel van Mallery (1571–c. 1635), and some of the plates have been ascribed to Jacob de Weert (b. 1569), a pupil of the Flemish engraver Hieronymus Wierix (1553–1619) (Norman, 1987, p. 50). Unfortunately, the plate in question does not show any signature or monogram.

Though Du Laurens' plate obviously depicts a horse's tail, the Franco-Danish anatomist Jacques-Bénigne Winslow (1669–1760) pointed out another possibility : "*Queue de Cheval, à cause de quelque ressemblance qu'il en paraît avec une chevelure, surtout quand il est détaché du Canal Osseux & mis dans de l'eau claire*" ["Pony tail, on account of some resemblance to a head of hair, especially when it is detached from the osseous canal and put into clear water"] (Winslow, 1752, Vol. 4, p. 188). To the best of our knowledge, it is the British general William Cadogan (1672–1726) who brought into fashion the pony tail tied by a ribbon (Boudet, 1998, pp. 971–972), a way to do one's hair referred to as "Cadogan" or "Catogan" since that time (Kybalová, Herbenová, & Lamarová, 1970, pp. 323–352). It may therefore be possible to assume that the metaphor *cauda equina*, in its neuroanatomical meaning, imperceptibly switched from comparative anatomy to hairstyle. Whatever the metaphor may have been, this term has come down through the successive revisions of the official anatomical terminology, from its 1895 outline to the present edition (His, 1895, p. 90; Kopsch, 1950, p. 16; Donáth, 1960, p. 233; Sobotta, 1977, p. 235; Terminologia Anatomica, 1998, p. 133).

Let us conclude with two anecdotes on terminological relationship between spinal cord and hair. Firstly, William Cadogan, who gave a name to the pony (and not horse) tail, never wrote anything about hairstyle nor hippology (Huth, 1887) but distinguished himself as colonel of a regiment. Of what arm? Of course the cavalry, the "6th (Cadogan's) Horse" (Ward, 1967, Vol. 4, pp. 565–566). Secondly, vertebrae—and especially cervical vertebrae and spinal chord—were in times past compared with "*chaînons*" (a French word meaning links), a term at the root of "*chignon*" (bun) with reference to the low implantation of hair (Castan, 1992, p. 85). The spinal cord therefore had a horse tail at its lower end and a bun at its upper end!

---

[1]Gerhard Wolf-Heidegger and Anna Maria Cetto refer to a 1589 edition (1967, p. 231). We compiled most medical bibliographies without finding any edition prior to 1593. To the best of our knowledge, the 1593 edition is really the first one but we would greatly appreciate the reader's remarks on this 1589 hypothetical bibliographical ghost.

References

Albert DM, Norton EWD, Hurtes E (1995): *Source Book of Ophthalmology*. Cambridge, Blackwell Science, Inc.

Boudet J (1998): *Les mots de l'histoire*. Paris, Larousse.

Castan P (1992): *L'anatomie masquée: Un essai sur la symbolique du langage anatomique*. Montpellier, no publisher name.

Choulant L (1852): *Geschichte und Bibliographie der anatomischen Abbildung nach ihrer Beziehung auf anatomische Wissenschaft und bildende Kunst*. Leipzig, Rudolph Weigel.

Colladon T (1615): *Adversaria, seu commentarii medicinales critici, dialytici, epanorthotici, exegematici ac didactici, ubi varii et multiplices neotericorum . . .* Coloniae Allobrogum, J. Stoer, 2 volumes.

Donáth T (1960): *Erläuterndes anatomisches Wörterbuch. Vergleichende Übersicht der Baseler, Jenaer und Pariser Nomenklaturen, gruppiert nach Organen*. Terra Budapest, Verlag Medicina Budapest.

Du Laurens A (1600): *Historia anatomica humani corporis & singularum eius partium multis controversiis & observationibus novis illustrata*. Parisiis, apud Marcum Orry.

Du Laurens A (1605): *Historia anatomica, humani corporis partes*. Lugduni, apud Horatium Cardon.

Dunn P (1916): A Sixteenth Century Oculist. *Proceedings of the Royal Society of Medicine* 9: 120–142.

Dupont M (1999): *Dictionnaire historique des Médecins dans et hors la médecine*. No place, Larousse-Bordas/HER.

Gintzburger BW (1743): *Disputatio inauguralis qua medicinam ex Talmudicis illustratam*. Gottingae, A. Vandenhoeck.

Hagelin O (1989): *Rare and Important Medical Books in the Library of the Swedish Society of Medicine: A Descriptive and Annotated Catalogue*. Stockholm, Svenska Läkaresällskapet.

Haller A von (1774–1777): *Bibliotheca anatomica. Qua scripta ad anatomen et physiologiam facientia a rerum initiis recensentur*. Tiguri, apud Orell, Gessner, Fuessli, et Socc.

Hirsch A (1884–1888): *Biographisches Lexikon der hervorragenden Aerzte aller Zeiten und Völker*. Wien und Leipzig, Urban & Schwarzenberg, 6 volumes.

His W (1895): Die anatomische Nomenclatur. Nomina anatomica. Verzeichniss der von der Commission der anatomischen Gesellschaft festgestellten Namen, eingeleitet und im Einverständniss mit dem Redactionsausschuss erläutert. *Archiv für Anatomie und Physiologie* (Supplement-Band).

Huth FH (1887): *A Bibliographical Record of Hippology*. London, Bernard Quaritch.

Hyrtl J (1880): *Onomatologia anatomica. Geschichte und Kritik der anatomischen Sprache der Gegenwart, mit besonderer Berücksichtigung ihrer Barbarismen, Widersinnigkeiten, Tropen, und grammatikalischen Fehler*. Wien, Wilhelm Braumüller.

Kopsch F (1950): *Die Nomina anatomica des Jahres 1895 (B.N.A.) nach der Buchstabenreihe geordnet und gegenübergestellt den Nomina anatomica des Jahres 1935 (I.N.A.)*. Leipzig, Georg Thieme, 4. Auflage.

Kybalová L, Herbenová O, Lamarová M (1970): *Encyclopédie illustrée du costume et de la mode*. Paris, Gründ.

Lauth T (1815): *Histoire de l'anatomie, Volume 1*. Strasbourg, F. G. Levrault.

Leyh F (1871): *Anatomie des animaux domestiques*. Paris, P. Asselin.

Nieuwenhuys R, Voogd J, van Huijzen C (2008): *The Human Central Nervous System*. Berlin, Springer-Verlag, 4th edition.

Norman J (1987): *Medicine and the Life Sciences: Catalogue Eighteen*. San Francisco, CA, Jeremy Norman & Company, Inc.

Rodrigues JBH (1842): *Notice sur Du Laurens, et analyse de ses oeuvres*. Montpellier, J. Martel, Snr.

Sobotta J (1977): *Atlas d'Anatomie Humaine, Volume 4*. Paris, Maloine S. A.: nomenclature anatomique française.

Terminologia Anatomica (1998): *International Anatomical Nomenclature Federative Committee on Anatomical Terminology*. Stuttgart, Thieme.

Turner E (1880): André Du Laurens. *Gazette hebdomadaire de Médecine et de Chirurgie* 17: 341–379.

Ward WR (1967): Cadogan, William Cadogan. In: *Encyclopaedia Britannica*. Chicago, William Benton, Publisher.

Winslow JB (1752): *Exposition anatomique de la structure du corps humain*. Amsterdam, Emanuel Tourneisen, nouvelle édition, 4 volumes.

Wolf-Heidegger G, Cetto AM (1967): *Die anatomische Sektion in bildlicher Darstellung*. Basel, New York, S. Karger.

Kanashibari (金縛り): A Ghost's Business

On July 1, 1976, the German student Anneliese Michel was found dead in her parents' house, in Klingenberg-am-Main, Bavaria. She was only 24 years old and the real nature of the disease from which she had been suffering during the last eight years of her life was—and continues to be—much written about: Some people say she had been struck down by a neurologic (epilepsy: generalized or uncinate) and/or psychiatric (psychosis) disorder (Goodman, 2005; Wolff, 2006; Wegner, 2009; Duffey, 2011), while others believe she had actually been possessed by the devil (Bullinger, 1983; Siegmund, 1985; Buttner, 1986; Fortea & LeBlanc, 2010). Such a differential diagnosis is of course not a matter for us (!), but the very first scary events Anneliese experienced in mid-September 1968 perfectly illustrate the topic of this column:

> That night, shortly after midnight, she woke up and could not move. A giant force was pinning her down. [. . .] Her breathing became labored. In utter panic, she wanted to call to her sisters, but no sound came out. Her tongue was as if paralyzed. "Holy Mother of God," she thought, "I must be dying." By the time the tower clock of the church sounded the quarter hour, it was over. All pressure ceased as if blown away. Only her tongue felt sore. (Goodman, 2005, p. 14)

On reading this paragraph, we think Anneliese Michel experienced what looks just like a phase of sleep paralysis.

First, from a historical point of view, early descriptions of sleep paralysis could be traced back to the late-first millennium—in Al-Akhawayni's (died 983 AD) Persian manuscript titled *Hidayat,* for example (Golzari et al., 2012). In 1664, Dutch physician and anatomist Isbrand van Diemerbroeck (1609–1674) presented an accurate case report of a 50-year-old woman (Kompanje, 2008). Publications about this strange disease increased from the early-nineteenth century (Pearce, 1993). However, the link between sleep paralysis and nightmares is usually ascribed to the English lexicographer Samuel Johnson (1709–1784). In his 1755 *Dictionary*, a masterpiece rightly remembered as "the most amazing, enduring and endearing one-man feat" (Bauman & Bauman, 2005, Item 106, p. 54), a nightmare is defined in these words:

NI'GHTMARE. *n. f.* [*night*, and according to *Temple, mara*, a spirit that, in the heathen mythology, was related to torment or suffocate sleepers.] A morbid oppression in the night, resembling the pressure of weight upon the breast.
Saint Withold footed thrice the would,
He met the *nightmare*, and her name he told;
Bid her alight, and her troth plight. *Shakes. K. Lear.*
The forerunners of an apoplexy are, dullness, drowsiness, vertigoes, tremblings, oppressions in sleep, and *night-mares.*
Arbuthnot on Aliments. (Johnson, 1755, p. 1363)

From a medical point of view, sleep paralysis may either be part of the tetrad of the narcoleptic syndrome (daytime sleepiness, cataplexy, sleep paralysis, and hypnagogic or hypnopompic hallucinations; Yoss & Daly, 1957) or be a more or less isolated manifestation (Fukuda et al., 1987), which

> sometimes intrudes into waking at a time that does not present any physical danger—just before or just after normal sleep, when a person is already lying down. This symptom of narcolepsy is referred to as sleep paralysis, an inability to move just before the onset of sleep or upon waking in the morning [. . .] the person dreams while lying awake, paralyzed. These episodes, called hypnagogic hallucinations, are often alarming, or even terrifying. (Carlson, 2010, pp. 302–303)

An isolated sleep paralysis, linked with the belief that deceased spirits are involved in "pressure on the body, hallucinations, breathing difficulty, and anxiety" (Arikawa et al., 1999, p. 372), is referred to as *kanashibari* experience.[1] The Japanese term *kanashibari* (金縛り) from *kane* (金, metal) and *shibaru* (縛る, to bind) means "to immobilize as if bound with metal chains" (Hufford, 1994, p. xiv; Ozeki, 2013, p. 181). It refers to "a Buddhist spell that renders an opponent immobile" (Bush, 2001, p. 93) by the power of *Fudô myô-ô* (不動明王) (Nakamura et al., 1989), a Japanese deity who "represents resolute and immovable determination" (Ashkenazi, 2003, p. 151). Unequivocally, the term *kanashibari* implies a spiritual nature (or at least a component) of the phenomenon. Knowing that "il n'est de meilleur moyen d'appréhender la culture d'un peuple que de s'abreuver à la source de sa mythologie" (There is no better way to apprehend the culture of people than to draw on the sources of its mythology: Féray, 2012, p. 7), we then have to set foot in the world of Japanese folktales, and especially those involving ghosts, for it seems that the *kanashibari* phenomenon may be caused by them (Drazen, 2011, p. 151).

Ghosts are ubiquitous in Asian culture, as pointed out by the writer Chandrani Warnasuriya, who writes: "Beliefs in Ghosts, Spirits, Demons and related creatures and phenomena are an integral part of Oriental and Far Eastern cultures" (Warnasuriya, 2009, p. 7). This is particularly true in Japan, where folklore (Mitford, 1876; Davis, 1913; Mayer, 1984; Lewinsky-Sträuli, 1989; Iwasaka & Toelken, 1994; Martin, 1996; Ross, 1996; Shirô Inouye, 1996, 2005; Faure, 2005; Hearn, 2007), art (Graf & Graf, 1925; Kondo, 1980; Stevenson, 1983; Addiss, 1985), theatre (Beck, 1933), literature (Ueda, 2010; Féray, 2012), and cinema (Meikle, 2005; Calorio, 2005; Kalat, 2007; McRoy, 2008; Galloway, 2006; Balmain, 2008; Harper, 2008; Lacefield, 2010; Scherer, 2011) are packed with this kind of

---

[1]Japanese and Korean words are Romanized using the Hepburn and the McCune-Reischauer systems, respectively.

story. Many describe a nocturnal thoracic oppression (e.g., a sense of compression) by a supernatural creature.

In the mid-twelfth century, 76th Japanese Emperor Konoe Tonnô (1139–1155) experienced this phenomenon: "Every night the emperor was oppressed by a mysterious agony which the holiest monks, working all their healing rites, seemed unable to relieve" (Tyler, 1987, pp. 292–293). The emperor was finally saved in 1153 by Minamoto no Yorimasa

Figure 1. A *Yamachichi*, taken from Volume 2 of Takehara Shunsen's 1841 *Ehon Hyaku Monogatari* (絵本百物語, Picture Book of a Hundred Stories). Source: Wikimedia Commons. File: ShunsenYamachichi.jpg. (Color figure available online.)

(1104–1180), who killed with an arrow a winged demon called *Nue* (夜鳥), which was responsible for the emperor's night oppression (Frédéric, 1996, pp. 648, 734).

Many artists were, of course, inspired by this subject. In 1841, Takehara Shunsen (竹原春泉) depicted a strange creature known as *Yamachichi* (山池乳), which inhales the breath of a sleeper (Graf & Graf, 1925, p. 55, Plate 65) (Figure 1). Also, in a picture rightly titled *Dream Ghost*, Utagawa Kuniyoshi (歌川国芳) (1798–1861) showed a ghost that puts its icy hand on the heart of a sleeping man (Graf & Graf, 1925, p. 60, Plate 119).

Japan is not the only Asian country to ascribe to ghosts in all kinds of manifestations. China (Hearn, 1949; Yun, 1998), Laos (Tossa & Nettavong, 2008), Vietnam (Khiêm, 1989; Viên & Ngoc, 1996), Korea (Jewett, 1953; Im & Yi, 1982; Kim, 2010), Indonesia, Philippines, Malaysia, and Thailand (Faurot, 1995) share similar beliefs. In Korean, sleep paralysis is known as *gawi nulim* (가위눌임) from *gawi* (가위, nightmare, incubus) and *nulida* (눌리다, to be pressed down), and the ghosts sitting on the sleeper's chest are specifically called *kwishin* (귀신, a departed soul). To cite another example, the Thai term for sleep paralysis, *ph ǐi am* (ผีอ๋า), includes the character (ผี, *ph ǐi*), meaning ghost. In Cambodia, sleep-paralysis-type panic attacks in a Khmer refugee population are described as "the ghost pushes you down" (Hinton et al., 2005a, 2005b). In a Chinese study, 37% of Hong Kong students answered they had experienced at least one "attack of ghost oppression" (Wing, Lee, & Chen, 1994), and the prevalence remains high (about 26%) even among Chinese living in the United States (Yeung, Xu, & Chang, 2005).

What about the rest of the world? In Mexico, sleep paralysis is believed to be caused by "a dead body [which] climbed on top of me" (Jiménez-Genchi et al., 2009, p. 546). In Southwest Nigeria, an acute nighttime disturbance that is culturally attributed to demonic infiltration is referred to as "Ogun Oru" (Aina & Famuyiwa, 2007). In Newfoundland, Canada, sleep paralysis is induced by an attack of "Old Hag" (Ness, 1978; Hufford, 1982). It is, therefore, also tinged with a hint of supernatural (Robbins, 1970, pp. 355–358; McGovern, 2007, p. 628).

Beware of Japanese ghosts, even in the Occident!

References

Addiss S, ed. (1985): *Japanese Ghosts & Demons: Art of the Supernatural*. New York, George Braziller, Inc.

Aina OF, Famuyiwa OO (2007): Ogun Oru: A traditional explanation for nocturnal neuropsychiatric disturbances among the Yoruba of southwest Nigeria. *Transcultural Psychiatry* 44(1): 44–54.

Arikawa H, Templer DI, Brown R, Cannon WG, Thomas-Dodson S (1999): The structure and correlates of Kanashibari. *Journal of Psychology* 133(4): 369–375.

Ashkenazi M (2003): *Handbook of Japanese Mythology*. Oxford, Oxford University Press.

Balmain C (2008): *Introduction to Japanese Horror Film*. Edinburgh, Edinburgh University Press.

Bauman D, Bauman V (2005): *Bauman Rare Books: Catalogue Wizard*. New York, Bauman.

Beck LA (1933): *The Ghost Plays of Japan*. New York, The Japan Society.

Bullinger K (1983): *Anneliese Michel und die Aussagen der Dämonen*. Altötting, A. Ruhland.

Bush LC (2001): *Asian Horror Encyclopedia: Asian Horror Culture in Literature, Manga, and Folklore*. San Jose, Writers Club Press.

Buttner W (1986): *Die deutsche Stimme des Himmels: Offenbarungen Christi und Mariens an Barbara Weigand von Schippach. 1975 zur Erfüllung angemahnt durch Anneliese Michel in Klingenberg*. Lippstadt, Verlag Claus P. Clausen.

Calorio G (2005): *Horror dal Giappone e dal resto dell'Asia*. Roma, Profondo Rosso.

Carlson NR (2010): *Physiology of Behavior*. Boston, Allyn & Bacon, 10th edition.

Davis FH (1913): *Myths and Legends of Japan*. London, George G. Harrap & Company.

Drazen P (2011): *A Gathering of Spirits: Japan's Ghost Story Tradition*. Bloomington, Universe Inc.

Duffey M (2011): *Lessons Learned: The Anneliese Michel Exorcism: The Implementation of a Safe and Thorough Examination, Determination, and Exorcism of Demonic Possession*. Eugene, Oregon, Wipf & Stock.

Faure E (2005): *Histoires japonaises d'esprits, de monstres et de fantômes*. Paris, L'Harmattan.

Faurot JL (1995): *Asian-Pacific Folktales and Legends*. New York, Touchstone.

Féray Y (2012): *Contes d'une grand-mère japonaise*. Arles, Philippe Picquier.

Fortea JA, LeBlanc LEU (2010): *Prawdziwa historia egzorcysmów Anneliese Michel*. Radom, Polskie Wydawnictwo Encyklopedyczne.

Frédéric L (1996): *Le Japon: Dictionnaire et civilisation*. Paris, Robert Laffont.

Fukuda K, Miyasita A, Inugami M, Ishihara K (1987): High prevalence of isolated sleep paralysis: Kanashibari phenomenon in Japan. *Sleep* 10(3): 279–286.

Galloway P (2006): *Asia Shock: Horror and Dark Cinema from Japan, Korea, Hong Kong, and Thailand*. Berkeley, Stone Bridge Press.

Golzari SEG, Khodadoust K, Alakbarli F, Ghabili K, Islambulchilar Z, Shoja MM, Khalili M, Abbasnejad F, Sheikholeslamzadeh N, Shahabi NM, Hosseini SF, Ansarin K (2012): Sleep paralysis in medieval Persia—The *Hidayat* of Akhawayni (?–983 AD). *Neuropsychiatric Disease and Treatment* 8: 229–234.

Goodman FD (2005): *The Exorcism of Anneliese Michel*. Eugene, Oregon, Resource Publications.

Graf O, Graf C (1925): *Japanisches Gespensterbuch*. Stuttgart Berlin Leipzig, Union Deutsche Verlagsgesellschaft.

Harper J (2008): *Flowers From Hell: The Modern Japanese Horror Film*. Hereford, Noir Publishing.

Hearn L (1949): *Kwaidan, Some Chinese Ghosts, Chita, and Other Stories and Essays*. New York, The Citadel Press.

Hearn L (2007): *Fantômes du Japon*. N.p., Privat/Le Rocher.

Hinton DE, Pich V, Chhean D, Pollack MH (2005a): "The ghost pushes you down": Sleep paralysis-type panic attacks in a Khmer refugee population. *Transcultural Psychiatry* 42(1): 46–77.

Hinton DE, Pich V, Chhean D, Pollack MH, McNally RJ (2005b): Sleep paralysis among Cambodian refugees: Association with PTSD diagnosis and severity. *Depression and Anxiety* 22: 47–51.

Hufford DJ (1982): *The Terror That Comes in the Night: An Experience-Centered Study of Supernatural Assault Traditions*. Philadelphia, University of Pennsylvania Press.

Hufford DJ (1994): Preface. In: Iwasaka M, Toelken B, eds., *Ghosts and the Japanese: Cultural Experience in Japanese Death Legends*. Logan, Utah, Utah University Press, pp. xi–xvi.

Im B, Yi R (1982): *Korean Folk Tales: Imps, Ghosts, and Fairies*. Rutland, Vermont & Tokyo, Charles E. Tuttle Company.

Iwasaka M, Toelken B (1994): *Ghosts and the Japanese: Cultural Experience in Japanese Death Legends*. Logan, Utah, Utah University Press.

Jewett EM (1953): *Which Was Witch?: Tales of Ghosts and Magic From Korea*. New York, The Viking Press.

Jiménez-Genchi A, Ávila-Rodríguez VM, Sánchez-Rojas F, Vargas Terrez BE, Nenclares-Portocarrero A (2009): Sleep paralysis in adolescents: The "a dead body climbed on top of me" phenomenon in Mexico. *Psychiatry and Clinical Neurosciences* 63: 546–549.

Johnson S (1755): *A Dictionary of the English Language: In which The Words are Deduced from their Originals, and Illustrated in their Different Significations by Examples from the Best Writers. To Which Are Prefixed A History of the Language And An English Grammar*. London, Printed for J. and P. Knapton; T. and T. Longman; C. Hitch and L. Hawes; A. Millar; and R. and J. Dodsley, 2 vols.

Kalat D (2007): *J-Horror: The Definitive Guide to The Ring, The Grudge and Beyond*. New York, Vertical, Inc.

Khiêm PD (1989): *Légendes des terres sereines*. Paris, Mercure de France.

Kim SP (2010): *The Curious Tale of Mandogi's Ghost*. New York, Columbia University Press.

Kompanje EJO (2008): "The devil lay upon her and held her down": Hypnagogic hallucinations and sleep paralysis described by the Dutch physician Isbrand van Diemerbroeck (1609–1674) in 1664. *Journal of Sleep Research* 17: 464–467.

Kondo E (1980): *Japanische Gespenster: Holzschnitte, Alben und Handzeichnungen des 18. und 19. Jh. Aus der Sammlung Felix Tikotin.* Köln, Museum für Ostasiatische Kunst.

Lacefield K, ed. (2010): *The Scary Screen: Media Anxiety in "The Ring."* Burlington, Ashgate.

Lewinsky-Sträuli M (1989): *Japanische Dämonen und Gespenster: Geschichten aus zwölf Jahrhunderten.* München, Eugen Diederichs Verlag.

Martin R (1996): *Mysterious Tales of Japan.* New York, G. P. Putnam's Sons.

Mayer FH (1984): *Ancient Tales in Modern Japan: An Anthology of Japanese Folk Tales.* Bloomington, IN, Indiana University Press.

McGovern U, ed. (2007): *Chambers Dictionary of the Unexplained.* Edinburgh, Chambers Harrap Publishers Ltd.

McRoy J (2008): *Nightmare Japan: Contemporary Japanese Horror Cinema.* Amsterdam and New York, Rodopi.

Meikle D (2005): *The Ring Companion.* London, Titan Books.

Mitford AB (1876): *Tales of Old Japan: Folklore, Fairy Tales, Ghost Stories, and Legends of the Samurai.* London, Macmillan and Company.

Nakamura H, Fukagawa K, Tamura Y, Imano T (1989): *Iwamani bukkyo jiten* [Iwamani's Buddhist Dictionary]. Tokyo, Iwamani shoten.

Ness RC (1978): The Old Hag phenomenon as sleep paralysis: A biocultural interpretation. *Culture, Medicine and Psychiatry* 2: 15–39.

Ozeki R (2013): *En même temps, toute la terre et tout le ciel.* Paris, Belfond.

Pearce JM (1993): Early descriptions of sleep paralysis. *Journal of Neurology, Neurosurgery and Psychiatry* 56: 1302.

Robbins RH (1970): *The Encyclopedia of Witchcraft and Demonology.* London, Spring Books.

Ross C (1996): *Japanese Ghost Stories.* Tokyo, Tuttle Publishing.

Scherer E (2011): *Spuk der Frauenseele: Weibliche Geister im japanischen Film und ihre kulturhistorischen Ursprünge.* Bielefeld, Transcript Verlag.

Shirô Inouye C (1996): *Japanese Gothic Tales: Izumi Kyôka.* Honolulu, University of Hawai'i Press.

Shirô Inouye C (2005): *In light of Shadows: More Gothic Tales by Izumi Kyôka.* Honolulu, University of Hawai'i Press.

Shunsen T (1841): *Ehon hyaku monogatari* (Chinese edition made available by Nanhi Publishing Company, 2011).

Siegmund G (1985): *Von Wemding nach Klingenberg.* Stein am Rhein, Christiana-Verlag.

Stevenson J (1983): *Yoshitoshi's Thirty-Six Ghosts.* New York, Weatherhill/Blue Tiger.

Tossa W, Nettavong K (2008): *Lao Folktales.* Westport, Connecticut, and London, Libraries Unlimited.

Tyler R (1987): *Japanese Tales.* New York, Pantheon Books.

Ueda A (2010): *Contes de pluie et de lune.* Paris, Gallimard/Unesco.

Viên NK, Ngoc H (1996): *Mille ans de littérature vietnamienne.* Arles, Philippe Picquier.

Warnasuriya C (2009): *Spooky Tales from the Orient: Tales of Ogres, Demons, Ghosts, Spells, Charms and the Enchanted.* Baltimore, PublishAmerica.

Wegner M (2009): *Exorzismus heute: Der Teufel spricht deutsch.* Gütersloh, Gütersloher Verlagshaus.

Wing YK, Lee ST, Chen CN (1994): Sleep paralysis in Chinese: Ghost oppression phenomenon in Hong Kong. *Sleep* 17(7): 609–613.

Wolff U (2006): *Der Teufel ist in mir: Der Fall Anneliese Michel, die letzte Teufelsaustreibung in Deutschland.* München, Wilhelm Heyne Verlag.

Yeung A, Xu Y, Chang DF (2005): Prevalence and illness beliefs of sleep paralysis among Chinese psychiatric patients in China and the United States. *Transcultural Psychiatry* 42(1): 135–145.

Yoss RE, Daly DD (1957): Criteria for the diagnosis of the narcoleptic syndrome. *Proceedings of Staff Meetings of the Mayo Clinic* 32: 320–328.

Yun J (1998) : *Des nouvelles de l'au-delà.* Paris, Gallimard.

"Magic Mirror in my Hand, Who is the Fairest in the Land . . . and, Incidentally, Are You Transparent or Shining?"

May brothers Jacob Ludwig Carl Grimm (1785–1863) and Wilhelm Carl Grimm (1786–1859) forgive us for this implied reference to one of their most celebrated fairy tales! But let's leave the Evil Queen and her Magic Mirror aside and concentrate on the *septum pellucidum* that was sometimes compared with—hence our title—a transparent or a shining mirror.

To start with the term *septum*, broadly speaking it consists of two parts. The ventral part, known as the *septum verum* (true or real septum), is situated within the paraterminal gyrus and contains two cell masses: the lateral septal nucleus and the medial septal complex (Nieuwenhuys, Voogd, & van Juijzen, 2008, p. 363). The dorsal part, or *septum pellucidum*, is a "bilateral laminae of fibres, sparse grey matter and neuroglia" (Standring, 2008, p. 352), interposed between the anterior part of the lateral ventricles (medially), the basal surface of the corpus callosum (rostrally), and the rostral convexity of the fornix (caudally). The Latin word *septum*, or more exactly *saeptum* (Quicherat, 1962, p. 254), does not present any etymological ambiguity: It means "partition" or "dividing wall" (between both lateral ventricles in this case) and also applies to a great number of other anatomical structures (33 different entries in the index of the current edition of the *Gray's Anatomy*: Standring, 2008, p. 1534; no less than 62 entries in Terra, 1913, pp. 491–494). According to the Danish anatomist Thomas Bartholin (1616–1680), Galen had used an equivalent term: the cerebral diaphragm (Galen as cited in Bartholin, 1677, p. 492). On the other hand, the etymology of the adjective *pellucidum* or *perlucidum* seems a little more questionable: *Per* may actually mean either "very" or "through," and *lucidus* either "to shine" or "to be transparent" (Joubert, 1738, pp. 698, 1237, 1240; Quicherat, 1962, pp. 833, 1460, 1463; Gaffiot, 1989, pp. 412, 337). Now something transparent is a medium through which light can travel, whereas something shining emits or reflects light. It seems therefore that a structure, whatever its physical properties may be, cannot be both transparent and shining.

French anatomist and medical examiner François Chaussier (1746–1828), pointing out that this septum is "presque entièrement opaque" [almost completely opaque] (Chaussier, 1807, p. 53), proposed the topographical adjective median rather than pellucid. Other synonyms were more recently coined, for example, supracommissural septum (Standring, 2008, p. 348, Fig. 23-13), telencephalic septum (Andy & Stefan, 1966, pp. 389–399), and *area lucida* (Stephan, 1975, p. 11).

We wondered whether the adjective pellucid was to be found elsewhere in medical sciences terminology. We could find only two other occurrences. The first one is in Ambroise Paré's (1509–1590) work: "Nostre oeil est une substance, de sa nature, pellucide et lumineuse" [Our eye is a substance, by its nature, pellucid and luminous] (Paré as cited in Littré, 1874, p. 1037). The second one in the description of the early stages of oogenesis: "As the primary follicle takes shape, a prominent, translucent, non cellular membrane called the zona pellucida forms between the primary oocyte and its enveloping follicular cells" (Carlson, 2004, p. 9). Let's point out that the term zona pellucida was coined by the discoverer of mammalian ovum, Karl Ernst von Baer (1792–1876), early in the nineteenth century (Baer, 1827, p. 19, Figs. 4–5).

Most French-speaking authors, especially before the publication of the first *Nomina anatomica* in 1895, used *lucidum* instead of *pellucidum* (e.g., Winslow, 1752, p. 155; Verdier, 1752, p. 277; Tarin, 1753, p. 24; Allouel, 1776, p. 60; Cloquet, 1816, p. 552; Cruveilhier, 1837, p. 299; Sappey, 1872, p. 76; Dejerine, 1895, p. 352), and many of them unfortunately keeping this bad habit since that time (e.g., Cossa & Paillas, 1944, p. 221; Rouvière, 1979, p. 593). The only officially acknowledged term has actually always been *septum pellucidum* (Donath, 1960, p. 212; Terminologia Anatomica, 1998, p. 127), as used by English-speaking authors (e.g., Strong & Elwyn, 1943, p. 297; Ranson, 1943, p. 252; Chusid, 1976, p. 25).

Let's now turn to the metaphor of the mirror (*speculum* in Latin) and its features: "Miroir luisant" [shining mirror] in Jean Riolan's (1580–1657) textbook (Riolan, 1672, p. 385) and in the 1606 German translation by Johann Andreas Schenck of Realdo Colombo's (ca. 1515–1559) *De re anatomica* (as cited by Hyrtl, 1884, p. 207); "*speculum lucidum*" [transparent or shining—once again this discrepancy!—mirror] in Isbrand van Diemerbroeck's (1609–1674) work (Diemerbroeck, 1695, p. 240). André Dulaurens (1558–1609) added the term "*lapis specularis*" (Dulaurens, 1605, p. 774) that, we must admit, caused us some trouble. We finally found that the ancients used the so-called specular stones, that is mica sheets (mica is one of the basic three components of granite), as panes because of their transparency.

In the 1990s, the Parma neurologist Giacomo Rizzolatti and his collaborators identified a very strange subpopulation of neurons they called mirror neurons (Gallese et al., 1996). These neurons are known to discharge when a monkey observes another individual performing an action that is similar to that encoded by this neuron. What a wonderful coincidence if mirror neurons had been observed in the transparent/shiny mirror! Unfortunately, mirror neurons were found only in the left inferior frontal cortex (opercular region) and the right superior parietal lobule (Iacoboni et al., 1999).

References

Allouel (1776): *Explication des mots d'usage en anatomie et en chirurgie*. Paris, Rémont.
Andy OJ, Stephan H (1966): Phylogeny of the primate septum telencephali. In: Hassler R, Stephan H, eds., *Evolution of the forebrain*. Stuttgart, Thieme, pp. 389–399.
Baer KE von (1827): *De ovi mammalium et hominis genesi*. Leipzig, Sumptibus Leopoldi Vossii.
Bartholin T (1677): *Anatome quartum renovata*. Lugduni, Sumpt. Joan. Ant. Huguetan, & Soc.
Carlson BM (2004): *Human Embryology and Developmental Biology*. Philadelphia, Mosby, third edition.

Chaussier F (1807): *Exposition sommaire de la structure et des différentes parties de l'encéphale ou cerveau; suivant la méthode adoptée à l'École de médecine de Paris*. Paris, Théophile Barrois.

Chusid JG (1976): *Correlative Neuroanatomy & Functional Neurology*. Los Altos, CA, Lange Medical Publications.

Cloquet H (1816): *Traité d'anatomie descriptive rédigé d'après l'ordre adopté à la faculté de médecine de Paris*. Paris, Crochard, Vol. 2.

Cossa P, Paillas JE (1944): *Anatomie des centres nerveux*. Paris, Amédée Legrand & Jean Bertrand.

Cruveilhier J (1837): *Anatomie descriptive*. Bruxelles, Meline, Cans et Compagnie, Vol. 2.

Dejerine J (1895): *Anatomie des centres nerveux*. Paris, Rueff et Cie, Vol. 1.

Diemerbroeck I Van (1695): *L'anatomie du corps humain*. Lyon, Anisson & Posuel, Vol. 2.

Donath T (1960): *Erläuterndes anatomisches Wörterbuch: Vergleichende Übersicht der Baseler, Jenaer und Pariser Nomenklaturen, gruppiert nach Organen*. Terra Budapest, Verlag Medicina Budapest.

Dulaurens A (1605): *Historia anatomica, humani corporis partes singulas uberrimè enodans, novisque controversiis et observationibus illustrata*. Lugduni, apud Horatium Cardon.

Gaffiot F (1989): *Dictionnaire latin-français abrégé*. Paris, Le Livre de Poche, nouvelle édition par Catherine Magnien.

Gallese V, Fadiga L, Fogassi L, Rizzolatti G (1996): Action recognition in the premotor cortex. *Brain* 119: 593–609.

Hyrtl J (1884): *Die alten deutschen Kunstworte der Anatomie*. Wien, Braumüller.

Iacoboni M, Woods RP, Brass M, Bekkering H, Mazziotta JC, Rizzolatti G (1999): Cortical mechanisms of human imitation. *Science* 286: 2526–2528.

Joubert J (1738): *Dictionnaire François et latin, tiré des auteurs originaux et classiques de l'une et de l'autre langue*. Lyon, Louis & Henry Declaustre.

Littré É (1874): *Dictionnaire de la langue française*. Paris, Hachette et Cie, Vol. 3.

Nieuwenhuys R, Voogd J, van Huijzen C (2008): *The Human Central Nervous System*. Berlin, Heidelberg, New York, Springer-Verlag, fourth edition.

Quicherat L (1962): *Dictionnaire français-latin*. Paris, Hachette, nouvelle édition par Émile Chatelain.

Ranson SW (1943): *The Anatomy of the Nervous System*. Philadelphia and London, W. B. Saunders Company, seventh edition.

Riolan J (1672): *Manuel anatomique et pathologique, ou abrégé de toute l'anatomie*. Lyon, Antoine Laurens.

Rouvière H (1979): *Anatomie humaine, topographique et fonctionnelle*. Paris, Masson, onzième édition, Vol. 3.

Sappey PC (1872): *Traité d'anatomie descriptive*. Paris, Adrien Delahaye, 2ème édition, Vol. 3.

Standring S, ed. (2008): *Gray's Anatomy: The Anatomical Basis of Clinical Practice*. N.p., Churchill Livingstone Elsevier, 40th edition.

Stephan H (1975): *Allocortex*. Berlin, Heidelberg, New York, Springer-Verlag.

Strong OS, Elwyn A (1943): *Human Neuroanatomy*. Baltimore, The Williams & Wilkins Company.

Tarin P (1753): *Dictionnaire anatomique suivi d'une bibliothèque anatomique et physiologique*. Paris, Briasson.

Terminologia Anatomica (1998): *International Anatomical Terminology*. Stuttgart, New York, Thieme.

Terra P de (1913): *Vademecum anatomicum. Kritisch-etymologisches Wörterbuch der systematischen Anatomie. Mit besonderer Berücksichtigung der Synonymen. Nebst einem Anhang: Die anatomischen Schriftsteller des Altertums bis zur Neuzeit*. Jena, Gustav Fischer.

Verdier C (1752): *Abrégé de l'anatomie du corps humain; Où l'on donne une description courte & exacte des Parties qui le composent, avec leurs usages*. Paris, Jean Leonard, nouvelle édition, Vol. 2.

Winslow JB (1752): *Exposition anatomique de la structure du corps humain*. Amsterdam, Emanuel Tourneisen, Vol. 4.

Trigeminal Neuralgia: Pleonasm and Miscalculation

The Bavarian physician Johann Lorenz Bausch was born in Schweinfurt on September 30, 1605. He studied medicine in Germany (Jena, Marburg), Italy (Padua) and then settled back in his native city where he died on November 17, 1665. Johann Lorenz Bausch is especially remembered for having founded on January 1, 1652, with his colleagues Johann Michael Fehr (1610–1688), Georg Balthasar Metzger (1623–1687), and Georg Balthasar Wohlfart (1607–1674), one of the very first European scientific societies, the *Academia Naturae Curiosum* (Hirsch, 1884–1888, vol. 1, p. 337; Keller, 1955). Johann Lorenz Bausch was probably never involved in neuroscience except by the (indirect) cause of his death: trigeminal neuralgia, the term we intend to study in this article.

Trigeminal neuralgia is characterized by "excruciating paroxysms of pain in the lips, gums, cheek, or chin and, very rarely, in the distribution of the ophthalmic division of the fifth nerve" (Beal & Hauser, 2012, p. 3360). It may be primary (demyelination of large myelinated trigeminal fibers potentially related to vascular — usually the superior cerebellar artery — compression, or by frank compression without demyelination by the same vessel) or symptomatic (multiple sclerosis, intracranial tumor, or aneurysm).

The very first description of trigeminal neuralgia probably happened ages ago, but ancient authors could not be rightly credited with accurate clinical descriptions of authentic cases. The characterization of headaches was too vague in the Hippocratic *corpus* (Hippocrates, 460–375 BC) (Lewy, 1938); Aretaeus of Cappadocia (81–ca. 138) described signs and symptoms that would more likely belong to migraine (Cole et al., 2005); and Avicenna's (980–1037) "*tortura faciei*" (or "*tortura oris*") was actually mistranslated by "*facial torture*," while the Arabian term "*lakwat*" should have been understood as the negation "*la*" and the substantive "*kuwwet*" (that is "*no*" and "*strength, power*"): What Avicenna described was therefore much more probably facial paralysis (Eboli et al., 2009). Actually, historians of neurology ascribe the very first authentic case report of trigeminal neuralgia to Johannes Michael Fehr and Elias Schmidt who, in the eulogy of their colleague Johann Lorenz Bausch, published a description of his disease (trigeminal neuralgia leading to limitation of dietary intake, emaciation, and finally stroke) in 1671 (Fehr & Schmidt, 1671), hence our introductory paragraph.

Among the numerous synonyms of trigeminal neuralgia, let us begin with the most common ones: *"prosopalgia," "tic douloureux," "névralgie épileptiforme,"* and *"Fothergill's disease."*

The term *"prosopalgia"* (from the Greek πρoσωπoν, *prosôpon*: face, and άλγoς, *algos*: pain) was coined by the Swiss physician Johann Jakob Wepfer (1620–1695) (Manuila et al., 1981, vol. 13, p. 426). Though mainly remembered as an anatomist (Nigst, 1947), the term prosopalgia was in all likelihood coined in Wepfer's 1727 posthumously published *Observations Medico-Practicae.*

Contrary to current and common thinking (Bousser & Baron, 1979, p. 163), the term *"tic douloureux"* was not coined by Armand Trousseau (1801–1867) but by a less well-known Versailles surgeon, Nicolas André (1704–1780), in a supplement inserted at the end of the 1756 edition of his *treatise on . . . urethral diseases* (André, 1756, p. 318). This surgeon, by the way of cauterization of the infraorbital nerve, had succeeded in curing a patient of a facial neuralgia that had been induced by the treatment of a lacrimal fistula (Dechaume & Huard, 1977, p. 250). The word *"tic"* was chosen "because of the facial grimaces the patient tends to make during the pain" (Sweet, 1987, p. 763). Armand Trousseau, Internist and member of the 1848 legislative body, also described the disease but coined another term: *"névralgie épileptiforme"* (epileptiform neuralgia; Trousseau, 1853).

English physician, botanist, philanthropist, and Quaker, John Fothergill (1712–1780) described trigeminal neuralgia in 1773 and accurately listed its distinguishing features: a condition affecting people of advanced age, women more than men, possible relation to tumors (intracranial, but also extracranial: hard tumor of the breast in 2 of the 14 cases he presented; Cole et al., 2005), and clinical features of the pain (sudden, excruciating, short-lasting, returning at irregular intervals) (Fothergill, 1773; Pearce, 2003). The eponym "Fothergill's neuralgia" is therefore justified (provided, of course, that medical eponyms go on being justified; see Olry 2014a, 2014b, for review). It should, however, be pointed out that a certain Samuel Fothergill, probably John's great nephew, also published a 105-page monograph devoted to trigeminal neuralgia in the early-nineteenth century (Fothergill, 1804).

So, to which Fothergill does the eponym Fothergill's disease really belong: John or Samuel? The answer is John, and it is very simple to prove. The name Fothergill already appears in Forstmann's Duisbourg 1794 dissertation (*De dolore faciei Fothergillii*) and Kunder's 1803 monograph (*Beobachtungen über das Fothergill's Gesichtschmerz*) and both were devoted to facial pain and published before 1804 (listed in Adelon et al., 1835, p. 596).

Other little known or uncommon synonyms — this short list does not claim to fully cover the subject — could be found here and there in medical or dental literature (e.g., Engelmann, 1848, 1867; Index Catalogue, 1880–1895, 1896–1916; Crowley, 1885; David, 1889; Weinberger, 1929), with some examples being: *"trismus dolorificus"* (painful trismus; Boissier de Sauvage, 1768, as cited by Dechaume & Huard, 1977, p. 250), *"dolore faciei convulsivo"* (convulsive facial pain; van Loenen, 1797), *"dolore faciei Fothergillii"* (Fothergill's facial pain; von Leuthner, 1810), *"neuralgia spasmodica"* (spasmodic neuralgia; Campbell, 1823), *"prosopalgia nervosa"* (nervous prosopalgia; Major, 1827), *"neuralgiae nervi quinti"* (neuralgias of the fifth nerve; Romberg, 1840), *"tic facial"* (facial tic; Fischlin, 1840), *"neuralgia intermittente nervi trigemini"* (intermittent neuralgia of the trigeminal nerve; Genenius, 1852), *"névralgie trifaciale"* (trifacial neuralgia; Ditandy, 1865), *"epileptiform tic douloureux"* (Bartholow, 1872), *"neuritis rami primi trigemini"* (neuritis of the first rami of trigeminal nerve; Abrahamsz, 1873), *"affectus spasmodico-convulsivus labiorum"* (labial spasmodic convulsive disorder; Troisier,

1877, p. 48), "*prosopalgia periódica*" (periodic prosopalgia; Aguilar y Venegas, 1878), "*névralgie trifaciale épileptiforme convulsive*" (trifacial convulsive epileptiform neuralgia; Liégeois, 1881), "*suicide disease*" (probably coined by Harvey Cushing, as cited in Adams et al., 2011), and "*trigeminalepsy*" (Miró & Ortiz, 2013).

The current (and most frequently used) name of this disorder is "trigeminal neuralgia." Let us consider some linguistic features of the common name on the one hand and of the adjective on the other hand.

Whatever dictionary we refer to, the definition of the term "*neuralgia*" (from the Greek νευρον, *neuron*, nerve and άλγος, *algos*, pain) always signifies pain (spontaneous or not, relentless or paroxysmal) extending along the course of one or more nerves (Friel, 1974, p. 1038; Garnier et al., 2009, p. 606). As far as we know, and except phantom (e.g., amputee) and mental (e.g., major depression) pains, pain necessarily requires nerves — in this case sensory nerves — to express itself! Neuralgia therefore appears to be a pleonasm.

Now the adjective "*trigeminal.*" It refers to the trigeminal nerve but, and it may be a surprise for many of our readers, there are two different nerves referred to as trigeminal in the human body. One of them — give honor where honor is due! — is the fifth cranial nerve (of course the one involved in the disease in question), accurately described for the first time by Italian anatomist Gabriele Falloppio (1523–1562; Lauth, 1815, p. 444), and named in 1732 by the Paris anatomist of Danish origin, Jacques-Bénigne Winslow (1669–1760; Winslow, 1732, vol. 3, p. 201). The other one can be found in Hermann von Jehring's 1878 monograph on the peripheral nervous system; this author called the ventral ramus of the second sacral spinal nerv a trigeminal nerve, because of its division into three branches: a superior one anastomosing with the first sacral nerve, an inferior one anastomosing with the third sacral nerve, and a middle one taking part into the constitution of the ischiatic nerve (as cited in Paturet, 1964, p. 1022).

The adjective *trigeminal* leads us to explain the different ways (at least for "in number") of introducing a notion of counting in medical terminology: (a) the insertion of a cardinal number into a term (a cardinal number is "a measure of the size of a set that does not take into account the order of its members": Borowski & Borwein, 1999, p. 67); in former times the hip bone, because of its three main initial components (ilium, ischium, pubis) was called "*Dreybeyn,*" an ancient German word meaning "three bones" (Hyrtl, 1884, pp. 33–34); (b) the insertion of an ordinal number (an ordinal number is "a measure of a set that takes account of the order as well as the number of its elements": Borowski & Borwein, 1999, p. 423); this is how the 12 (actually 13: see Olry & Haines, 1998, for review) pairs of cranial nerves were numbered, from the first (olfactory nerve) to the twelfth (hypoglossal nerve) by the celebrated German anatomist Samuel Thomas von Soemmering (1755–1830) in his 1778 dissertation (Plates I–III); (c) the addition of the Latin prefixes "*bis,*" "*tris,*" or "*quadra*" to a root describing the similar parts (of an organ) to be counted; some muscles of the limbs, taking into consideration the number of their heads or bellies, are therefore called "*biceps,*" "*triceps,*" or "*quadriceps*" (a "*pentaceps*" muscle has been described in human, but it belongs to anatomical variations: Testut, 1884, p. 387); and, lastly, (d) the borrowing of the concept (and Latinized term "*geminus*" or "*gemellus*") of twins from embryology and obstetrics; so did mathematicians ("*twin primes [are] a pair of prime numbers that differ by two,*" see Caldwell & Honaker, 2009, p. 265), heraldists (twins are "*barrulets in pairs*": Galbreath & Jéquier, 1977, p. 102), astronomers (the twins refer to the constellation Gemini that was named after Zeus' sons Castor and Pollux: Commelin, 1960, pp. 352–354), and neurologists. This notion of twins ("*gemellus*" or "*geminus*") is worth being examined in more detail.

French anatomist and lexicographer Pierre Tarin (died 1761) defined *"jumeau"* (*geminus, gemellus*) as *"deux parties qui se tiennent ou sont voisines l'une de l'autre"* [two parts that stand next to each other] (Tarin, 1753, pp. 47–48); the first anatomical structures to have been called *gemellus* belong to the myology of the lower limb (Tassin, 1688, pp. 300–302 and 308; Disdier, 1753, pp. 94 and 112; Chaussier, 1789, pp. 25–26 and 35; Dumas, 1797, pp. 150 and 190). In neuroscience, the twins may be two in number (bigeminal tubercle of the comparative anatomy of the brain: Vimont, 1833, Plate LXXIV: in domestic duck and cuckoo), three in number (trigeminal nerve and all structures in topographical/functional relationship with it: trigeminal cavum or Meckel cavum, described by Johann Friedrich Meckel in 1748; trigeminal ganglion or Gasser ganglion, though not discovered by the Austrian anatomist Johann Lorenz Gasser but by his pupil Anton Balthazard Raymund Hirsch in his 1765 dissertation; trigeminal impression, a shallow impression in the floor of the middle cranial fossa lodging the trigeminal ganglion; trigeminal lemniscus, part of the medial lemniscus arising from the contralateral spinal and principal sensory nuclei of the trigeminal nerve; and trigeminal triangle, described in 1923 by André Latarjet and Pierre Wertheimer as the triangular space between the anterior aspect of the cerebellar hemisphere and the rostral border of the petrous part of temporal bone), or four in number (quadrigeminal plate and surrounding structures: quadrigeminal cistern, pedunculogeminal artery of Alezais and d'Astros [1892]). In a similar manner, the *corpora bigemina* of the developing midbrain becomes the *corpora quadrigemina* of the mature form.

Our title alluded to a miscalculation and, in the light of these explanations, the error becomes obvious: the adjective *trigeminal* wrongly superimposes two different counting linguistic elements: the prefix *tri* and the root *geminus*, leading to the misinterpretation that three times two is . . . three. To the best of our knowledge, the famous anatomist Joseph Hyrtl (1810–1894) was the very first — and since that time the only one? — to point out this mistake: *"Der schlichte Verstand meint, dass, wenn geminus doppelt ist, bigeminus vierfach bedeutet, und quadrigeminus achtfach. Wenn dem so wäre, müsste allerdings das Corpus quadrigeminum, richtiger bigeminum genannt werden"* [it is easy to understand that if geminus means doubled, bigeminus means quadruplicate, and quadrigeminus octuplicate. In that case, the corpus quadrigeminum (i.e., superior and inferior colliculi) should more rightly be called bigeminum] (Hyrtl, 1880, p. 437). As pointed out by the mathematicians John H. Conway (Princeton, USA) and Richard K. Guy (Calgary, Canada) in the first chapter of their 1996 *Book of Numbers*:

> Throughout history, *number* and *numbers* have had a tremendous influence on our culture and on our language. Thousands of words are obviously associated with numbers [. . .] but in many [. . .] cases the connections [. . .] have been obscured by the passage of time and changes in meaning. (Conway & Guy, 1996, p. 1)

How could such a mistake have so steadily escaped notice? Remember: "let him who is without sin among you to be the first to throw a stone . . . to the neurologists" (John 8: 7. biblia.com/bible/esv/Jn8.3-11, consulted on December 23, 2014, modified, with respect). Obstetricians made the same mistake: on ventôse 7, an II (that is February 25, 1794), a certain Mrs. d'Anguillon gave birth to one boy and three girls: Her pregnancy was described as a case report of *"quadrigéméllité,"* a term that would have implied the birth of (four times two) eight babies and not four (Mercier, 1936, p. 200). And cardiologists go on calling *"bigeminal pulse"* the occurrence of two beats (and not four) of the pulse in rapid succession (Hurst & Schlant, 1974, p. 177).

REFERENCES

Abrahamsz T (1873): *Neuritis rami primi trigemini*. Utrecht, P.W. van de Weijer.

Adams H, Pendleton C, Latimer K, Cohen-Gadol AA, Carson BS, Quinones-Hinojosa A (2011): Harvey Cushing's case series of trigeminal neuralgia at the Johns Hopkins Hospital: A surgeon's quest to advance the treatment of the "suicide disease." *Acta Neurochirurgica (Wien)* 153(5): 1043–1050.

Adelon NP et al. (1835): *Dictionnaire de médecine ou répertoire général des sciences médicales considérées sous les rapports théorique et pratique*. Paris, Béchet Jeune, 2nd edition, Vol. 12.

Aguilar y Venegas LJ (1878): Prosopalgia periódica refractoria à los antitípicos usuales, curacion por el licor de Labarraque. *La Andalucía médica Córdoba* 3: 27–32.

Alezais H, d'Astros L (1892): La circulation artérielle du pédoncule cérébral. *Journal de l'Anatomie et de la Physiologie* 28: 522–523.

André N (1756): *Observations pratiques sur les maladies de l'urèthre et sur plusieurs faits convulsifs, et la guérison de plusieurs maladies chirurgicales*. Paris, Delaguette.

Bartholow R (1872): Epileptiform tic douloureux of six years' duration cured by the hypodermic injection of morphine and by the iodide and bromide of potassium. *The Clinic, Cincinnati* 2: 253–256.

Beal MF, Hauser SL (2012): Trigeminal Neuralgia, Bell's Palsy, and other cranial nerve disorders. In: DL Longo, AS Fauci, DL Kasper, SL Hauser, JL Jameson, J Loscalzo, eds., *Harrison's Principles of Internal Medicine*. New York, McGraw-Hill, 18th edition, pp. 3360–3365.

Borowski EJ, Borwein JM (1999): *Dictionary of Mathematics*. Leicester, Bookmart Ltd.

Bousser MG, Baron JC (1979): *Migraines et algies vasculaires de la face*. N.p., Sandoz Éditions.

Caldwell CK, Honaker GL (2009): *Prime Curios! The Dictionary of Prime Number Trivia*. n.p., CreateSpace.

Campbell J (1823): *An Essay on Neuralgia Spasmodica, or Tic Douloureux; Submitted by Authority of the President and his Council, to the Examination of the Royal College of Surgeons of Edinburgh, When Candidate for Admission into their Corporation*. Edinburgh, printer unknown.

Chaussier F (1789): *Exposition sommaire des muscles du corps humain, suivant la classification & la nomenclature méthodiques adoptées au Cours public d'Anatomie de Dijon*. Dijon, Chez l'Auteur, Paris, Barrois le jeune, Méquignon l'aîné, Croullebois.

Cole CD, Liu JK, Apfelbaum RI (2005): Historical perspectives on the diagnosis and treatment of trigeminal neuralgia. *Neurosurgical Focus* 18: 1–10.

Commelin P (1960): *Mythologie grecque et romaine*. Paris, Garnier Frères.

Conway JH, Guy RK (1996): *The Book of Numbers*. New York, Copernicus.

Crowley CG (1885): *Dental Bibliography: A Standard Reference List of Books on Dentistry Published Throughout the World from 1536 to 1885*. Philadelphia, The S. S. White Dental Mfg. Co.

David T (1889): *Bibliographie française de l'art dentaire*. Paris, Félix Alcan.

Dechaume M, Huard P (1977): *Histoire illustrée de l'art dentaire. Stomatologie et Odontologie*. Paris, Roger Dacosta.

Disdier FM (1753): *Sarcologie; ou traité des parties molles. Première partie: De la myologie, ou description de tous les muscles du corps humain*. Paris, printer unknown.

Ditandy E (1865): *Réflexions sur un cas de névralgie trifaciale traitée par la névrotomie*. Strasbourg, Thesis.

Dumas CL (1797): *Système méthodique de nomenclature et de classification des muscles du corps humain*. Montpellier, Bonnariq, Avignon et Migueyron.

Eboli P, Stone JL, Aydin S, Slavin KV (2009): Historical characterization of trigeminal neuralgia. *Neurosurgery* 64(6): 1183–1187.

Engelmann W (1848): *Bibliotheca medico-chirurgica et anatomico-physiologica*. Leipzig, W. Engelmann.

Engelmann W (1867): *Bibliotheca medico-chirurgica et anatomico-physiologica. Supplement*. Leipzig, W. Engelmann.

Fehr JM, Schmidt E (1671): Naturae genius, medicorum Celsus, Jason Argonautarum, Bauschius occubuit. *Miscellanea Curiosa medico-physica Academiae naturae curiosorum Jenae* 2: sig. d 3 and both following pages.

Fischlin M (1840): *Mémoire sur le tic facial*. Rouen, Mégard.

Fothergill J (1773): Of a painful affection of the face. *Medical Observations and Inquiries by a Society of Physicians in London* 5: 129–142.

Fothergill S (1804): *A Concise and systematic Account of a Painful Affection of the Nerves of the Face; Commonly Called Tic Douloureux*. London, J. Murray.

Friel JP (1974): *Dorland's Illustrated Medical Dictionary*. Philadelphia, W.B. Saunders, 25th edition.

Galbreath DL, Jéquier L (1977): *Manuel du Blason*. Lausanne, Spes, nouvelle édition.

Garnier M, Delamare V, Delamare J, Delamare T (2009): *Dictionnaire illustré des termes de médecine*. Paris, Maloine, 30th edition.

Genenius HPV (1852): *De neuralgia intermittente nervi trigemini*. Halis Sax., Thesis.

Hirsch A (ed.) (1884–1888): *Biographisches Lexicon der hervorragenden Aerzte aller Zeiten und Völker*. Wien und Leipzig, Urban & Schwarzenberg, 6 vols.

Hirsch ABR (1765): *Paris quinti nervorum encephali disquisition anatomica, in quantum ad ganglion sibi proprium semilunare et ad originem nervi intercostalis pertinet*. Viennae, printer unknown.

Hurst JW, Schlant RC (1974): Examination of the arterial pulse. In: Hurst JW, Logue RB, Schlant RC, Wenger NK, eds., *The Heart, Arteries and Veins*. New York, McGraw-Hill Book Company, 3rd edition, pp. 170–179.

Hyrtl J (1880): *Onomatologia anatomica. Geschichte und Kritik der anatomischen Sprache der Gegenwart, mit besonderer Berücksichtigung ihrer Barbarismen, Widersinnigkeiten, Tropen, und grammatikalischen Fehler*. Wien, Wilhelm Braumüller.

Hyrtl J (1884): *Die alten deutschen Kunstworte der Anatomie*. Wien, Wilhelm Braumüller.

Index-Catalogue (1880–1895): *Library of the Surgeon General's Office, United States Army*. Washington, Government Printing Office, 1st series, 16 vols.

Index-Catalogue (1896–1916): *Library of the Surgeon General's Office, United States Army*. Washington, Government Printing Office, 2nd series, 21 vols.

Keller H (1955): *Dr. Johann Laurentius Bausch, 1605–1665, Gründer der Academia Naturae Curiosum*. Würzburg, Thesis.

Latarjet A, Wertheimer P (1923): Note sur les rapports de la portion rétrogassérienne du trijumeau intracrânien. *Comptes-Rendus de l'Association des Anatomistes* 18: 299–308.

Lauth T (1815): *Histoire de l'Anatomie*. Strasbourg, F. G. Levrault, vol. 1 (all published).

Lewy FH (1938): The first authentic case of major trigeminal neuralgia and some comments on the history of this disease. *Annals of Medical History* 10: 247–250.

Liégeois C (1881): Sur un cas de névralgie trifaciale épileptiforme convulsive. *Revue médicale de l'Est (Nancy)* 8: 179–183.

Major JC (1827): *De prosopalgia nervosa*. Pragae, typ. Sommerianis.

Manuila A, Manuila L, Nicole M, Lambert H (1981): *Dictionnaire français de médecine et de biologie*. Paris, Masson, 20 vol.

Meckel JF (1748): *De quinto pare nervorum cerebri*. Goettingae, A. Vandenhoeck.

Mercier R (1936): *Le monde médical de Touraine sous la Révolution*. Tours, Arrault & Cie.

Miró C, Ortiz T (2013): Neurological pictures. Trigeminalepsy. *Journal of Neurology Neurosurgery and Psychiatry* 84(8): 857–858.

Nigst H (1947): *Das anatomische Werk Johann Jakob Wepfers (1620–1695)*. Aarau, H. R. Sauerländer & Co.

Olry R (2014a): Anatomical eponyms, Part 1: To look on the bright side. *Clinical Anatomy* 27: 1142–1144.

Olry R (2014b): Anatomical eponyms, Part 2: The other side of the coin. *Clinical Anatomy* 27: 1145–1148.

Olry R, Haines DE (1998): The three musketeers and the twelve cranial nerves. *Journal of the History of the Neurosciences* 7: 248–249.

Paturet G (1964): *Traité d'anatomie humaine*. Paris, Masson & Cie, vol. 4 (*Système nerveux*).

Pearce JMS (2003): Trigeminal neuralgia (Fothergill's disease) in the 17th and 18th centuries. *Journal of Neurology Neurosurgery and Psychiatry* 74: 1668.

Romberg MH (1840): *Neuralgiae nervi quinti specimen. Prolusio academica.* Berolini, A. Duncker.

Soemmering ST von (1778): *De basi encephali et originibus nervorum cranio egredientium libri quinque.* Goettingae, apud Abr. Vandenhoeck viduam.

Sweet WH (1987): Neuralgia, trigeminal. In: G. Adelman, ed., *Encyclopedia of Neuroscience.* Boston, Birkhäuser, vol. 2, pp. 763–764.

Tarin P (1753): *Dictionnaire anatomique suivi d'une bibliothèque anatomique et physiologique.* Paris, Briasson.

Tassin L (1688): *Les administrations anatomiques et la myologie.* Paris, Michel Vaugon, 3rd edition.

Testut L (1884): *Les anomalies musculaires chez l'homme expliquées par l'anatomie comparée. Leur importance en anthropologie.* Paris, G. Masson.

Troisier EC (1877): Face (pathologie médicale). In: Dechambre, A, ed., *Dictionnaire encyclopédique des sciences médicales.* Paris, P. Asselin, G. Masson, sér. 4, vol. 1.

Trousseau A (1853): De la névralgie épileptiforme. *Archives générales de médecine* 1: 33–44.

Van Loenen R (1797): *De dolore faciei convulsivo.* Groningae, J. Oomkens.

Vimont J (1833): *Treatise on Human and Comparative Phrenology.* London, J. B. Baillière, Explanation of the Plates.

Von Leuthner FXJ (1810): *De dolore faciei Fothergillii; comment. Med.-chirurg.* Wirceburgi, typ. F.E. Nitribitti.

Weinberger BW (1929): *Dental Bibliography: A Reference Index to the Literature of Dental Science and Art as Found in the Libraries of the New York Academy of Medicine.* New York, The First District Dental Society, 2nd edition.

Wepfer JJ (1727): *Observationes medico-practicae, de affectibus capitis internis et externis. Studio et opera Bernhardini et Georgii Mich. Wepferi.* Scaphusii, typ. et imp. J. A. Ziegleri.

Winslow JB (1732): *Exposition anatomique de la structure du corps humain.* Paris, Guillaume Desprez et Jean Dessesartz, 4 vol.

Hallervorden-Spatz Disease:
Did One Set the Fox to Mind the Geese?

There is a recent trend in the history of medicine that considers shedding more light on the great human tragedies of WWII, particularly those related to the Nazi party. Research has also been conducted to identify the victims, especially those whose bodies were used for anatomical/pathological purposes (Hildebrandt, 2014, with a very detailed bibliography), including teaching materials: Eduard Pernkopf's (1888–1955) atlas of anatomy has probably been the most debated example (Israel & Seidelman, 1996; Hubbard, 2001). This trend is also expressed in another way, consisting of in-depth analyses of the biographies of some physicians in the era in exquisite detail, in order to decide whether his or her name deserves — on the basis of his or her behavior and not of his or her contributions to science — to be kept or to be eliminated from medical terminology (Strous & Edelman, 2007). These so-called "tainted" eponyms (Woywodt, Lefrak, & Matteson, 2010) are the topic of this article.

Fully aware of the sensitivity surrounding this subject and of the deep scar left on humankind by these historical events, we want to make clear to the reader that this article does not necessarily object to, or endorse, this trend. Our only goal is to provide food for thought from a linguistic point of view, especially as similar matters of conscience might well mushroom throughout other scientific (and even popular) vocabulary.

Let's start with a well-documented example taken from the field of neurosciences: the physician and neuroscientist Julius Hallervorden (1882–1965) and the neuropathologist Hugo Spatz (1888–1969). In 1922, these scientists described a hereditary (autosomal recessive) disorder characterized by accumulation of iron pigment in the globus pallidus and substantia nigra, leading to rigidity (beginning in the lower extremities), choreoathetoid movements, dysarthria, progressive mental deterioration, with death usually occurring before the thirtieth year (Hallervorden & Spatz, 1922). As usual in the history of medicine, this condition was subsequently referred to as Hallervorden-Spatz disease. In the following years, Hallervorden and Spatz held high positions at the *Kaiser-Wilhelm Institut für Hirnforschung* (Head of Neuropathology Department in 1938, and Director in 1937, respectively). Biographical studies have revealed their sympathies with the Nazi Party and (at least) their moral complicity towards what would be today called a crime against humanity (Shevell & Peiffer, 2001). Consequently, it was decided to abandon the term Hallervorden-Spatz disease and to replace it with pantothenate kinase-associated neurodegeneration (PKAN) or neurodegeneration with brain iron accumulation 1 (NBIA 1).

Bernfried Leiber and Theodor Olbert have shown that neurology was, about 150 years ago, the first area of medicine to resort to a great number of eponyms (Leiber & Olbert, 1968, p. v): Predictably enough, other neurological diseases were given alternative names. Because Franz Seitelberger (1916–2007) earned his PhD in 1954 under the supervision of Julius Hallervorden (Neugebauer & Stacher, 1999), Seitelberger disease became infantile neuroaxonal dystrophy. Similarly, because Joachim Scherer (1906–1945) had conducted research on children's brains supplied by the Loben Institute (Peiffer & Kleihes, 1999), van Bogaert-Scherer-Epstein syndrome became cerebrotendineous xanthomatosis. Many other examples have been recorded in the neurosciences (see Kondziella, 2009), but other areas of medicine are not wholly immune from these tainted eponyms.[1]

What Eponyms Are and, Perhaps Even More Importantly, What They Are Not

Eponyms are generally regarded as a way to pay tribute to a discoverer or to remember a name our collective memory should be proud of. Alternatively, they may function to simplify a complex medical term or condition. Hence, there are some names to worship — "Masters [. . .] Whose Names Have Adorned" (Kemper, 1905, Title), "Notable Names in Medicine & Surgery" (Bailey & Bishop, 1946, Title) — and others to pillory — "a man [Max Clara] who does not deserve our respect" (Woywodt, Lefrak, & Matteson, 2010, p. 708).

Such orientations are actually mistakes. The primary (and we may even add "only") meaning of an eponym is nothing but a "historical-becoming-semantic" link between something and someone. To coin (and to use) an eponym does not amount to applauding everything this person did/said/believed/thought/hoped for in his or her life. This is why we disagree, for example, with Daniel Kondziella when he writes that Julius Hallervorden was "honored with a neurological eponym" (Kondziella, 2009, p. 57). The neuroscientist in question was actually not "honored" but only "remembered" with this eponym, a difference that should not escape notice. Did the Finns and the Germans congratulate the famous Soviet dictator and his foreign minister by coining the terms Stalin's organs and Molotov cocktail, respectively (Zaloga & Grandsen, 1984, p. 153; Lloyd & Mitchinson, 2011, p. 76)? Four other examples of famous pivotal figures in support of the important distinction that should be drawn between use and approval are Machiavelli, Sade, Buffon, and Guillotin.

Italian statesman and writer Niccolò Machiavelli (1469–1527; Brion, 1948) wrote his famous 26-chapter *Il Principe* in the last months of 1513 (first published in 1532), after having been disgraced, put in jail and even tortured by order of the Medicis (Heers, 1985, pp. 226–233). This *"chef-d'oeuvre bref et fulgurant"* [brief and dazzling masterpiece] (Lévy, 1992, p. 5), rightly or wrongly, has always been considered as a masterpiece "that [has however] too often been misjudged as immoral or cynical" (Ridolfi, 1967, p. 518). Hence, the term Machiavellian really honors neither the memory of Machiavelli nor the one

---

[1]For example, congenital cutaneous candidiasis (formerly Beck-Ibrahim disease), portal vein thrombosis (formerly Cauchy-Eppinger-Frugoni disease), reactive arthritis (formerly Reiter syndrome), granulomatosis with polyangiitis (formerly Wegener granulomatosis).

at whom this word is aimed. The same remark, of course, applies to Donatien-Alphonse-François de Sade (1740–1814), this writer *"impie et débauché"* [impious and debauched] (Lacombe, 1974, p. 183) whose name gave rise to the term "sadism."

In the mid-eighteenth century, the famous naturalist Georges-Louis Leclerc, also known as the Count of Buffon (1707–1788), sharply criticized his colleague Carl von Linné (1707–778) for the superfluous complexity of his nomenclature (Roger, 1989, p. 409). Feeling the object of ridicule, the Swedish scientist found a way to have his revenge on the Frenchman (Bayle & Thillaye, 1855, p. 352). Linné coined the term *"Buffonia"* to refer to plants of the *Caryophyllaceae* family (*Buffonia tenuifolia* or LINN 168.1, *Buffonia sp.* or LINN 168.2) (Collective, 1817, p. 412), acknowledged not as wonderful but as awfully foul-smelling!

Without a shadow of a doubt, the French physician Joseph-Ignace Guillotin (1738–1814) would have wished to add another legacy to his important family name, with roots dating back to the sixteenth century (Pigaillem, 2004, p. 9). However, *"L'image de la justice révolutionnaire que la postérité a généralement retenue est celle de la guillotine"* [The image of revolutionary justice the posterity has generally remembered is the one of the guillotine] (Allen, 2005, p. 9). From its very first victim, Nicolas-Jacques Pelletier on April 25, 1792 (Cortequisse, 1988, pp. 20–24) to the abrogation of the death penalty in France by the Senate on September 30, 1981 (Badinter, 2000, p. 314), the term *"décapité"* [beheaded, decapitated] (Stahl, 1986) was replaced with *"guillotiné"* [guillotined]. It would be difficult to consider the term "guillotine" as a tribute paid to Dr. Guillotin, especially as he was a humanist not even the inventor of this instrument (see Soubiran, 1962; Carol, 2012, for reviews). Machiavellianism, sadism, Buffonia, and guillotine could hardly be described as laudatory.

To Remember or To Forget?

As rightly pointed out by Kurt Gilliland and Royce Montgomery, the use of eponyms is "a desire to perpetuate the *memory* of original investigators" (Gilliland & Montgomery, 2011, p. v, emphasis added). We question if leaving some names off the collective memory might not be the best way to remember what they did.

Once again some examples are in support of this question. Ugolino de Anagni, also known as Pope Gregory IX (ca. 1145–1241), never had his name crossed off the list of the Popes, although he was the principal founder of the Holy Inquisition in the 1230s (Lea, 1997, pp. 273–319). General officer Louis-Marie Turreau de Linières (1756–1816), the notorious organizer of the *"colonnes infernales"* [infernal columns] that slaughtered 40,000 Vendeans (including women and children) in early 1794 (Clénet, 1993, p. 221), today still has his name inscribed under the Arc de Triomphe in Paris (Eastern pillar, Column 15, first line).

To Separate Art and Morality?

The works of the French writer Pierre Eugène Drieu la Rochelle (1893–1945; Desanti, 1978) recently entered *"La Pléiade,"* one of the most renowned literature collection in the world (Drieu la Rochelle, 2012). This was nothing less than to drop a bombshell, because Drieu la Rochelle, who committed suicide on March 15, 1945 before being tried by the *"Commission d'épuration"* (Lottman, 1986, p. 410), was a fascist, an anti-Semitic, and collaborationist. Many wondered how the celebrated publishing house Gallimard could have got to the point of accepting Drieu la Rochelle in its collection. In the May 2012 issue of *Le Magazine Littéraire*, the journalist Cécile Guilbert, however, approved of this decision. She points out that it is "*l'occasion de mesurer ses réels états de service littéraires, si l'on accepte de dissocier art et moralité*" [the opportunity to measure his real literary service record, if one accepts to separate art and morality] (Guilbert, 2012, p. 92). Might this observation also apply to our subject, that is, "the opportunity to measure his [or her] real scientific service record, if one accepts to separate science and morality?" This, once again, is only a question.

What About the Body Snatchers?

Should some other eponyms be abandoned just because some physicians resorted to body snatchers for their medical research? Joseph Guichard du Verney (1648–1730), William Hunter (1718–1783), John Hunter (1728–1793), Sir Astley Cooper (1768–1841), Charles Bell (1774–1842), and Robert Knox (1791–1862), among many others, have been found guilty of business relationships with grave robbers (Wolf-Heidegger & Cetto, 1967, pp. 71–84; Jack, 1981, pp. 245–246; French, 1993, pp. 99–100; Persaud, 1997, pp. 254–268). Some physicians were actually regarded as dangerous torturers, a fear that even spread into vernacular language. In Germany, prisoners under sentence of death implored their executioners "*nach dem Richten nicht gerolfinckt zu werden*" [not to be "rolfincked" after the execution] (Fröber et al., 1996, pp. 9–10), the past participle "rolfincked" referring to the Jena anatomist Werner Rolfinck (1599–1673). In England, the practice of murder to obtain bodies for the physicians was called "Burking" (Cohen, 1977, p. 75) in reference to the body snatcher William Burke (see below).

We think, however, that one should be very careful not to fall into this trap, because both situations — mass extermination politics and body snatching — should never be compared with each other. Firstly, body snatchers were spurred on by financial gain and not by anthropological ravings. The medical researchers for whom they provided anatomical material were driven by their perception of scientific and medical need. Secondly, they only rarely murdered people to sell their bodies; even the most (in)famous case of William Burke (1792–1829) and William Hare (*fl.* 1829) brought the number of victims only to 16 (Cohen, 1977, pp. 61–77), a number that cannot possibly be compared with the "bookkeeping" of the concentration camps. That is, body snatching has never been shown to be a large-scale phenomenon. And thirdly, social and moral values have changed.

There is a strong link between terminology — scientific or not — and history. Now history leaves nobody unmoved — neither the ones who suffer it, nor the others who cause it. Some medical terms may rightly be labelled "handle with care," but does this require one to erase names from the collective memory? The status of some eponyms call for a further discussion, which is far from being as simple as it appears, given the sensitivities involved, is most certainly not about to end with any author's opinion piece.

References

Allen R (2005): *Les tribunaux criminels sous la Révolution et l'Empire 1792–1811*. Rennes, Presses Universitaires de Rennes.

Badinter R (2000): *L'Abolition*. Paris, Fayard.

Bailey H, Bishop WJ (1946): *Notable Names in Medicine & Surgery*. London, H. K. Lewis & Co., second edition.

Bayle ALJ, Thillaye AM (1855): *Biographie médicale*. Paris, Adolphe Delahays, vol. 2.

Brion M (1948): *Génie & destinée: Machiavel*. Paris, Albin Michel.

Carol A (2012): *Physiologie de la veuve: Une histoire médicale de la guillotine*. Seyssel, Champ Vallon.

Clénet LM (1993): *Les colonnes infernales*. Paris, Perrin.

Cohen D (1977): *The Body Snatchers*. London, Toronto, Melbourne, J. M. Dent & Sons Ltd.

Collective (1817): *Dictionnaire de sciences naturelles*. Strasbourg, F. G. Levrault; Paris, Le Normant, vol. 5.

Cortequisse B (1988): *La Sainte Guillotine*. Paris, France-Empire.

Desanti D (1978): *Drieu la Rochelle: Le séducteur mystifié*. Paris, Flammarion.

Drieu la Rochelle P (2012): *Romans, nouvelles, récits*. Paris, Gallimard, Bibliothèque de la Pléiade.

French R (1993): The anatomical tradition. In: Bynum WF, Porter R, eds., *Companion Encyclopedia of the History of Medicine*. London and New York, Routledge, vol. 1, pp. 81–101.

Fröber R, Pester T, Unger J, Linβ W, Burkhard E (1996): *Museum anatomicum Jenense: Die anatomische Sammlung in Jena und die Rolle Goethes bei ihrer Entstehung*. Jena, Gabriele Köhler.

Gilliland K, Montgomery R (2011): *Anatomists and Eponyms: The Spirit of Anatomy Past*. Nottingham, Nottingham University Press.

Guilbert C (2012): Drieu, un peu d'azur dans la fange. *Le Magazine Littéraire* 519: 92–93.

Hallervorden J, Spatz H (1922): Eigenartige Erkrankung in extrapyramidalen System mit besonderer Beteiligung des Globus pallidus und der Substantia nigra. *Zeitschrift für die gesamte Neurologie und Psychiatrie* 79: 254–302.

Heers J (1985): *Machiavel*. Paris, Fayard.

Hildebrandt S (2014): Current status of identification of victims of the National Socialist regime whose bodies were used for anatomical purposes. *Clinical Anatomy* 27: 514–536.

Hubbard C (2001): Eduard Pernkopf's atlas of topographical and applied human anatomy: The continuing ethical controversy. *Anatomical Record* 265: 207–211.

Israel HA, Seidelman WE (1996): Nazi origins of an anatomy text: The Pernkopf atlas. *Journal of the American Medical Association* 276: 1633.

Jack D (1981): *Rogues, Rebels, and Geniuses: The Story of Canadian Medicine*. Toronto, Doubleday Canada Limited.

Kemper GWH (1905): *The World's Anatomists: Concise Biographies of Anatomic Masters, from 300 B.C. to the Present Time, Whose Names Have adorned the Literature of the Medical Profession*. Philadelphia, P. Blakiston's Son & Co., revised edition.

Kondziella D (2009): Thirty neurological eponyms associated with the Nazi Era. *European Neurology* 62: 56–64.

Lacombe RG (1974): *Sade et ses masques*. Paris, Payot.

Lea HC (1997): *Histoire de l'Inquisition au Moyen Âge. Tome 1: Origines et procédures de l'Inquisition*. Grenoble, Jérôme Million (translation of the New York 1887 edition).

Leiber B, Olbert T (1968): *Die klinischen Eponyme: Medizinische Eigennamenbegriffe in Klinik und Praxis*. Munich, Berlin, Vienna, Urban & Schwarzenberg.

Lévy Y (1992): Introduction. In: Machiavel, ed., *Le Prince*. Paris, Flammarion, pp. 5–59.

Lloyd J, Mitchinson J (2011): *The Second Book of General Ignorance*. London, Faber and Faber.

Lottman H (1986): *L'Épuration 1943–1953*. Paris, Fayard.

Machiavelli N (1532): *Il Principe*. Firenze, Antonio Blado d'Asola.

Neugebauer W, Stacher G (1999): Nazi child "euthanasia" in Vienna and the scientific exploitation of victims before and after 1945. *Digestive Diseases* 17: 279–285.

Peiffer J, Kleihes P (1999): Hans-Joachim Scherer (1906–1945), pioneer in glioma research. *Brain Pathology* 9: 241–245.

Persaud TVN (1997): *A History of Anatomy*. Springfield, IL, Charles C. Thomas.

Pigaillem H (2004): *Le docteur Guillotin. Bienfaiteur de l'humanité*. Paris, Pygmalion.

Ridolfi R (1967): Macchiavelli, Niccolò. In: *Encyclopedia Britannica*. Chicago, London, Toronto, Geneva, Sydney, Tokyo, Manila, William Benton, vol. 14, pp. 518–521.

Roger J (1989): *Buffon: Un philosophe au Jardin du Roi*. Paris, Fayard.

Shevell M, Peiffer J (2001): Julius Hallervorden's wartime activities: Implications for science under dictatorship. *Pediatric Neurology* 25(2): 162–165.

Soubiran A (1962): *Ce bon docteur Guillotin et sa simple mécanique.* Paris, Librairie Académique Perrin.

Stahl PH (1986): *Histoire de la décapitation.* Paris, Presses Universitaires de France.

Strous RD, Edelman MC (2007): Eponyms and the Nazi era: Time to remember and time for change. *The Israel Medical Association Journal* 9(3): 207–214.

Wolf-Heidegger G, Cetto AM (1967): *Die anatomische Sektion in bildlicher Darstellung.* Basel, New York, S. Karger.

Woywodt A, Lefrak S, Matteson E (2010): Tainted eponyms in medicine: the "Clara" cell joins the list. *European Respiratory Journal* 36(4): 706–708.

Zaloga SJ, Grandsen J (1984): *Soviet Tanks and Combat Vehicles of World War Two.* London, Arms and Armours Press.

The sleeping brain: Extenuating circumstances of the Marquis de La Fayette on October 6, 1789

During the night of October 5 to 6, 1789, a crowd of threatening people besieged the Versailles Palace. The Marquis de La Fayette (1757–1834), a major of the newly created *Gardes nationales*, and hence in charge of public safety, told King Louis XVI that he vouched for tranquillity of the assailants and went to bed. Some hours later, the royal family was forced to leave Versailles: The Revolution had just scored one of its most important victories, while La Fayette, as if unconcerned about the future of the French monarchy, was sleeping quietly. Antoine de Rivarol (1753–1801), the "king of polemicists" (Faÿ, 1978, p. 115), could not help jumping at the opportunity, and he nicknamed La Fayette "General Morpheus" (Rivarol, 1824, p. 300) with, of course, reference to the god of sleep.

Today, many regions of the brain are known to be more or less directly involved in the neural control of sleep, including the hypothalamic preoptic area (ventrolateral preoptic area and median preoptic nucleus: Saper, Chou, & Scammell, 2001) for the control of slow-wave sleep and the dorsal pons (sublaterodorsal nucleus: El Mansari, Sakai, & Jouvet, 1989) and dorsal midbrain (ventrolateral periaqueductal gray matter: Carlson, 2010, p. 318) for the control of rapid eye movement (REM) sleep. In this article, we will analyze the origins of some neuroanatomical terms referring to sleep, broadly speaking.

First, the bedroom

To the best of our knowledge, the very first monograph devoted to the anatomy of the thalamus (*Thalamus*) was a doctoral thesis submitted at the University of Copenhagen in 1834 by Sophus August Vilhelm Stein (1797–1868) (Stein, 1834). Since that time, the origin of the term thalamus is a topic about which much has been written (Hyrtl, 1880, pp. 539–541; Walker, 1938, pp. 1–19). It is derived from the Greek term θάλαμος (*thalamos*), which could be translated in many ways: "bedroom," "women bedroom," "wedding bedroom," "wedding," "wedding bed," "food store," "den of animal," "sanctuary of a temple," "enclosure where sheep sleep," "bee cells," "tabernacle," and even "last bench of oarsmen in a galley" (Hyrtl, 1880, pp. 539–541; Pessonneaux, 1959, p. 690; Georgin, 1961, p. 378). In most cases, the etymology refers to a soothing place propitious for rest or sleep, sometimes also alluding to a wedding ceremony (hence, the "epithalam" and, by extension, epithalamus, meaning a poem or a song written to celebrate a marriage: Olry and Haines, 2012). Sixteenth-century anatomists also used the term thalamus to refer to cardiac cavities, pericardium, and *corpora carvernosa* (*Thalami cordis*, *Thalamus regalis*, and *Thalami penis*, respectively). These obsolete synonyms confirm that the term thalamus metaphorically applies to something hollow.

Second, the bed

The bed nucleus of the stria terminalis, *Nucleus striae terminalis*—surprisingly the "bed" has never appeared in the Latin, but it has appeared in its English equivalent in the *Terminologia Anatomica* (Federative Committee on Anatomical Terminology, 1998, p. 129) — is an arch-shaped neuronal mass that belongs to the so-called "extended amygdala" (Alheid, De Olmos, & Beltramino, 1995). It is comprised of three parts: caudolateral (dorsal to the amygdaloid complex), intermediate (along and among the *stria terminalis*), and rostrome-dial (enveloping the anterior commissure) (Nieuwenhuys, Voogd, & van Huijzen, 2008, p. 414). In his 2015 lexicon, Swanson refers the entry, "bed nuclei of terminal stria," to a 1925 paper by Gurdjian (Swanson, 2015, p. 63). Nonetheless, this neurosurgeon of Turkish origin, Elisha Stephens Gurdjian (1900–1985), acknowledged a predecessor in John Black Johnston (1868–1939), writing that "Johnston has described [in 1923] this [the bed nucleus of the *stria terminalis*] for the rat" (Gurdjian, 1925, p. 160).

Third, the pillow

The massive caudal pole of the thalamus is known as the pulvinar (*Pulvinar thalami*), a term probably coined by German physiologist Carl Friedrich Burdach (1776–1847) in 1822: "*Hinten liegt das Polster (pulvinar), eine Anschwellung am hintern Ende des inner Randes der obern Fläche [...] wie ein Kissen*" [Posteriorly is the cushion [pulvinar], a swelling of the posterior extremity of the internal edge of the superior surface [...] like a cushion" (Burdach, 1822, p. 117, emphasis in original).

Burdach used the German terms *Polster* and *Kissen*, meaning cushion (or something padded, broadly speaking), whereas the term *pulvinar* refers either to a cushion or more precisely to a pillow (Joubert, 1738, pp. 313 and 805; Chatelain, 1962, p. 965). Only one other anatomical structure is referred to as the pulvinar: the fibroelastic fat contained in the central nonarticular area of the acetabulum, the *Pulvinar acetabulare* (Leonhardt et al., 1987, vol. 1, p. 499). Though Latin, the term *Pulvinar acetabulare* has never belonged to any official anatomical terminology.

Fourth, a soporific, if necessary

The compression of carotid arteries has been known as a way to lose consciousness ages ago. A possible origin — and this question remains debated — of the adjective carotid may therefore be found in the Greek verb καρόω (*karo-o*), meaning to make drowsy or sleepy (Pessonneaux, 1959, p. 761). The same origin would explain the French term *coma carus*, referring to deep or Stage III coma (Mathé & Richet, 1981, p. 857). Other obsolete synonyms of carotid are more easily understood: *soporariae "ainsi nommées de ce qu'on croyait autrefois que ces artères étaient le siège du sommeil*" [so called, because one believed in the past these arteries to be the seat of sleep] (Tarin, 1753, p. 8, emphasis in original), *lethargicae* ("deep doze which removes the use of all senses, and is usually lethal": Joubert, 1738, p. 680), and *soporiferae* and *apoplecticae* (Andreas

Vesalius and Carolus Stephanus, respectively, as cited by Hyrtl, 1880, p. 94). Sometimes the reference to sleep is even more obvious: *arteria somni* or its German translation *Schlaffader* (Hyrtl, 1884, p. 182).

Finally the sleeper

The nomenclature of the numerous thalamic nuclear groups may more or less vary from a reference to another (Nieuwenhuys, Voogd, & van Huijzen, 2008, pp. 255–259). However, there always exists a midline (or median) nuclear group, including the nucleus reuniens. This nucleus is often referred to as nucleus endymalis in research papers (Strenge et al., 1981) and in textbooks as well (Leonhardt et al., 1987, Volume 3, pp. 358–359). The term endymalis, coined by Hassler in the late 1950s (Hassler, 1959), reminds us of a little-known Greek mythological character named Endymion. As usual in mythology, different versions of the same story more or less overlap with each other. Endymion is described either as a young shepherd, a grandson of Zeus, or as a son of Aëthlius and King of Elis (Grégoire, 1877, p. 678; Augé, 1930, Volume 3, p. 159; Anonymous, 1967, Volume 8, p. 383). He is even sometimes regarded as the very first astrologer to have observed the movements of the moon (Anonymous, 1783, Volume 3, p. 310). But neither his profession nor his ancestry matter to us here. Much more pertinent "biographical" data are his relationship with Selene, the goddess of the moon. Having been loved by her, he obtained from Zeus (as a reward or punishment?) the right to an everlasting sleep in a cave of Mount Latmus in Caria. This is why Endymion is often referred to as the "everlasting sleeper" (Commelin, 1960, p. 179).

In her memoirs, the famous French writer Louise-Marie-Victoire de Chastenay (1771–1855) accused La Fayette of having had a "*sommeil coupable*" (i.e., guilty sleep: as cited by Taillemite, 1989, p. 195) on October 6, 1789. He was certainly guilty from the historical point of view but with lexicological extenuating circumstances!

References

Alheid GF, De Olmos JS, Beltramino CA (1995): Amygdala and extended amygdala. In: Paxinos G, ed., *The Rat Nervous System*. San Diego, Academic Press, 2nd edition, pp. 495–578.

Anonymous (1783): *Nouveau Dictionnaire Historique*. Caen, G. Le Roy, cinquième édition.

Anonymous (1967): Endymion. In: Preece WE, ed., *Encyclopedia Britannica*. Chicago, London, Toronto, Geneva, Sydney, Tokyo, Manilla, William Benton, pp. 90–91.

Augé P (1930): *Larousse du XXe siècle*. Paris, Librairie Larousse.

Burdach CF (1822): *Vom Baue und Leben des Gehirns*. Leipzig, in der Dyk'schen Buchhandlung, Band 2.

Carlson NR (2010): *Physiology of Behavior*. Boston, Allyn & Bacon, 10th edition.

Chatelain E (1962): *Dictionnaire français-latin*. Paris, Hachette.

Commelin P (1960): *Mythologie grecque et romaine*. Paris, Garnier Frères.

El Mansari M, Sakai K, Jouvet M (1989): Unitary characteristics of presumptive cholinergic tegmental neurons during the sleep-waking cycle in freely moving cats. *Experimental Brain Research* 76: 519–529.

Faÿ B (1978): *Rivarol et la Révolution*. Paris, Librairie Académique Perrin.

Federative Committee on Anatomical Terminology (1998): *Terminologia Anatomica: International Anatomical Terminology*. Stuttgart, New York, Thieme.

Georgin C (1961): *Dictionnaire Grec-Français*. Paris, A. Hatier, nouvelle édition.

Grégoire L (1877): *Dictionnaire Encyclopédique D'histoire, de Biographie, de Mythologie et de Géographie.* Paris, Garnier Frères, nouvelle édition.

Gurdjian ES (1925): Olfactory connections in the albino rat, with special reference to the stria medullaris and the anterior commissure. *Journal of Comparative Neurology* 38: 127–163.

Hassler R (1959): Anatomy of the thalamus. In: Schaltenbrand G, Bailey P, eds., *Introduction to Stereotaxis with an Atlas of the Human Brain.* Stuttgart, Georg thieme, pp. 230–290.

Hyrtl J (1880): *Onomatologia anatomica: Geschichte und Kritik der anatomischen Sprache der Gegenwart, mit besonderer Berücksichtigung ihrer Barbarismen, Widdersinnigkeiten, Tropen, und grammatikalischen Fehler.* Wien, Wilhem Braumüller.

Hyrtl J (1884): *Die alten deutschen Kunstworte der Anatomie.* Wien, Wilhelm Braumüller.

Joubert J (1738): *Dictionnaire françois et latin, tiré des auteurs originaux et classiques de l'une et l'autre langue.* Lyon, H. Declaustre, cinquième èdition.

Leonhardt H, Tillmann B, Töndury G, Zilles K (1987): *Rauber/Kopsch Anatomie des Menschen.* Stuttgart, New York, Georg Thieme Verlag.

Mathé G, Richet G, eds. (1981): *Sémiologie Médicale.* Paris, Flammarion Médecine-Sciences, 4ème édition.

Nieuwenhuys R, Voogd J, van Huijzen C (2008): *The Human Central Nervous System.* Berlin, Heidelberg, Springer, 4th edition.

Olry R, Haines DE (2012): Is poetry a disease of the brain, as Alfred de Vigny said? *Journal of the History of the Neurosciences*: 228–231.

Pessonneaux E (1959): *Dictionnaire Grec-Français Rédigé Spécialement à L'usage des Classes D'après les Travaux et les Textes les Plus Récents.* Paris, Eugène Belin, 29ème édition.

Rivarol A (1824): *Mémoires de Rivarol, Avec Des Notes et des Éclaircissements Historiques: Précédés d'une Notice, par M. Berville.* Paris, Baudoin Frères.

Saper CB, Chou TC, Scammell TE (2001): The sleep switch: Hypothalamic control of sleep and wakefulness. *Trends in Neurosciences* 24: 726–731.

Stein SAW (1834): *De Thalamo et Origine Nervi Optici in Homine et Animalibus Vertebratis Dissertatio Anatomica.* Hauniae, Typis Excudebat S. Trier.

Strenge H, Braak E, Braak H, Muhtaroglu U (1981): On the nucleus endymalis of the human thalamus. *Journal für Hirnforschung* 22(3): 243–252.

Swanson LW (2015): *Neuroanatomical Terminology: A Lexicon of Classical Origins and Historical Foundations.* Oxford, Oxford University Press.

Taillemite E (1989): *La Fayette.* Paris, Fayard.

Tarin P (1753): *Dictionnaire Anatomique, Suivi d'une Bibliothèque Anatomique et Physiologique.* Paris, Briasson.

Walker AE (1938): *The Primate Thalamus.* Chicago, The University of Chicago Press.

The devil always experienced malicious pleasure in imposing himself in neuropsychiatric nosology

In 1911, the Swiss psychiatrist Paul Eugen Bleuler (1857–1939) became a pivotal figure of psychiatry by placing the so-called *dementia praecox* in the brand new mold of schizophrenia (Bleuler, 1911). However, several psychiatrists have cast doubt on the reality of this disease. The present-day Paris psychiatrist Barthold Bierens de Haan regards schizophrenia as a:

> psychosis invented by Eugen Bleuler [...]. Behind this spectacular term [...] hides, like behind their impenetrable language, the whole trickery of psychiatrists. [...] The truth about schizophrenia is that it doesn't exist. (Bierens de Haan, 1980, pp. 230–231)

Similarly, his colleague of Hungarian origin, Thomas Stephen Szasz (1920–2012), writes that it is "a wonderfully vague concept [...] a disease medicine [could not] list" (Szasz, 1983, p. 12). Both deny the existence of schizophrenia itself but, in their arguments, are compelled to use the term schizophrenia. Hence, to use a term might not imply a belief in the reality to what it applies. We previously approached this paradox with an anatomical example, Reissner's fiber (Olry & Haines, 2003), but this article centers on a much trickier problem in neuropsychiatry nomenclature.

Having an inquiring mind by nature, the Devil[1] always managed to interfere in all spheres of human activity, including the sciences. In 1831, the German mycologist Harald Othmar Lenz (1798–1870) coined the term "Satan's bolete" (*Rubroboletus satanas*) to refer to a poisonous mushroom (Lenz, 1831, p. 67). Biologists use an enzyme called "luciferase" — Lucifer has been described as the "light-bearing" fallen angel, hence the bioluminescence — to spot certain proteins by chromogenous reactions (Lodish et al., 2005, p. 92). Mathematicians do not follow far behind: The "devil's stair" is obtained by fractal partition of a rectangle (Sapoval, 2001, pp. 263–264), and "diabolical numbers" are real numbers in which the sum of the first n decimals is equal to 666 (Lignon, 2012, p. 451). Some very large numbers have, in fact, been named after other well-known "figures" of medieval demonology: Leviathan (the Leviathan number = $[10^{666}]!$; Pickover, 2001, p. 196), Behemoth (Behemoth numbers are any extremely large numbers; Pickover, 1995, p. 102), and Belphegor (Belphegor prime is the large palindromic prime $10^{13}[666]0^{13}1$; http://googology.wikia.com/wiki/Belphegor's_prime, consulted May 14, 2016).

---

[1] The capital is a convention used by most historians of demonology (Russell, 1981, p. 23; Migrenne, 2010, p. 31).

But how did the Devil get a foot — of course cloven (!) — into the door of the neurosciences?

The concept of demonic possession has been mainly of theological (Omand, 1970; Balducci, 1975; Rodewyk, 1988; Amorth, 1999, 2002; Bamonte, 2006; Fortea, 2006, 2008) and/or historical concern (Villeneuve, 1975; Pigin, 1998; Kelly, 2010; Kiely & McKenna, 2007). However, literature and the movie industry — let's remember William Peter Blatty's *The Exorcist* (Blatty, 1971) (see Fig. 1) and the sociological impact of William Friedkin's screen adaptation two years later (Bozzuto, 1975) — not only generated impassioned movie critics (Newman, 1974; McCabe, 1999; Wolff, 1999; Kermode, 2010) but also brought back scientific discussions involving neurosciences and, more specifically, psychology, neurology, and psychiatry (Montgomery, 1976).

Although conservative theologians might not question the reality of diabolical possession (see Haag, 1969; Cortès & Gatti, 1975, for the few exceptions), many psychiatrists and psychologists admit being interested in the concept though, of course, not declaring themselves in favor of a supernatural etiology (Stevenson, 1974, 1984; Davis, 1979; Schendel & Kourany, 1980; Naegeli-Osjord, 1983; Noll, 1992; Ferracuti, Sacco, & Lazzari, 1996; Peck, 2005; Kochko & Si Ahmed, 2009). As pointed out by Trethowan, 40 years ago:

> There are several reasons why the medical profession in general, and psychiatrists in particular, should continue to interest themselves in exorcism. While many might insist

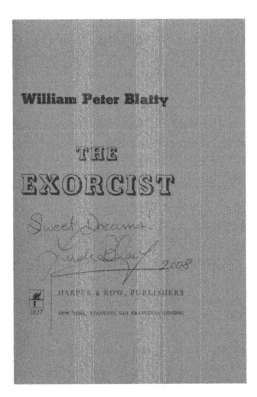

Figure 1. Title page of William Peter Blatty's *The Exorcist*, with signed dedication by the actress Linda Blair. Author's (R. O.) copy.

that the time is long past for such nonsense [...] the matter still crops up, occasionally with
disastrous consequences. (Trethowan, 1976, p. 127)

The Church itself involved physicians many centuries ago in the differential diagnosis
between possession and mental disease, as exemplified by the 1583 Rheims National
Synod:

Devant que le prêtre entreprenne d'exorciser, il doit diligemment s'enquérir de la vie du
possédé [...], de sa santé [...], car souvent des mélancoliques, lunatiques [...] ont plus besoin
de remèdes du médecin, que du ministère des exorcistes.

[Before he undertakes to exorcize, the priest has to inquire diligently about the life of the
possessed [...], of his health [...], because melancholics, lunatics often need much more cures
of the physician than the ministry of exorcists.] (Tonquédec, 1948, p. 330)

Physicians, and in actual fact, clinical neuroscientists, then had to name a phenomenon — nosology oblige — about which most did not believe.

The term possession

The term possession sometimes appears in the title of medical papers (Ehrenwald, 1975;
Kiraly, 1975; Henderson, 1976). However, neuropsychiatrists are quite justified in having
reservations about this term, and even some theologians want to rule it out. C. Fred
Dickason, former professor of theology at the Moody Bible Institute in Chicago, explains:

The word possession implies ownership. Actually, demons own nothing. The New Testament
regards them as squatters or invaders of territory that does not belong to them. In reality,
God owns them, for He is their Creator and their Judge. (Dickason, 1989, p. 38)

This opinion is shared by Paris doctorate in Canon Law, Claude Nicolas, who writes: "If
God does not possess us, all the more so we cannot be the unclean spirit's property"
(Nicolas, 1997, p. 74).

Some lexicological compromises

By this heading, we wish to point out that neuropsychiatrists sometimes allow themselves
the use of theological concepts (e.g., possession, diabolical, demonological), provided that
an additional term — medical or not — grants them a little more scientific credibility. This
addition may be "neurosis" (demonological neurosis: Hélot, 1898; Freud, 1923), "psychosis" (diabolical possession psychosis: Lhermitte, 1944), "delirium" (diabolical possession
delirium: Gayral, 1944; Delay, 1945), "syndrome" (possession syndrome: Yap, 1960),
"phenomenon" (phenomenon of possession: Bron, 1975), "state" (possession state:
Wittkower, 1970), or "experience" (possession experience: Pattison, 1969, p. 323).

In his last published book, esteemed French neuropsychiatrist and member of the
Académie de Médecine, Jean Lhermitte (1877–1959) proposed a simple but highly ques-
tionable solution: There are "true possessions" and "false possessions," he wrote
(Lhermite, 1956, note his title), using a terminology he had previously applied to mystics
(Lhermitte, 1952, again note the title).

Energumen

Among the countless letters of Marchioness Marie de Rabutin-Chantal (1626–1696), the celebrated *Madame de Sévigné*, to her daughter, Countess Françoise-Marguerite de Grignan (1646–1705), we find in the letter dated July 9, 1690 that:

> [Madame de Sévigné connaît] le mot d'énergumène pour l'avoir lu en bon lieu; c'est dans le Nouveau Testament: quand notre seigneur fait sortir les démons de ces possédés, on les appelle énergumènes.

> [[Madame de Sévigné knows] the term energumen which she read in the right place: it's in the New Testament: when our lord expels the demons from these possessed persons, one calls them energumens]. (Capmas, 1876, pp. 426–427)

Actually, the French term *énergumène* [energumen] was coined by the jurist, political philosopher, and demonologist Jean Bodin (1530–1596) in his *De la démonomanie des sorciers* [*Of the Demon-mania of the Sorcerers*] (Bodin, 1582, p. 153). Some decades later, the Latin translation *energumenus* was used to signify a person possessed in the *Rituale Romanum* published at Pope Paul V's (1552–1621) request (*Rituale Romanum*, 1617, p. 343). The Latin term *energumenus* derives from the Greek ἐνεργούμενος [*energoumenos*], which itself comes from the verb ἐνεργέω [*energeo*], meaning to influence and, by extension, to possess (Joubert, 1738, p. 459; Pessonneaux, 1959, pp. 513–514; Quicherat & Chatelain, 1962, p. 514).

Arctic hysteria and olonism

In 1970, American anthropologist Weston LaBarre (1911–1996) used the terms "arctic hysteria" (a passive state of possession during which the person is helplessly exploited by the spirits) and "olonism" (an active and self-induced state of possession). The term "olonism" probably derives from the Greek ὅλος [*olos*], which can be translated as "entirely" — meaning the responsibility for this altered state of consciousness is entirely that of the patient. As for the expression "arctic hysteria," it seems to be linked to the ethnological researches Weston LaBarre made in Alaska and eastern Siberia (Ebon, 1974, p. 18). Arctic hysteria, also known as *Pibloktoq* meaning "not himself" (Foulks, 1973; Dick, 1995), is a condition that most commonly appears in Inuit societies within the Arctic Circle. American explorer Robert Edwin Peary (1856–1920) observed this condition in 1892 and his wife and coadventurer, Josephine Diebitsch-Peary (1863–1955), described it in print two years later (Diebitsch-Peary, 1894).

The root demon — And all kinds of suffixes

The Greek radical δαίμων [*daimôn*], meaning demon, has been used to coin many terms by adding different suffixes to it. The term "demoniac" itself goes back to the thirteenth century (Bloch & Wartburg, 2002, p. 186). It derives from the Latin *daemoniacus* and refers to "one who has or seems to have relations with the devil" (Bénac, 1956, p. 314). It is mostly used as an adjective but sometimes as a common noun to refer to a possessed person. Jean-Martin Charcot (1825–1893) and Paul Richer (1849–1933), in fact, chose the term "demoniacs" for the title of their historical work how demon possession has been portrayed in the graphic arts (Charcot & Richer, 1887).

Some related terms are the following: "Demonomania" ($\mu\alpha\nu\iota\alpha$, *mania* or delirium), a monomania in which the patient considers oneself possessed of devils; "demonophobia" ($\phi\acute{o}\beta o\varsigma$, *phobos* or fear), a morbid fear of demons; "demonopathy" ($\pi\acute{\alpha}\theta o\varsigma$, *pathos* or disease) and "demonopathology" (Ebon, 1974, p. 22), mental disorders involving the concept of demons; "demonization" (Unger, 1971, p. 87), including the suffix "tion," which is used to point out the action expressed by a verb (Bossy, 1999, p. 29); and "demonolatry" ($\lambda\acute{\alpha}\tau\rho\iota\varsigma$, *latris* or servant), a morbid admiration of the demons. We also found the term "demonosis" ($\acute{\omega}\sigma\iota\varsigma$, *ôsis* or noninflammatory chronic disease), obviously comparing this term with psychosis and neurosis (McAll, 1971).

In 2010, Sherbrooke neuropediatrician, Guillaume Sébire, wrote that clinical manifestations of so-called demonic possession might sometimes be consistent with recently individualized autoimmune limbic encephalitis with anti-N-methyl-D-aspartate receptor antibodies (Tüzun & Dalmau, 2007; see Sébire, 2010). Contrary to what San Bernardo di Chiaravalle (1090–1153), the French abbot and reformer for the Cistercian order, might have thought, perhaps the road to hell is not paved with good intentions but with anti-NMDA-r antibodies!

References

Amorth G (1999): *An Exorcist Tells His Story*. San Francisco, Ignatius Press.

Amorth G (2002): *An Exorcist: More Stories*. San Francisco, Ignatius Press.

Balducci C (1975): *La possessione diabolica*. Roma, Edizioni Mediterranee.

Bamonte F (2006): *Possessioni diaboliche ed esorcismo: Come riconoscere l'astuto ingannatore*. Milano, Paoline.

Bénac H (1956): *Dictionnaire des synonymes*. Paris, Hachette.

Bierens de Haan B (1980): *Dictionnaire critique de psychiatrie*. Paris, Le Hameau Éditeur.

Blatty WP (1971): *The Exorcist*. New York, Evanston, San Francisco, London, Harper & Row.

Bleuler PE (1911): *Dementia praecox oder die Gruppe der Schizophrenien*. Leipzig, Wien, F. Deuticke.

Bloch O, Wartburg W von (2002): *Dictionnaire étymologique de la langue française*. Paris, Quadrige/PUF.

Bodin J (1582): *De la démonomanie des sorciers*. Paris, Jacques Du Puys.

Bossy J (1999): *La grande aventure du terme médical: Filiation et valeurs actuelles*. Montpellier, Sauramps Médical.

Bron B (1975): Zum Phänomen der Besessenheit. *Confinia Psychiatrica* 18: 16–29.

Bozzuto JC (1975): Cinematic neurosis following "The Exorcist": Report of four cases. *The Journal of Nervous and Mental Disease* 161: 43–48.

Capmas C (1876): *Lettres inédites de madame de Sévigné à madame de Grignan sa fille*. Paris, Hachette et Cie, Vol. 2.

Charcot JM, Richer P (1887): *Les démoniaques dans l'art*. Paris, Adrien Delahaye et Émile Lecrosnier.

Cortès JB, Gatti FM (1975): *The Case Against Possessions and Exorcisms*. New York, Vantage Press.

Davis DR (1979): Symposium: Exorcism: Dismiss or make whole? *Journal of the Royal Society of Medicine* 72: 215–218.

Delay J (1945): Délire de possession diabolique. *Presse Médicale* 11: 143.

Dick L (1995): "Pibloktoq" (Arctic Hysteria): A construction of European-Inuit relations? *Arctic Anthropology* 32(2): 1–42.

Diebitsch-Peary J (1894): *My Arctic Journal: A Year Among Ice-Fields and Eskimos*. London, Longmans, Green, and Co.

Dickason CF (1989): *Demon Possession & the Christian*. Westchester, IL: Crossway Books.

Ebon M (1974): *The Devil's Bride: Exorcism: Past and Present*. New York, Evanston, San Francisco, London: Harper & Row.

Ehrenwald J (1975): Possession and exorcism: Delusion shared and compounded. *Journal of the American Academy of Psychoanalysis* 3: 105–109.

Ferracuti S, Sacco R, Lazzari R (1996): Dissociative Trance Disorder: Clinical and Rorschach findings in ten persons reporting demon possession and treated by exorcism. *Journal of Personality Assessment* 66(3): 525–539.

Fortea JA (2006): *Interview with an Exorcist*. West Chester, PA, Ascencion Press.

Fortea JA (2008): *Memorias de un Exorcista*. Madrid, Ediciones Martinez Roca.

Foulks E (1973): The Arctic hysterias of the North Alaskan Eskimo. *Abstracts International* 33: 2905B.

Freud S (1923): Eine Teufelsneurose im siebzehnten Jahrhundert. *Zeitschrift für Anwendung der Psychoanalyse auf die Geisteswissenschaften* 9(1): 1–34.

Gayral J (1944): *Les Délires de Possession Diabolique*. Toulouse, Imprimerie du Commerce.

Haag H (1969): *Abschied vom Teufel*. N.p., Benziger Verlag.

Hélot C (1898): *Névroses et possessions diaboliques*. Paris, Bloud et Barral, 2ème édition.

Henderson DJ (1976): Exorcism, possession and the Dracula cult. *Bulletin of the Menninger Clinic* 40: 603–628.

Joubert J (1738): *Dictionnaire françois et latin tiré des auteurs originaux et classiques de l'une et l'autre langue*. Lyon, Louis & Henry Declaustre, 5ème édition.

Kelly HA (2010): *Satan: Une biographie*. Paris, Seuil.

Kermode M (2010): *The Exorcist*. N.p., Palgrave MacMillan, 2nd edition.

Kiely DM, McKenna C (2007):^ *The Dark Sacrament: True Stories of Modern-Day Demon Possession and Exorcism*. New York, HarperOne.

Kiraly SJ (1975): Folie à deux: A case of "demonic possession" involving mother and daughter. *Canadian Psychiatric Association Journal* 20: 223–227.

Kochko I de, Si Ahmed D (2009): Expériences de hantise et de possession. In: Allix S, Bernstein P, eds., *Manuel clinique des expériences extraordinaires*. Paris, InterÉditions-Dunod, pp. 331–365.

Lenz HO (1831): *Die nützlichen und schädlichen Schwämme, nebst einem Anhange über die islandische Flechte*. Gotha, Beckersche Buchhandlung.

Lhermitte J (1944): Les psychoses de possession diabolique. *Revue Médicale Française* 4: 51–54.

Lhermitte J (1952): *Mystiques et faux mystiques*. N.p., Bloud & Gay.

Lhermitte J (1956): *Vrais et faux possédés*. Paris, Fayard.

Lignon D (2012): *Dictionnaire de (presque) tous les nombres entiers*. Paris, Ellipses.

Lodish H, Berk A, Matsudaira P, Kaider CA, Kriegetr M, Scott MP, Darnell J, Zipursky L (2005): *Biologie moléculaire de la cellule*. Bruxelles, de Boeck, 3ème édition.

McAll RK (1971): Demonosis or the possession syndrome. *International Journal of the Society of Psychiatry* 17: 150–158.

McCabe B (1999): *The Exorcist: Out of the Shadows: The Full Story of the Film*. London, New York, Sydney, Omnibus Press.

Migrenne J (2010): Introduction. In: Jacques VI, ed., *Démonologie*. Grenoble, Jérôme Million (translation with notes of the 1597 edition), p. 31.

Montgomery JW, ed. (1976): *Demon Possession: A Medical, Historical, Anthropological and Theological Symposium*. Minneapolis, MN, Bethany Fellowship, Inc.

Naegeli-Osjord H (1983): *Besessenheit und Exorzismus*. Remagen, Otto Reichl Verlag.

Newman H (1974): *The Exorcist: The Strange Story Behind the Film*. New York, Pinnacle Books.

Nicolas C (1997): *Le démon de l'angoisse*. Paris, Bayard Éditions/Centurion.

Noll R (1992): *Vampires, Werewolves, and Demons: Twentieth Century Reports in the Psychiatric Literature*. New York, Brunner/Mazel.

Olry R, Haines DE (2003): Reissner's Fibre: The exception which proves the rule, or the Devil according to Charles Baudelaire. *Journal of the History of the Neurosciences* 12(1): 73–75.

Omand D (1970): *Experiences of a Present Day Exorcist*. London, William Kimber.

Pattison EM, ed. (1969): *Clinical Psychiatry and Religion*. Boston, Little, Brown and Company.

RHINENCEPHALON, TABES DORSALIS, ETC

Peck MS (2005): *Glimpses of the Devil: A Psychiatrist's Personal Accounts of Possession, Exorcism, and Redemption.* New York, Free Press.

Pessonneaux E (1959): *Dictionnaire grec-français.* Paris, Eugène Belin, 29e édition.

Pickover CA (1995): *Keys to Infinity.* New York, John Wiley & Sons, Inc.

Pickover CA (2001): *Wonders of Numbers: Adventures in Mathematics, Mind, and Meaning.* Oxford, Oxford University Press.

Pigin AV (1998): *Aus der Geschichte der Russischen Dämonologie des 17: Jahrhunderts. Erzählung von der besessenen Frau Solomonija.* Köln, Weimar, Wien, Böhlau Verlag.

Quicherat L, Chatelain E (1962): *Dictionnaire français-latin.* Paris, Hachette, nouvelle édition.

Rituale Romanum (1617): Romae, Ex Typographia Camerae Apostolicae.

Rodewyk A (1988): *Dämonische Besessenheit: Tatsachen und Deutungen.* Augsburg, Pattloch Verlag.

Russell JB (1981): *Satan: The Early Christian Tradition.* Ithaca and London, Cornell University Press.

Sapoval B (2001): *Universalités et fractales.* Paris, Flammarion.

Schendel E, Kourany RFC (1980): Cacodemonomania and exorcism in children. *Journal of Clinical Psychiatry* 41(4): 119–123.

Sébire G (2010): In search of lost time: From "demonic possession" to anti-N-Methyl-D-Aspartate receptor encephalitis. *Annals of Neurology* 67(1): 141–142.

Stevenson I (1974): *Xenoglossy: A Review and Report of a Case.* Charlottesville, University Press of Virginia.

Stevenson I (1984): *Unlearned Language: New Studies in Xenoglossy.* Charlottesville, University Press of Virginia.

Szasz TS (1983): *La schizophrénie.* Paris, Payot.

Tonquédec J de (1948): L'exorciste devant les manifestations diaboliques. In: *Satan: Études carmélitaines.* Paris, Desclée de Brouwer, pp. 328–351.

Trethowan WH (1976): Exorcism: A psychiatric viewpoint. *Journal of Medical Ethics* 2: 127–137.

Tüzün E, Dalmau J (2007): Limbic encephalitis and variants: Classification, diagnosis, and treatment. *Neurologist* 13: 261–271.

Unger MF (1971): *Demons in the World Today: A Study of Occultism in the Light of God's Word.* Wheaton, IL: Tyndale House Publishers, Inc.

Villeneuve R (1975): *Les possessions diaboliques.* Paris, Pygmalion.

Wittkower ED (1970): Trance and possession states. *International Journal of the Society of Psychiatry* 16: 153–160.

Wolff U (1999): *Das bricht dem Bischof das Kreuz: Die letzte Teufelsaustreibung in Deutschland 1975/76.* Reinbek bei Hamburg, Rowohlt Taschenbuch Verlag.

Yap PM (1960): The Possession syndrome: A comparison of Hong Kong and French findings. *Journal of Mental Science* 106: 114–137.

Tabes dorsalis: Not, at all, "Elementary my dear Watson!"

Let us begin this column with two slices of life of the celebrated Sir Arthur Conan Doyle (1859–1930). First, he studied medicine at Edinburgh University in Scotland where he defended, in April 1885, his MD thesis devoted to the vasomotor changes in *tabes dorsalis* (Doyle, 1885)—hence, the first part of our title. Second, he is, of course, chiefly remembered for his creation of the "subtle, hawk-eyed amateur detective Sherlock Holmes" (Drabble, 1996, p. 292). The first work featuring Sherlock Holmes and Dr. (John H.) Watson, *A Study in Scarlet*, was published in 1887,[1] followed by three novels and 56 short stories until 1927. Commonplaces are hard to get rid of: contrary to what some quite reliable references still convey (Demougin, 1992, p. 722), Sherlock Holmes never said word for word to his foil: "Elementary my dear Watson!"; this famous but apocryphal exclamation only appeared in later screen adaptations of Holmes' adventures. Hence, the second part of our title: We would actually never describe the historical roots of the term *"tabes dorsalis"* as "Elementary my dear Watson!" Since our first "Neurowords Column" almost 20 years ago (Olry & Haines, 1997), this term caused us no end of trouble.

Tabes dorsalis belongs, with general paresis, to the late (tertiary, the onset of symptoms usually occurring 25–30 years after infection) manifestations of parenchymatous neuro-syphilis. It is histologically characterized by a demyelination of the posterior columns, posterior roots, and posterior root ganglia. Its clinical manifestations include ataxic wide-based gait, paresthesia, loss of some sensations (position sense, deep-pain, thermal sense), bladder disturbances, trophic joint degeneration—the famous French neurologist Charcot's (1825–1893) arthropathy[2] (Charcot, 1868)—and the Argyll Robertson (1837–1909) pupil (Robertson, 1869), among others (Cabanne & Bonenfant, 1986, p. 1282; Lukehart, 2015, p. 1136).

Tabes: Etymology and lexicology

The Latin term *"tabes"* means wasting, consumption (Quicherat, 1962, p. 302; Gaffiot, 1989, p. 565), "disease which rots the blood" (Joubert, 1738, p. 284). In the same family of words, we could quote *"tabesco"* (to rot, to be consumed), *"tabidus"* (corrupted, rotted), and *"tabificus"* (dissolving, pestilential). Another one, *"tabitudo,"* is all the more interesting given that it also refers to phthisis, a "disease which dries the whole body" (Joubert,

---

[1]The first book edition was published in 1888, but the first publication of this story appeared in the November 1887 issue of *Beeton's Christmas Annual*, a paperback magazine published from 1860 (Volume 1) through 1898 (Volume 39).
[2]The term "Charcot's Arthropathy" was coined after the 1881 London Medical International Conference (Thuillier, 1993, p. 83).

1738, p. 863). The distinction between *tabes* and phthisis, "*convenientia ac differentia*" (common points as well as differences), was discussed in the mid-1700s by German physician and apothecary Johann Christophor Fimmler (1676–1753; see Fimmler, 1744), and the term phthisis, as more or less synonymous with *tabes*, remained in use in the first half of the nineteenth century in the German medical literature (Loewenhardt, 1817; Oertel, 1846; Geyer, 1848).

The English philologist Walter William Skeat (1835–1912) added an obsolete French verb, "*tabifier*," meaning to waste (Skeat, 1882, p. 620), but we could not find this verb in Greimas' *Dictionnaire de l'ancien Français* (Greimas, 1969).

We could also encounter the term *tabes* without the "s," which is a normal spelling in Italian ("*tabe dorsale*" is the Italian translation of *tabes dorsalis*; cited by Tonini, 1994, Item 10, p. 6) but is difficult to explain in Latin: "*tabe*" (Hoogeveen, 1616, in the title), "*tabe dorsuali*" (Chemnitz, 1749, in the title), "*tabe nervosa*" (Schaper, 1825, in the title), or "*tabe dorsali*" (Gossow, 1825, in the title).

Finally, some authors did not consider the term *tabes* as pathological in itself and, therefore, added the notion of disease: "*morbis tabificis*" (Berends, 1829, in the title).

Tabes: Historical and bibliographical roots

In their etymological dictionary, the French linguist Oscar Bloch (1877–1937) and the Swiss philologist Walther von Wartburg (1888–1971) wrote that the term *tabes* appeared in English medical terminology in 1651 and in French in 1752 (Bloch & Wartburg, 2002, p. 620). In all likelihood, the 1651 reference is the first and probably only edition (Wing, 1945–1951, p. 153) of a book written by a certain Noah Biggs (*fl.* 1651), an English medical reformer and alchemical writer (Debus, 1990, pp. 177–178):

> As intolerable and whimsicall also are Fontanells in Tabes, or consumptions, distempers of the lungs, head, eyes. (Biggs, 1651, § 258, p. 190)

As for the French 1752 reference, we think that Bloch and Wartburg referred to the 1752 supplement to the 1743 edition of the *Dictionnaire de Trévoux* (Weil, 1991). These assumptions will not be discussed further for, as it turns out, the term *tabes* actually appeared much earlier in medical writings.

The "Ortolang" Web site of the *Centre National de Ressources Textuelles et Lexicales* (National Center of Textual and Lexical Resources) ascribes the very first use of the term *tabes* to J. Falcon's 1520 edition of *Le Guidon en François*. We had then to answer three questions: Who was J. Falcon? What does the term "*Guidon*" in the title of this book actually mean? Where could we find a copy of this book, precisely this 1520 edition, in order to make sure that the information taken from the above Web site is accurate.

Who was J. Falcon? Biographical data were not easy to find. Jean Falcon, born in Catalonia in 1491, studied medicine at Montpellier where he took over for the royal physician Jean Garcin (who died in 1502) in the early 1500s. He probably died in 1540 or 1541 (Nicaise, 1890, p. cxxxvi; Tsoucalas et al., 2013). Most of, if not all of, his printed medical contributions were new editions of, or additions to, Guy de Chauliac's (ca. 1300–1368) *Grande Chirurgie* on the one hand and Antonio Guainerio's (who died ca. 1448) *Practica* on the other hand. That is probably why he is never found under the letter "F" in medical bibliographies or famous collection catalogues.

What does the term *"Guidon"* mean in the title of the book? We first believed it might be related to Chauliac's given name Guy. In the genitive, the Latin translation Guido actually reads Guidonis, as can be seen in the title of a 1546 translation of his *Grande Chirurgie*: *"Ars chirurgica Guidonis Cauliaci"* (listed in Durling, 1967, p. 271). The genitive form of a given name was usual at that time in book titles: Guido de Vigevano's (or de Papia, born ca. 1300) *Liber notabilium* includes in its title *"Francorum Regis, a libris Galieni per me Guidonem de Papia, medicorum"* (as cited in Wickersheimer, 1926, p. 71, underline added). Guy de Chauliac is even referred to by the only surname Guidon in Raoul du Montvert's *Les fleurs et secretz de Medicine* published ca. 1530 (as cited in Davies, 1961, p. 554, No. 390). But our first hypothesis proved to be wrong. Some authors actually consider his real full name to have been Guigue de Chauliac (or Guigo de Caulliaco), as mentioned in St-Just Chapter's *Actes capitulaires* (as cited by Allut, 1859/1972, pp. 128–129). In that case, *"Guidon"*—which should have been spelled *"guion"* since its appearance ca. 1160 (Greimas, 1969, p. 326) —would not be related to Chauliac's given name. This would support another hypothesis suggested by the celebrated German biographer August Hirsch (1817–1894): The *"Guidon"* would simply be the French word meaning "handlebars" (and more largely guide or driver, as in Jean Hennequin's 1631 treatise on economics), because Chauliac's *Grande Chirurgie*

> mehrere Jahrhunderte lang der hauptsächlichste Führer ("Guidon") in diesem Fache wurde [was for many centuries the principal guidebook in this field]. (Hirsch, 1884–1888, p. 710)

Where could we find a copy of Joannes Falcon's 1520 *Le Guidon en françoys*? The bibliography of Guy de Chauliac is of outstanding complexity, and it may be difficult to find one's way from its very first printed edition by Barthélemy Buyer on March 28, 1478 (Osler, 1923, p. 107, No. 164) to the numerous subsequent translations, reprints, and comments. In 1890, the French surgeon Edouard Nicaise (1838–1896) published a detailed list of 56 manuscripts and 93 printed editions of Chauliac's works (Nicaise, 1890, pp. cviii–clxiv). The 1520 edition for which we were looking is actually described on pages cxxxviii–cxxix: It was, therefore, not the kind of bibliographical ghost we sometimes come across in the history of medicine. This edition also contains additions by Symphorien Champier (ca. 1471–1537), a remote cousin and one of the very first biographers of Pierre Terrail, the famous chevalier de Bayard (1473–1524) (Jacquart, 1987, p. 8), and by Anthoine Romari, one of Montpellier Falcon's colleagues. Copies of this book seem, however, to be of utmost rarity: Nicaise could only find two copies (*Bibliothèque Nationale de France* and Erlangen University Library), and we could find only one more copy in the Glasgow Hunterian Museum (Ferguson, 1930, p. 163). Being unable to consult this edition in person, we had to make do with a later Latin edition (Falcon, 1559) in which, unfortunately, we could not find the term *tabes*.

Tabes dorsalis

Some authors ascribe the very first use of the term *"tabes dorsalis"* to the German neurologist Robert Remak (1815–1865) (Pryse-Phillips, 2003, p. 919), when others write that it is the term *"tabes cervicalis"* that has been coined by him (Raymond, 1894, p. 86). However that may be, this term should not have been coined before Sir William Withey

Gull (1816–1890), one of the Physicians-in-Ordinary to Her Majesty Queen Victoria (1819–1901) (Pearce, 2006), showed in 1856 and 1858 the lesions of *tabes dorsalis* to be located in the posterior columns of the spinal cord (Gull, 1856, 1858).

It's not so simple. As far back as the early 1700s, the English writer Edward Phillips (1630–ca. 1696), a nephew of the famous poet John Milton, already gave a definition of *tabes dorsalis* in the 1706 sixth edition of his dictionary:

> Tabes dorsalis, a Consumption in the Marrow of the Back-bone, which happens to those that are to much given to Venery. (Phillips, 1706, n.p.)

What the author exactly meant with "Marrow of the Back-bone" is not clear: Did he refer to the bone marrow of thoracic vertebrae? Or could he have been referring to the *marrow* (*medulla, medulla spinalis*) of the back-bone (*vertebral column*) or the soft structure within the vertebral column? This directly describes the involvement of the spinal cord in the disease condition.

Furthermore, Edward Phillips has been accused—probably wrongly (Considine, 2015)—of plagiarizing from an earlier dictionary, Thomas Blount's *Glossographia*, first published in 1656. The 1707 edition of Blount's *Glossographia* includes the following definition:

> Tabes dorsalis, a Consumption in the Spinal Marrow; incident to those who are to much addicted to Venery. (B[lount], 1707, p. 557)

Maybe this time "Spinal Marrow" refers to the spinal cord as noted above? Unfortunately, we could not consult the first edition of these two dictionaries (1656 and 1658, respectively). We cannot therefore say definitively who—and why—Edward Phillips or Thomas Blount probably coined the term *tabes dorsalis* in the seventeenth century.

The nonsyphilitic *tabes*

Being originally a term of general histopathology, the term *tabes* also referred to diseases others than those caused by *Treponema pallidum*.

The celebrated French neurologist Jules Dejerine (1849–1917) coined, in 1883, the term "nervo-tabes" to describe peripheral neuritis related to alcoholism (as cited in Gauckler, 1922, p. 181).

The "tabes mesenterica" (or sometimes "tabes mesaraica"), nowadays referred to intestinal tuberculosis (Kumar, Abbas, & Aster, 2013, p. 497), is the mycobacterial infection of mesenteric lymph nodes in children. To the best of our knowledge, this term was coined by Gulielmus Ball in his 30-page Edinburgh 1773 dissertation (Ball, 1773). Some other (obsolete?) examples could be found in the twenty-fifth edition of the *Dorland's Illustrated Medical Dictionary*: "Cerebral tabes" (dementia paralytica), "tabes ergotica" (due to ergotism), and "vessel tabes" (due to obliterative endarteritis) (Friel, 1974, p. 1536). In the nineteenth century, the term "tabes metallurgica" referred to the pulmonary disease of mineworkers (Dechambre, 1864–1889, Vol. 8, p. 227).

We could, unfortunately, not lift the curtain on some historical roots of the term *tabes dorsalis*. As Dr. (John H.) Watson said in a fictitious biography of Sherlock Holmes:

> To think that an important secret may be hidden in this inscription, and that it's impossible to decipher. (Baring-Gould, 1964, p. 102)

References

Allut P (1859/1972): *Étude biographique & bibliographique sur Symphorien Champier.* Nieuwkoop, B. de Graaf.

Ball G (1773): *Dissertatio medica inauguralis, de tabe mesenterica.* Edinburgi, apud Balfour et Smellie.

Baring-Gould WS (1964): *Moi, Sherlock Holmes.* Paris, Buchet/Chastel.

Berends CAG (1829): *Lectiones de morbis tabificis. Edidit et praefatus est Aug. Guil. A. Stosch.* Berolini, typis et impensis G. Reimeri.

Biggs N (1651): *Mataeotechnia medicinae praxews. The vanity of the craft of physick; or, A new dispensatory. Wherein is dissected the errors, ignorance, impostures and supinities of the schools, in their main pillars or purges, blood-letting, fontanels or issues, and diet, &c. and the particular medicines of the shops. With an humble motion for the reformation of the universities, and the whole landscape of physick, and discovering the terra incognita of chymistrie. To the Parliament of England.* London, Giles Calvert.

Bloch O, Wartburg W von, eds. (2002): *Dictionnaire étymologique de la langue française.* Paris, Presses Universitaires de France.

B[lount] T (1707): *Glossographia Anglicana Nova.* London, printed for D. Brown.

Cabanne F, Bonenfant JL (1986): *Anatomie pathologique. Principes de pathologie générale, de pathologie spéciale et d'aetopathologie.* Québec, Paris, Les presses de l'Université Laval, Maloine S.A., deuxième édition.

Charcot JM (1868): Sur quelques arthropathies qui paraissent dépendre d'une lésion du cerveau ou de la moëlle épinière. *Archives de Physiologie normale et pathologique* 1: 161–178.

Chemnitz JH (1749): *De tabe dorsuali.* Gottingae, typis J. C. Schulzii.

Considine J (2015): In praise of Edward Phillips. *Studia Linguistica Universitatis Iagellonicae Carcoviensis* 132: 211–218.

Davies HWM (1961): *Catalogue of a Collection of Early French Books in the Library of C. Fairfax Murray.* London, The Holland Press, Volume 1.

Debus A (1990): Chemistry and the universities in the seventeenth century. *Estudos Avançados* 4 (10): 173–196.

Dechambre A, ed. (1864–1889): *Dictionnaire encyclopédique des sciences médicales.* Paris, G. Masson et P. Asselin, Volume 8.

Demougin J, ed. (1992): *Dictionnaire des Littératures française et étrangères.* Paris, Larousse.

Doyle AC, Sir (1885): *An Essay upon the vasomotor changes in tabes dorsalis and on the influence which is exerted by the sympathetic nervous system in that disease, being a thesis presented in the hope of obtaining the degree of the Doctorship of medicine of the University of Edinburgh.* Edinburgh, MD thesis.

Doyle AC, Sir (1887): A study in scarlet. *Beeton's Christmas Annual* 28: 1–95.

Doyle AC, Sir (1888): *A Study in Scarlet.* London, Ward Lock & Co.

Drabble M, ed. (1996): *The Oxford Companion to English Literature.* Oxford, New York, Oxford University Press, revised edition.

Durling RJ (1967): *A Catalogue of Sixteenth Century Printed Books in the National Library of Medicine.* Bethesda, National Library of Medicine.

Falcon J (1520): *Le Guidon en Francoys, nouvellement imprimé, avec les gloses de Jehan Falcon. Et spécialement sus le Tracte des playes et ulcères. Et... le texte: et aussi les additions de Maistre Simphorien Champiel [sic] avec les additions de maistre Anthoine Romari sus Lantidotaire...* Lyon, Constantin Fradin.

Falcon J (1559): *Notabilia supra Guidonem.* Lyon, Ian de Tournes.

Ferguson M (1930): *The Printed Books in the Library of the Hunterian Museum in the University of Glasgow.* Glasgow, Jackson, Wylie & Company.

Fimmler JC (1744): *De tabis et phthiseos convenientia ac differentia.* Vitembergae, prelo E. G. Eichsfeldi.

Friel JP (1974): *Dorland's Illustrated Medical Dictionary.* Philadelphia, W. B. Saunders, 25th edition.

Gaffiot F (1989): *Dictionnaire Latin-Français*. Paris, Hachette, nouvelle édition par Catherine Magnien.

Gauckler E (1922): *Le Professeur J. Dejerine 1849–1917*. Paris, Masson et cie.

Geyer RB (1848): *Die Rückenmarkschwindsucht, ihre Beschreibung, Erklärung und Heilung*. Leipzig, Arnold.

Gossow AFA (1825): *De tabe dorsali*. Berolini, lit. A. Petschii.

Greimas AJ (1969): *Dictionnaire de l'ancien Français*. Paris, Librairie Larousse.

Gull WW (1856): Cases of paraplegia. *Guy's Hospital Reports* 2: 143–190.

Gull WW (1858): Cases of paraplegia (second series). *Guy's Hospital Reports* 4: 169–216.

Hennequin J (1631): *Le guidon général des finances*. Paris, Toussaint Quinet.

Hirsch A (1884–1888): *Biographisches Lexicon der hervorragenden Aerzte aller Zeiten und Völker*. Wien und Leipzig, Urban & Schwarzenberg, Volume 1.

Hoogeveen G ab (1616): *De tabe*. Lugduni-Batavorum, ex officina J. Boudewini.

Jacquart J (1987): *Bayard*. Paris, Fayard.

Joubert J (1738): *Dictionnaire François et latin, tiré des auteurs originaux et classiques de l'une et de l'autre langue*. Lyon, Declaustre.

Kumar V, Abbas AK, Aster JC (2013): *Robbins Basic Pathology*. Philadelphia, Elsevier-Saunders, 9th edition.

Loewenhardt SE (1817): *De myelophthisi chronica vera et notha*. Berolini, typ. Haynianis.

Lukehart SA (2015): Syphilis. In Kasper DL, Fauci AS, Hauser SL, Longo DL, Jameson JL, Loscalzo J, eds., *Harrison's Principles of Internal Medicine*. New York, McGraw-Hill, 19th edition, pp. 1132–1140.

Nicaise E (1890): *La Grande Chirurgie de Guy de Chauliac, chirurgien, maistre en médicine de l'Université de Montpellier, composée en l'an 1363*. Paris, Félix Alcan.

Oertel C (1846): *De myelophthisi sicca*. Berolini, G. Schade.

Olry R, Haines DE (1997): Rhinencephalon: A brain for the nose? *Journal of the History of the Neurosciences* 6: 217–218.

Osler W (1923): *Incunabula Medica: A Study of the Earliest Printed Medical Books 1467–1480*. Oxford, Oxford University Press.

Pearce JMS (2006): Sir William Withey Gull (1816–1890). *European Neurology* 55: 53–56.

Phillips E (1706): *The New World of Words, or Universal English Dictionary*. London, J. Phillips, N. Rhodes and J. Taylor, 6th edition.

Pryse-Phillips W (2003): *Companion to Clinical Neurology*. Oxford, Oxford University Press, 2nd edition.

Quicherat L (1962): *Dictionnaire Français-Latin*. Paris, Hachette, nouvelle édition par Émile Chatelain.

Raymond F (1894): *Maladies du système nerveux. Scléroses systématiques de la moelle*. Paris, Octave Doin.

Robertson DMCLA (1869): On an interesting series of eye symptoms in a case of spinal disease, with remarks on the action of belladonna on the iris. *Edinburgh Medical Journal* 14: 696–708.

Schaper CWL (1825): *De tabe nervosa*. Berolini, typis Brüschckianis.

Skeat WW (1882): *An Etymological Dictionary of the English Language*. Oxford, Clarendon Press.

Thuillier J (1993): *Monsieur Charcot de la Salpêtrière*. Paris, Robert Laffont.

Tonini M (1994): *Catalogo 64. Medicina antica. Ritratti di medici. Curiosa. Dorè. "Collezione diamante." Vedute e piante di città*. Ravenna, Tipolitografia Scaletta.

Tsoucalas G, Karamanou M, Piagkou M, Skandalakis P, Androustos G (2013): Jean Falcon (1491–1541), a great surgeon and anatomist of the 16th century. *Italian Journal of Anatomy and Embryology* 118 (2): 172–176.

Weil F (1991): Les libraires parisiens et le Dictionnaire de Trévoux. *Recherches sur Diderot et sur l'Encyclopédie* 10(1): 155–158.

Wickersheimer E (1926): *Anatomies de Mondino dei Luzzi et de Guido de Vigevano*. Paris, E. Droz.

Wing D (1945–1951): *Short-Title Catalogue of Books Printed in* England, Scotland, Ireland, Wales, and British America and of English Books Printed in Other Countries *1641–1700*. New York, Columbia University Press, Volume 1.

Ondine's curse: With Jean Giraudoux's finishing touches

Monday February 12, 1883, Vendramin-Calergi Palace, Venice:

In an apartment rented by Duke della Grazia, the fourth of that line,[1] a 69-year-old man reads a book while his friend, the German painter of Russian origin Paul von Joukowsky (1813–1883), sketches a pencil drawing of him. Late that evening, the old man tells his wife Cosima (née von Bülow): "I love them, these creatures of the depths." And he asks: "And you, aren't you one of these creatures?" (Mistler, 1962, p. 230).

The creatures (*ondines*) and the book (*Undine*) in question led two Californian physicians to coin a new term in neurological nomenclature over 50 years ago. As for the old man, he was famed composer Richard Wagner (see Fig. 1), and he would die the next day.

Ondine's curse in neurology

"Ondine's curse," or congenital[2] central alveolar hypoventilation syndrome, is one of the strangest diseases in the history of neurology. It is a kind of disease one might think came straight out of a fairy tale, and this would not be wrong! Characterized by the loss of automatic respiration during sleep but with preserved voluntary breathing (Pedroso et al., 2009), this rare and still quite mysterious disease seems to be related to abnormalities in the gene encoding the transcription factor paired-like homeobox 2b (PHOX2b), which is known to be involved in neuronal development (McConville, Mokhlesi, & Solway, 2015, p. 1722).

John Wendell Severinghaus and Robert A. Mitchell, physicians at the Cardiovascular Research Institute of the University of California Medical School, coined the term "Ondine's curse" in 1962. Three of their patients had exhibited long periods of apnea, even when awake, yet could control their breathing on demand. The authors explained the choice of this new term:

> The syndrome was first described in German legend. The water nymph, Ondine, having been jilted by her mortal husband, took from him all automatic functions, requiring him to remember to breathe. When he finally fell asleep, he died. (Severinghaus & Mitchell, 1962, p. 122)

But who is Ondine, and which is the German legend in question?

---

[1]Maria Adinolfo Leopoldo Antonio Ettore (1840–1911), fourth Duke della Grazia, was the son of Marie Caroline Ferdinande Louise of Naples and Sicily, Duchess of Berry (1798–1870) and Ettore Carlo Lucchesi-Palli (1806–1864) (*Almanach de Gotha*, 1842, pp. 21 and 25).

[2]The adjective "congenital" is actually too restrictive: Many case reports are acquired diseases, caused by a brain-stem infarction for example (Shih, Hong, & Wong, 2003).

Figure 1. Richard Wagner (1813–1883) reading *Undine* the day before he died, drawn by his friend Paul von Joukowsky (1845–1912). From Günzel K (1995): *Die Deutschen Romantiker*. Zürich, Artemis. Source: Wikicommon (public domain).

Ondines and other water creatures

Legends portraying all kinds of water creatures go back to the dawn of time. Oceans, seas, and ponds are swarming with nymphs, nereids, sirens, naiads, oceanids, limnads, mermaids, and ondines. Mythology did not seem to spare the slightest puddle. Even the famous Swiss physician and naturalist Conrad Gesner (1516–1565) depicted a mermaid in one of his books, referred to her as *Meerfräulein*, meaning "young lady of the sea" (Gesner, 1670, p. 153; see Heuvelmans, 1965, and Bessler, 1995 for reviews).

As a common name, the term "ondine" is believed to have been coined in the sixteenth century, as synonymous with nymph. The man behind the name seems to have been Theophrastus Philippus Aureolus Bombastus von Hohenheim, also known as Paracelsus (1493–1541) (Zidaric, 2003). For unknown reasons, the masculine noun "ondin" appeared only much later in the eighteenth century (Bloch & Wartburg, 2002, p. 445).

What about Ondine as a given name? In his 1982 thesis, Ferlan wrote that La Motte-Fouqué was the first one to use Ondine as a given name (Ferlan, 1982, p. 6). Nonetheless, we found that a nymph named Ondine appeared over two centuries earlier, in Pierre de Ronsard's (1524–1585) poem *Hylas*[3]:

> Près de la nymphe au plus profond des ondes / Estoit Antrine aux belles tresses blondes / Et Azuine aux tetins descouverts / Verdine, Ondine, et Bordine aux yeux verts
>
> [Near the nymph in the depths of waters / Was Antrine with beautiful blond plaits / And Azuine with uncovered nipples / Verdine, Ondine, and Bordine with green eyes]. (see Ronsard, 1569, p. 28, Verses 273–276; underline added)

---

[3] In Greek mythology, Hylas, the squire of Heracles, was drowned by a dryad who wanted to kiss him (Hamilton, 1978, p. 144). The source of this story is to be found in Appolonios of Rhodes' *Argonautics* (Nassichuk, 1999).

In their study of the roots of the term Ondine's curse, Nannapaneni et al. (2005) explain that a water nymph could become a human only if she falls in love with a mortal man. But to fall in love was neither a sufficient nor as a necessary condition. Water nymphs, whether in love or not, had to marry to a mortal man to be so transformed. In his *Liber de nymphis*, Paracelsus was perfectly clear about it:

> [Elles] sont des filles de roi ... On pense qu'elles vivent sans âme raisonnable dans un corps fantastique [et ne peuvent échapper au jugement dernier] à moins qu'elles ne se marient avec un homme.
> [(They) are daughters of a king ... One thinks they live without any sensible soul in a fantastic body (and cannot escape the Last Judgment) unless they get married to a man].
> (Translated and cited in Lancner, 1988, p. 1003)

Ondine may, therefore, be regarded as an exemplar of the concept of "betrothed-animal." This concept was, in fact, developed by American psychoanalyst of Austrian origin, Bruno Bettelheim (1903–1990; 1976, pp. 461–466). A human in love with a nonhuman creature may help it obtain a soul and achieve the status of a human being.

La Motte-Fouqué and his *Undine* (1811)

Friedrich Heinrich Karl, Freiherr de La Motte-Fouqué (see Fig. 2), was born in Brandenburg (Prussia) on February 12, 1777. The grandson of Heinrich August de la Motte-Fouqué (1698–1774), one of the most famous generals of King Friedrich II (1712–1786), he started a military career but soon set his sights on literature. One of his first publications, *Dramatische Spiele* [Dramatic Plays], was written under the patronage of the German writer

Figure 2. Friedrich Heinrich Karl, Freiherr de La Motte-Fouqué (1777–1843). L. Staub, from Günzel K (1995): *Die Deutschen Romantiker.* Zürich, Artemis. Source: Wikicommon (public domain).

August Wilhelm von Schlegel (1767–1845) and was published in 1801. A fierce opponent of Napoléon, he lived out his last years with the help of a pension granted by King of Prussia Friedrich-Wilhelm IV (1795–1861) and died in Berlin on January 23, 1843 (Mourre, 1989, p. 26; Demougin, 1992, p. 867).

La Motte-Fouqué always drew his inspiration from ancient German sagas and French romances of chivalry. He is a pivotal figure of German romanticism, a movement opposed to the eighteenth-century rationalism (Guillemain, 1948, p. 191; see Richter & Richter, 1973, for review). His 189-page *Undine*, heavily influenced by Paracelsus' *Liber de nymphis*[4] (Gallagher, 2009, p. 351), was published in 1811 in *Die Jahreszeiten*, a literary journal published by La Motte-Fouqué himself (Alexandre, 1963, p. 1589).

Let's start by summarizing the plot of the story. An 18-year-old water nymph called Ondine had been adopted at the age of 3 by an old fisherman and his wife. One evening, she met the knight Huldbrand von Ringstetten who instantly fell in love and married her, albeit without worrying too much about the fact that he had previously been more or less betrothed to a certain princess, Bertalda. But the knight gradually grew away from Ondine, who in her despair leaped into the Danube and disappeared under the water. Princess Bertalda now became Huldbrand's second wife. One night, "a pale woman, completely dressed with white veils" emerged from the well of the castle and made her way to the knight (Alexandre, 1963, p. 1433). The apparition was, of course, Ondine's ghost.

> *Bebend vor Liebe ... neigte sich der Ritter ihr entgegen, sie küßte ihn mit einem himmlischen Kusse, aber sie ließ ihn nicht mehr los, sie drückte ihn inniger an sich und weinte ... bis ihm endlich der Atem entging und er aus den schönen Armen als ein Leichnam sanft auf die Kissen des Ruhebettes zurücksank.* [Trembling with love ... the knight leaned in her direction, she gave him a wonderful kiss, but she did not let him go, she clasped him to her bosom with all her might and cried ... until finally he could no more breathe, and peacefully collapsed, dead, onto the bed]. (La Motte-Fouqué, 1811, pp. 183–184)

The knight, Huldbrand von Ringstetten, died of suffocation in Ondine's arms. Revenge, no doubt, but as pointed out by David Goldblatt: "[S]omething is missing from that tale: it is, of course, The Curse" (Goldblatt, 1995, p. 219). He is right. There is not the slightest evidence of a curse in La Motte-Fouqué's novel. For this, we have to investigate elsewhere.

Jean Giraudoux and his *Ondine* (1939)

What led French writer Jean Giraudoux (1882–1944) (see Fig. 3) to adapt La Motte-Fouqué's *Undine* for the stage is interesting. In 1937, actress Madeleine Ozeray (1908–1989) no longer wanted to play *Agathe* in Giraudoux' adapted version of *Electra*; instead, she "dreamt of a role worthy of her" (Weil, 1990, p. 8). She suggested a tale of La Motte-Fouqué, and the famous actor Louis Jouvet (1887–1951), who was to stage the opening night of the play on May 4, 1939 at the *Théâtre de l'Athénée*, slipped a copy of *Undine* in Jean Giraudoux' pocket.

Giraudoux, in an interview with journalist Annie de Méredieu, acknowledged that he has "kept from the novel its title, its subject and the general line [but] as for the rest, everything was modified" (Méredieu, 1939). Characters, names, and even the plot are different from the original. But above all, the death circumstances of the knight are more detailed and revealed exactly what we were looking for:

---

[4]Though the title of this book is in Latin, its content was written in German.

Figure 3. Jean Giraudoux (1882–1944). Anonymous (1926). *Rozpravy Aventina* 2(16–17): 189. Source: Wikicommon (public domain).

Depuis que tu es partie, tout ce que mon corps faisait de lui-même, il faut que je le lui ordonne. Je ne vois que si je dis à mes yeux de voir…] J'ai à commander à cinq sens, à trente muscles, à mes os eux-mêmes. Un moment d'inattention, et j'oublierai d'entendre, de respirer. [Since you left, everything my body made by itself, I have now to order it to do it. I can see only if I say to my eyes to see … I have to command five senses, thirty muscles, my bones themselves. A momentary lapse of concentration, and I would forget to hear, to breathe]. (Hans, Act III, Scene 6; in Giraudoux, 1990, p. 123)

Ondine's revenge is actually to be found in Friedrich La Motte-Fouqué's 1811 *Undine*, but Ondine's curse appeared 128 years later in Jean Giraudoux's 1939 stage adaptation of this novel.

Undine was the last book Richard Wagner read before dying, supposedly the "victim of a heart attack" (Cross & Even, 1962, p. 859). On July 29, 1817, the young German actress Johann Eunicke (1798–1856) played *Ondine* in Ernst Theodor Amadeus Hoffmann's (1776–1822) homonymous Opera in the Berlin *Deutsches Nationaltheater*. During the performance, the theatre burst into flames and the next day only six Ionic columns were left (Mistler, 1950, p. 196). Aloysius Bertrand's (1807–1841) *Gaspard de la Nuit* included a chapter called *Ondine* (Bertrand, 2002, pp. 135–136). This book, published one year after the author's death, was a resounding flop. French writer Victor Pavie (1808–1886) wrote how "*[o]n ne vit jamais plus beau désastre de librairie*" [One never saw such a bookshop disaster] (Victor Pavie, as cited in Steinmetz, 2002, p. 16).

So be careful, Ondine's ghost might still be skulking around!

References

Alexandre M, ed. (1963): *Romantiques allemands*. Paris, Gallimard, Bibliothèque de la Pléiade, Volume 1.
Almanach de Gotha (1842): Gotha, Justus Perthes.

Bessler G (1995): *Von Nixen und Wasserfrauen*. Köln, DuMont Buchverlag.

Bettelheim B (1976): *Psychanalyse des contes de fées*. Paris, Robert Laffont.

Bertrand A (2002): *Gaspard de la Nuit. Fantaisies à la manière de Rembrandt et de Callot*. Paris, Librairie Générale Française.

Bloch O, Wartburg W von (2002): *Dictionnaire étymologique de la langue française*. Paris, Quadrige.

Cross M, Ewen D (1962): *Encyclopedia of the Great Composers and Their Music*. New York, Doubleday & Company, new edition, Volume 2.

Demougin J, ed. (1992): *Dictionnaire des Littératures française et étrangères*. Paris, Larousse.

Ferlan F (1982): *Le Thème d'Ondine dans la littérature et l'opéra allemand au XIXe siècle*. Paris, Thesis.

Gallagher D (2009): *Metamorphosis: Transformations of the Body and the Influence of Ovid's* Metamorphoses *on Germanic Literature of the Nineteenth and Twentieth Centuries*. Amsterdam, Rodopi.

Gesner C (1670): *Fisch-Buch*. Francfurt am Main, Wilhelm Gerlins.

Giraudoux J (1990): *Ondine*. Paris, Librairie Générale Française.

Goldblatt D (1995): Undine's course. *Seminars in Neurology* 15(2): 218–223.

Guillemain H (1948): *Notions de littératures étrangères*. Paris, J. de Gigord, 6ème édition.

Hamilton E (1978): *La mythologie*. Verviers, Marabout.

Heuvelmans B (1965): *Histoire des bêtes ignorées de la mer. Le grand serpent-de-mer. Le problème zoologique et sa solution*. Paris, Plon.

La Motte-Fouqué F de (1811): Undine. Eine Erzählung. *Die Jahreszeiten. Eine Vierteljahrsschrift für romantische Dichtungen* 1: 1–189.

Lancner LH (1988): Mélusine. In: Brunel, P, ed., *Dictionnaire des mythes littéraires*. Monaco, Éditions du Rocher, pp. 999–1004.

McConville JF, Mokhlesi B, Solway J (2015): Disorders of ventilation. In: Kasper DL, Fauci AS, Hauser SL, Longo DL, Jameson JL, Loscalzo J, eds., *Harrison's Principles of Internal Medicine*. New York, McGraw-Hill Education, 19th edition, pp. 1720–1723.

(1939)Méredieu A de: Une conférence qu'il fit en Sorbonne inspire à Jean Giraudoux "Ondine" créée en soirée à l'Athénée. *Paris-Soir* 4: 11.

Mistler J (1950): *Hoffmann le fantastique*. Paris, Albin Michel.

Mistler J (1962): La mort à Venise. In: Beaufils M, Brion M, Dumesnil R, Gavoty B, Goléa A, Huguenin JR, Mistler J, Panofsky, Rovan J, Witold J, eds., *Richard Wagner*. Paris, Hachette, Collection Génies et Réalités, pp. 213–232.

Mourre M (1989): La Motte Fouqué. In: Laffont-Bompiani, *Dictionnaire des auteurs de tous les temps et de tous les pays*. S.l., Robert Laffont, Volume 3, pp. 26–27.

Nannapaneni R, Behari S, Todd NV, Mendelow AD (2005): Retracing "Ondine's curse." *Neurosurgery* 57(2): 354–363.

Nassichuk J (1999): Ronsard lecteur de Flaminio: note sur quelques vers de "Hylas." *Bibliothèque d'Humanisme et de Renaissance* 61(3): 729–736.

Pedroso JL, Baiense RF, Scalzaretto AP, Neto PB, Texeira de Góis AF, Ferraz ME : Ondine's curse after brainstem infarction.(2009) *Neurology India* 57(2): 206–207.

Richter A, Richter H (1973): *L'Allemagne fantastique de Goethe à Meyrink*. Verviers, André Gérard.

(1569): Ronsard P de Hylas. In: *Le septieme Livre des poemes*. Paris, Jean Dallier, pp. 24–31.

Severinghaus JW, Mitchell RA (1962): Ondine's curse—Failure of respiratory center automaticity while awake. *Clinical Research* 10: 122.

Shih HN, Hong CT, Wong HY (2003): Medullary infarction with central hypoventilation (Ondine's Curse): A case report. *Acta Neurologica Taiwanica* 12(4): 201–204.

Steinmetz JL (2002): Preface. In: Bertrand A, *Gaspard de la Nuit. Fantaisies à la manière de Rembrandt et de Callot*. Paris, Librairie Générale Française, pp. 7–36.

Weil C (1990): Preface. In: Giraudoux J, *Ondine*. Paris, Librairie Générale Française, pp. 7–12.

Zidaric W (2003): Ondines et roussalkas: littérature et opéra au XIXe siècle en Allemagne et en Russie. *Revue de Littérature comparée* 305: 5–22.

Moyamoya (もやもや): When cerebral arteries go up in smoke

In 2014, we devoted a column to the *Kanashibari* phenomenon (Olry & Haines, 2014). The present article takes us again to the "Land of the Rising Sun," this time to analyze the roots of a strange Japanese term, *moyamoya*, coined some decades ago to refer to a hitherto undescribed cerebral vascular pathology.

Initiated in 1612 by Tokugawa Ieyasu (1543–1616), the first *shogun* of the Edo era, the proscription of the Christians (Dickson, 1898, pp. 176–192), and especially the Jesuits (Lacouture, 1991, p. 269), was later extended to the Portuguese by his successors, Tokugawa Hidetada (1579–1632) and Tokugawa Iemitsu (1604–1651; anonymous, 1680, p. 23). From the mid-seventeenth century, the Dutch became the only Europeans to have a relationship with the Japanese. Hence, the influence of Western medical knowledge over Japanese anatomy (Aramata, 1991), medicine, and surgery (Huard et al., 1974) at that time was essentially nonexistent.

Between 1853 and 1867, Japan put an end to its isolationist foreign policy (Hérail, 2009, pp. 929–984), a decision that allowed what we would call a cross-fertilization between cultures, as can be seen, for example, in medicine. Many terms of Southeast Asian origin have actually been taken up in the current Western medical terminology. We found many of these terms in two reference books: the 2017 edition of the "bestseller" of French medical dictionaries (Garnier et al., 2017), and the 2015 edition of a classic English medical treatise (Kasper et al., 2015). There were 59 terms of this kind. Most (48) originate from Japan; others came from China (6), Korea (1), Cambodia (1), Vietnam (1), Laos (1), and Malaya (1). More medical terms of Southeast Asian origin can be found in other places; our list (see Table 1) is merely a sampling to introduce the present column.

Moyamoya (Fig. 1) is a uni- or bilateral progressive occlusive disease involving the supraclinoid segment of the internal carotid artery, and often the proximal anterior and middle cerebral arteries. Different types of moyamoya have been defined (Gosalakkal, 2002), including ethmoidal moyamoya (blood supply by branches of the ophthalmic artery), posterior basal moyamoya (blood supply by perforating branches of the posterior cerebral artery), and vault moyamoya (blood supply by transmeningeal collaterals between pial vessels and branches of the external carotid artery). Although originally believed to be restricted to Japan (Kudo, 1968), this condition has been observed in South Korea (Ikezaki et al., 1997), Europe (Yonekawa et al., 1997), and the United States (Chiu et al., 1998). However, its incidence remains higher in Japan than in other countries (Uchino et al., 2005).

Table 1. Some medical terms of Southeast Asian origin.

Ekiri syndrome (J)	Kedani disease (J)	MASUGI nephritis (J)	SENDAI virus (J)
FUKUHARA disease (J)	KESHAN disease (Ch)	MINAMATA disease (J)	Shiatsu (J)
FUKUYAMA disease (J)	Khi-Huen (V)	Miyagawanella (J)	SHIGA toxin (J)
Ginkgo (Ch)	Khmer haemoglobin (Ca)	MIZUO phenomenon (J)	Sodoku (J)
Ginseng (Ch)	Ki-Mo (L)	Moya-Moya (J)	Sokosho (J)
HANTAAN virus (K)	KIKKAWA syndrome (J)	NIPAH virus (M)	TAKAHARA disease (J)
HARADA disease (J)	KIKUCHI Disease (J)	NISHIMOTO disease (J)	TAKATSUKI syndrome (J)
HASHIMOTO disease (J)	KIMURA disease (J)	OGUCHI disease (J)	TAKAYASHU disease (J)
HIRATA disease (J)	KITAHARA disease (J)	OHARA disease (J)	Tako-Tsubo (J)
IKAWA fever (J)	KOGA staging (J)	OKUDA staging (J)	TARUI disease (J)
ISHIHARA test (J)	KOYANAGI disease (J)	OTA naevus (J)	TAWARA node (J)
IZUMI fever (J)	Kubisagari (J)	Purupuru (J)	Umami taste sensation (J)
KANAGAWA phenomenon (J)	KUMAZAI-INOUE test (J)	Qinghaosu (Ch)	YAMAGUSHI syndrome (J)
KATAYAMA disease (J)	LI syndrome (Ch)	SATAYOSHI syndrome (J)	YANG-TSE fever (Ch)
KAWASAKI disease (J)	MASAOGA staging (J)	SEGAWA syndrome (J)	

Note: Based on Garnier et al. (2017) and Kasper et al. (2015). Capital letters indicate proper names (either authors or geographical locations); small letters indicate common names. Abbreviations in parentheses indicate countries: Ca = Cambodia; Ch = China; J = Japan; K = Korea; L = Laos; M = Malaya; V = Vietnam.

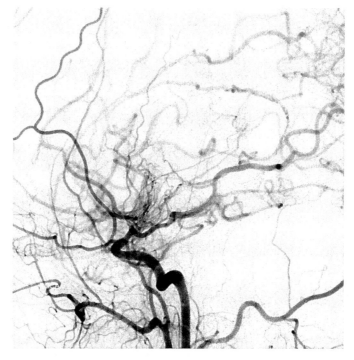

Figure 1. Carotid angiography showing the "smoke" of the supraclinoid segment of the internal carotid artery.

The etiology of this disease is still debated. Neither inflammatory nor arteriosclerotic lesions could be found in the affected vessels (Kono et al., 1990; Fukui et al., 2000). But genetic factors are known to be involved, especially a mutation affecting TIMP-2 (tissue inhibitor of matrix metalloproteinase type 2) on chromosome 17 (Mineharu et al., 2008). Chromosomes 3, 6, and 8 have also been implicated in genetic studies (Ikeda et al., 1999; Inoue et al., 2000; Sakurai et al., 2004, respectively).

The major clinical manifestations of moyamoya include brain ischemia (stroke, seizures, transient ischemic attacks), intracranial hemorrhage (intraventricular, intraparenchymal, subarachnoid) and migraine-like headache (Scott & Smith, 2009). The standard treatment is based on surgical revascularization, either direct bypass (via the superficial temporal or occipital arteries) or indirect bypass (EMAS, or encephalo-myo-arterio-synangiosis; EDAMS, or encephalo-duro-arterio-myo-synangiosis; EGS, or encephalo-galeo-synangiosis; Golby et al., 1999; Kim et al., 2016).

Moyamoya is a kind of word frequently encountered in the Japanese language: a two-syllable word concatenated with itself. These terms may be written in *Katakana* (most onomatopoeias, such as ペコペコ, *pekopeko*, to be very hungry; ガンガン, *gangan*, headache), or in *Hiragana* like moyamoya and some everyday expressions (もしもし, *moshi-moshi*, hello on the phone). The term *moya* (もや) refers to something hazy (mist, fog); and the verb derived therefrom, *moyasu* (燃やす), means to set on fire. What could that be linking mist with fire? Smoke, of course!

In 1969, two physicians of the Tohoku University School of Medicine, Suzuki Jiro and Takaku Akira, explained:

> The disease which produces an abnormal net-like blood vessel picture (hereinafter referred to as "moyamoya" [a Japanese expression for something hazy just like a puff of cigarette smoke drifting in the air"]) in the base of the brain might have been observed in our country during these ten years. However, visualization of such an angiogram seems not to have been noticed as indicating a disease with characteristic features. (Suzuki & Takaku, 1969, p. 288)

The diagnosis of moyamoya may be suggested on the basis of clinical manifestations (cerebral hemorrhage in children for example), but the "smoke" being formed by the abnormal vascular collateral networks that develop adjacent to the stenotic vessels has to be confirmed by imagery: at the present time, carotid angiography. The term moyamoya could not, therefore, have been coined before the use of percutaneous carotid angiography in the 1930s (Wilkinson et al., 1949). The first publication by a Japanese physician on this subject appeared shortly before the outbreak of World War II (Shimizu, 1937). Carotid angiography was popularized among neurosurgeons in Japan in the late 1950s (Poór & Gács, 1974; Oshima & Katayama, 2012).

Although moyamoya has been acknowledged as the specific name for this condition (Fukui, 1997), other synonyms, as usual, appeared in neurological and radiological literature, including "hypoplasia of the bilateral internal carotid arteries" (Takeuchi & Shimizu, 1957), Nishimoto disease (Simon et al., 1968), "spontaneous occlusion of the circle of Willis" (Kudo, 1968), and Nishimoto-Takeuchi-Kudo disease (Urvanek et al., 1970). Moreover, we encountered incorrect spellings: *moya-moya* with a hyphen (Garnier et al., 2017, p. 618), and "syndrome ou maladie de *Moya-Moya*" as though it was an eponym, which it definitely is not (Gaston et al., 1986, p. 283; Vignaud & Cosnard, 1991, p. 344).

Brain arteries like a puff of cigarette smoke. This just goes to show that sometimes there is smoke without fire.

References

Anonymous (1680): *Ambassades mémorables de la Compagnie des Indes Orientales des Provinces Unies vers les Empereurs du Japon*. Amsterdam, Jacob de Meurs.
Aramata H (1991): *Kaibu no Bigaku [Art of Anatomy]*. Tokyo, LibroPort Co.

RHINENCEPHALON, TABES DORSALIS, ETC

Chiu D, Shedden P, Bratina P, Grotta JC (1998): Clinical features of moyamoya disease in the United States. *Stroke* 29: 1347–1351.

Dickson W (1898): *Japan*. New York, Peter Fenelon Collier.

Fukui M (1997): Guidelines for the diagnosis and treatment of spontaneous occlusion of the circle of Willis ("moyamoya disease"). *Clinical Neurology Neurosurgery* 99 (Suppl 2): S238–S240.

Fukui M, Kono S, Sueishi K, Ikezaki K (2000): Moyamoya disease. *Neuropathology* 20 (Suppl): S61–S64.

Garnier M, Delamare V, Delamare J, Delamare T, Delamare J (2017): *Dictionnaire illustré des termes de médecine*. Paris, Maloine, 32ᵉ édition.

Gaston A, Le Bras F, Marsault C (1986): *Imagerie du système nerveux. L'encéphale*. Chevilly-Larue, Flammarion Médecine-Sciences.

Golby AJ, Marks MP, Thompson RC (1999): Direct and combined revascularization in pediatric moyamoya disease. *Neurosurgery* 45: 50–58.

Gosalakkal JA (2002): Moyamoya disease: A review. *Neurology India* 50: 6–10.

Hérail F (Ed.) (2009): *Histoire du Japon des origines à nos jours*. Paris, Hermann.

Huard P, Ohya Z, Wong M (1974): *La Médecine Japonaise des origines à nos jours*. Paris, Roger Dacosta.

Ikeda H, Sasaki T, Yoshimoto T, Fukui M, Arinami T (1999): Mapping of a familial moyamoya disease gene to chromosome 3p24.2-p26. *American Journal of Human Genetics* 64: 533–537.

Ikezaki K, Han DH, Kawano T, Kinukawa N, Fukui M (1997): Clinical comparison of definite moyamoya diseases between South Korea and Japan. *Stroke* 28: 2513–2517.

Inoue TK, Ikezaki K, Sasazuki T, Matsushima T, Fukui M (2000): Linkage analysis of moyamoya disease on chromosome 6. *Journal of Child Neurology* 15: 179–182.

Kasper DL, Hauser SL, Jameson JL, Fauci AS, Longo DL, Loscalzo J (Eds.) (2015): *Harrison's Principles of Internal Medicine*. New York, McGraw-Hill, 19th ed.

Kim T, Oh CW, Bang JS, Kim JE, Cho WS (2016): Moyamoya disease: Treatment and outcomes. *Journal of Stroke* 18 (1): 21–30.

Kono S, Oka K, Sueishi K (1990): Histopathologic and morphometric studies of leptomeningeal vessels in moyamoya disease. *Stroke* 12: 1044–1050.

Kudo T (1968): Spontaneous occlusion of the circle of Willis: A disease apparently confined to Japanese. *Neurology* 18: 485–496.

Lacouture J (1991): *Jésuites*. Paris, Seuil, vol. 1.

Mineharu Y, Liu W, Inoue K, Matsuura N, Inoue S, Takenata K, Ikeda H, Houkin K, Takagi Y, Kikuta K,Nozaki K, Hashimoto N, Koizumi A (2008): Autosomal dominant moyamoya disease maps to chromosome 17q25. *Neurology* 70: 2357–2363.

Olry R, Haines DE (2014) Kanashibari (金縛り): A ghost's business. *Journal of the History of the Neurosciences* 23: 192–197.

Oshima H, Katayama Y (2012): Discovery of cerebrovascular moyamoya disease: Research during the late 1950s and early 1960s. *Child's Nervous System* 28 (4): 497–500.

Poór G, Gács G (1974): The so-called "moyamoya disease." *Journal of Neurology, Neurosurgery, and Psychiatry* 37: 370–377.

Sakurai K, Horiuchi Y, Ikeda H, Ikezaki K, Yoshimoto T, Fukui M, Arinami T (2004): A novel susceptibility locus for moyamoya disease on chromosome 8q23. *Journal of Human Genetics* 49: 278–281.

Scott RM, Smith ER (2009): Moyamoya disease and moyamoya syndrome. *New England Journal of Medicine* 360: 1226–1237.

Shimizu K (1937): Beiträge zur Arteriographie des Gehirns—Einfache perkutane Methode. *Archiv für Klinische Chirurgie* 188: 295–316.

Simon J, Sabouraud O, Guy G, Turpin J (1968): Un cas de maladie de Nishimoto. A propos d'une maladie rare et bilatérale de la carotide interne. *Revue Neurologique* 119: 376–383.

Suzuki J, Takaku A (1969): Cerebrovascular "moyamoya" disease: Disease showing abnormal net-like vessels in base of brain. *Archives of Neurology* 20: 288–299.

Takeuchi K, Shimizu K (1957): Hypoplasia of the bilateral internal carotid arteries. *Brain Nerve* 9: 37–43.

Uchino K, Johnston SC, Becker KJ, Tirschwell DL (2005): Moyamoya disease in Washington State and California. *Neurology* 65: 956–958.

Urvanek K, Farkova H, Klaus E (1970): Nishimoto-Takeuchi-Kudo disease. *Journal of Neurology, Neurosurgery, and Psychiatry* 33: 671–673.

Vignaud J., Cosnard G. (Eds.) (1991) *Imagerie par résonance magnétique crânio-encéphalique.* Paris, Vigot.

Wilkinson M, Stanton JB, Jones DP, Spalding JMK (1949): Percutaneous carotid angiography: A team technique with a report of the results in seventy cases. *Journal of Neurology, Neurosurgery, and Psychiatry* 12: 183–186.

Yonekawa Y, Ogata N, Kaku Y, Taub E, Imhof HG (1997): Moyamoya disease in Europe, past and present status. *Clinical Neurology Neurosurgery* 99 (Suppl 2): S39–S44.

Migraine: Between headache, pomegranate, seed of cochineal, and unidentified fish

A lot has been written about the roots of the term "migraine" (see Lardreau, 2012, 2014). However, as recently pointed out by historian Annie Jourdan (2018, p. 9), "Rien n'est définitivement écrit: En histoire, plus qu'ailleurs" [Nothing is definitely written: In history, more than anywhere else]. We think that the term migraine still holds unexpected surprises, and that this issue has actually not yet been considered from all linguistic angles. We therefore decided to go more thoroughly into this, at first sight, very simple term that, however, refers to "the most famous [disease] in our profession" (Castaigne, 1979).

The sacrosanct one-sidedness

In Émile Zola's (1840–1902) *La Conquête de Plassans*, Mrs. Octavie Condamin complained to her physician, Dr. Porquier, "Oh! Docteur, j'ai une migraine, mais une migraine! Dit-elle avec des mines charmantes. Ça me tient là, dans le sourcil gauche." [Oh! Doctor, I've got a migraine, such a migraine! She said with charming expressions. It takes place here, in the left eyebrow] (Zola, 1972, p. 223).

Alfred Dreyfus's most celebrated supporter adhered to orthodoxy. Actually, most dictionaries (Huguet, 1961, vol. 4, p. 466, vol. 5, p. 267; Godefroy, 1969, p. 330; Simpson & Weiner, 1989, vol. 9, pp. 757 758; Bloch & von Wartburg, 2002, p. 408) and books (Bossy, 1999, p. 330) on medical etymology explain both the terms "migraine" and "hemicrania" by the fact that pain is limited to half the head. However, although unilateral pain remains one the simplified diagnostic criteria for migraine (Goadsby & Raskin, 2015, Table 447–3, p. 2590), it had been shown many decades ago that pain is bilateral in 23% of the cases (either from the outset or secondarily; Selby & Lance, 1960), and about 50% are not strictly unilateral (Critchley & Ferguson, 1933). But habits are hard to dismiss, as confirmed by three ancient synonyms covering migraine: *halbseitige Kopfwehe* [one-sided headache] (Anonymous, 1792), *hémipéricranalgie* [hemipericranalgia] (Tamin, 1860), and *Hemikephalie* [hemicephalia] (Lindemann, 1862).

The phonological link between hemicrania and migraine rests on two principles of descriptive/theoretical linguistics. First, the term migraine is an aphetism—that is, a new term coined by apheresis[1] of vowels: "Hemi" (HEMIcrania), having lost its HE became "mi" (Migraine; Brachet, n.d.a, p. 113). Second, the consonnant "c" (hemiCrania) was

---

[1]An apheresis is the loss of one (or more) sounds from the beginning of a word, especially of an unstressed vowel.

From Pharaonic Egypt to Western seventeenth century

Migraine was mentioned in the Papyrus Ebers (von Klein, 1905, p. 8), an Egyptian medical papyrus dating from ca. 1550 BCE, but it was based on much older material. The German historian Jürgen Thorwald (1915–2006) pointed out that it was referred to as "maladie de la demi-tête" [disease of half the head] (Thorwald, 1966, p. 80). Aretaeus, one of the most celebrated of the ancient Greek physicians, distinguished three types of headache: cephalalgia (short-lasting, mild headache), cephalea (chronic type of headache, more severe), and heterocrania (one-sided paroxysmal headache; Koehler & van de Wiel, 2001).

During the late-fourteenth century, French poet Eustache Deschamps (1346–ca. 1406), a prolific author of more than 1400 poems (Lagarde & Michard, 1970, p. 158), was considered "inexhaustible about the topic of the death" (Abraham & Desné, 1974, p. 376). In a short, three-stanza ballad, he also wrote about migraine:

> Pour mon costé crie: "Hahay!"
> Mainte fois, et a l'aventure
> Une migrayne ou chief array.

(Deschamps, 1893, p. 134, verses 9–11)

Let us clarify some terms of this sentence written in medieval French: (a) *costé* meant *côté* [side] (Greimas, 1969, p.145); (b) *Hahay* was a warning cry coined by the *trouvère* and Benedictine monk Gauthier de Coincy (1177–1236) in about 1220 (Greimas, 1969, p. 327); (c) *migrayne* was one of the variant spellings of migraine, another one being *migraigne* used by the French minstrel Gautier le Leu (born ca. 1210; Tobler & Lommatzsch, 1963, vol. 6, col. 41); (d) *chief* referred to the top of a mountain (Paré, 1947, p. 120) and, by extension, to the extremities of a body—that is, the head but also the feet (Henry, 1965, p. 177); and (e) *array* was the conditional present tense of the verb "to have." To sum up, Eustache Deschamps described unilateral headache.

In the second half of the seventeenth century, the famous anatomist Jean Riolan (1577–1657) took a stand on this question. Writing in French, he maintained that *céphalalgie* [cephalalgia] affects the whole head and is relentless, whereas migraine is limited in location (half the head) and in time (recurring) (Riolan, 1672, pp. 410–411).

The *Académie française* gives its opinion

The *Dictionnaire* of the French Academy is acknowledged for "sa qualité et [de] son utilité lexicographique" [its quality and its lexicographical usefulness] (Prévost, 1935, p. 115). In its 1694 first edition, migraine is defined as a "mal, douleur de teste qui occupe la moitié de la teste" [pain, headache located in half the head] (*Dictionnaire de l'Académie françoise*, 1694, p. 69). From the sixth edition in 1835, this one-sidedness was no longer an essential criterion: "la moitié ou une moindre partie de la tête" [half the head or less] (p. 205). This criterion totally disappeared from the eighth edition in 1935.

---

[2]JuGer (judiCare, to judge), draGon (draConem, dragon), Gonfler (Conflare, to inflate), ciGale (ciCadula, cicada), etc.

Since the Age of Enlightenment

The *Grande Encyclopédie*, sometimes considered as the "hypertext ancestor" (Brian, 1998, p. 29), questioned the one-sidedness of the migrainous pain: "[La migraine est une] espèce de douleur de tête qu'on a cru n'occuper que la moitié de cette partie" [(Migraine is a) type of headache one believed to be limited to half this region] (Diderot & d'Alembert, 1751, p. 498). Twenty-five years later, French lexicographer Allouel accurately differentiated between the meanings of the three terms cephalalgia, cephalia, and hemicrania:

> La céphalalgie est prise pour toutes sortes de douleurs de tête: mais dans un sens plus resserré on nomme céphalalgie la douleur de tête commençante; lorsqu'elle est invétérée, céphalie; enfin quand la douleur ne prend qu'un côté de la tête, c'est une hémicranie.

> [Cephalalgia refers to all kinds of headaches: but in a more restricted meaning, one calls cephalalgia the beginning headache; when it is ingrained, cephalia; finally, when it affects only half the head, it is a hemicrania]. (Allouel, 1776, pp. 230–231)

Some amazing homonyms

Migraine is an obsolete synonym for pomegranate (Zylberstein, 1996, p. 209). There are at least two possible explanations. French naturalist and lexicographer Pierre-Augustin Boissier de Sauvages (1710–1795), in his dictionary of the *langue d'oc*, referred to the pomegranate as *miougrano*, meaning "mille graines" [a thousand seeds] (Boissier de Sauvages, 1820–1821, vol. 2, p. 84). Anyone who has opened a pomegranate will admit to the truth of this metaphor! Additionally pomegranate might derive from the Latin *malum granatum*, a granulate (i.e., seeded) apple (Augé, 1931, vol. 4, p. 871).

A particular type of headache called cluster headache is known to be associated with conjunctival injection, and sometimes with ipsilateral redness of half the face (Bousser & Baron, 1979, p. 152). Might it explain the fact that migraine was also referred to as a "scarlet" or even "red migraine" (Lardreau, 2014, p. 101)?

Some historians have credited Gerard van Swieten (1700–1772) in his 1745 *Commentaria* with the first clinical description of cluster headache (e.g., Isler, 1993). Others have pointed to Nicolaas Tulp (1593–1674) in his 1641 *Observationes medicae* (e.g., Kohler, 1993). Nonetheless, the synonym migraine/scarlet was already in use prior to even the seventeenth century. In *Lib. 1 Cap. 56* of his masterpiece *Gargantua*, French Renaissance humanist François Rabelais (1494–1553) wrote that the nuns of the Abbey of Theleme "portaient chausses d'écarlate, ou de migraine" [wore hoses of scarlet, or of migraine] (Rabelais, 1857, vol. 1, p. 207). This Abbey was, however, only a utopian idea imagined by Rabelais himself — in reality, it was more of "anticonvent" with the motto, "Do whatever you want" (Febvre, 1962, p. 165; see Marin, 1976, for review). Importantly, Rabelais obviously knew the two synonyms.

The link between scarlet and migraine can be found in an hemiptera insect named cochineal of nopal, a Mexican cactus (Diguet, 1909). A scarlet dye can be extracted from this insect: "graine de cochenille" [seed of cochineal]. When a dyer used only half a dose of the grain, it was logically called "mi-graine" (half-seed). And over time, the hyphen disappeared.

In a posthumous edition of Gilbert Ménage's (1613–1692) *Dictionnaire étymologique*, we found that the term migraine also referred to a fish, *Ursus marinus*, apparently discovered by a certain Nicot (Ménage, 1750, vol. 2, p. 209). Unfortunately, we could not identify Nicot with any certainty, and we were not successful in finding a link between this fish and headache. Swiss naturalist Conrad Gesner (1516–1565) indeed mentioned a fish species named *Ursus* or *Wasserbär* [water-bear] (Gesner, 1670, p. 28), and later French scholar Antoine Mongez (1747–1835) described it as "quelque cétacé ou quelque grand poisson très vorace" [some cetacean or some very voracious tall fish] (Mongez, 1833, p. 453). To the best of our knowledge, the mystery surrounding a putative correlation between migraine and this fish has never been properly elucidated, the only putative link being the use of torpedo's electric discharge for headache recommended by Scribonius Largus in the first century CE (Koehler & Boes, 2010).

Clearly, "migraine" still has not yielded all of its linguistic secrets!

References

Abraham P, Desné R, eds. (1974): *Histoire de la littérature de la France. 1. Des origines à 1492*. Paris, Éditions sociales.
Allouel M (1776): *Explication des mots d'usage en anatomie et en chirurgie*. Paris, Rémont.
Anonymous (1792): Vom halbseitigen Kopfwehe. *Tirolische Arzt (Innsbruck)* 2: 113–126.
Augé P, ed. (1931): *Larousse du XXe siècle*. Paris, Larousse.
Bloch O, Wartburg W von (2002): *Dictionnaire étymologique de la langue française*. Paris, Quadrige/PUF.
Boissier de Sauvages PA (1820–1821): *Dictionnaire languedocien-français*. Alais, J. Martin, new edition.
Bossy J (1999): *La grande aventure du terme médical: Filiation et valeurs actuelles*. Montpellier, Sauramps Médical.
Bousser MG, Baron JC (1979): *Migraines et algies vasculaires de la face*. Rueil-Malmaison, Laboratoires Sandoz S.A.R.L.
Brachet A (n.d.a): *Grammaire historique de la langue française*. Paris, J. Hetzel et Cie, 11th edition.
Brachet A (n.d.b): *Dictionnaire étymologique de la langue française*. Paris, J. Hetzel et Cie, 8th edition.
Brian E (1998): L'ancêtre de l'hypertexte. *Les Cahiers de Science & Vie* 47: 28–38.
Castaigne P (1979): Preface. In: Bousser MG, Baron JC, eds., *Migraines et algies vasculaires de la face*. Rueil-Malmaison, Éditions Sandoz, p. 5.
Critchley M, Ferguson FR (1933): Migraine. *Lancet* 1: 123–126, 182–187.
Deschamps E (1893): De doloir pour jeunesse qui s'en va ailleurs. In: *Œuvres complètes. Publiées par Gaston Raynaud*. Paris, Firmin Didot et Cie, vol. 8.
Dictionnaire de l'Académie françoise (1694): Paris, Jean-Baptiste Coignard, vol. 2.
Dictionnaire de l'Académie françoise (1835): Paris, Firmin Didot Frères, 6th edition, vol. 2.
Diderot D, d'Alembert J le Rond (1751): *Encyclopédie, ou dictionnaire raisonné des sciences, des arts et des métiers, par une société de gens de lettres*. Paris, Briasson, David l'aîné, Le Breton, Durand, vol. 10.
Diguet L (1909): Histoire de la cochenille au Mexique. *Journal de la Société des Américanistes* 6: 75–99.
Febvre L (1962): *Le problème de l'incroyance au XVIe siècle: La religion de Rabelais*. Paris, Albin Michel.
Gesner C (1670): *Fisch-Buch*. Frankfurt, In Verlegung Wilhelm Serlins, Tomus V, Zweyter Theil.
Goadsby PJ, Raskin NH (2015): Migraine and other primary headache disorders. In: Kasper DL, Fauci AS, Hauser SL, Longo DL, Jameson JL, Loscalzo J, eds., *Harrison's Principles of Internal Medicine*. New York, McGraw-Hill, 19th ed., vol. 2, chap. 447, pp. 2586–2598.
Godefroy F (1969): *Dictionnaire de l'ancienne langue française et de tous ses dialectes du XIe au XVe siècle*. Nendeln/Liechtenstein, Kraus Reprint.
Greimas AJ (1969): *Dictionnaire de l'ancien français jusqu'au milieu du XIVe siècle*. Paris, Larousse.
Henry A (1965): *Chrestomathie de la littérature en ancien français: Textes*. Berne, A. Francke Verlag, 3rd edition.

Huguet E (1961): *Dictionnaire de la langue française du seizième siècle*. Paris, Didier.

Isler H (1993): Episodic cluster headache from a textbook of 1745: van Swieten classic description. *Cephalalgia* 13(3); 172–174.

Jourdan A (2018): *Nouvelle histoire de la Révolution*. Paris, Flammarion.

Klein CH von (1905): *The Medical Features of the Papyrus Ebers*. Chicago, Press of the American Medical Association.

Koehler PJ (1993): Prevalence of headache in Tulp's *Observationes Medicae* (1641) with a description of cluster headache. *Cephalalgia* 13(5): 318–320.

Koehler PJ, van de Wiel TWM (2001): Aretaeus on migraine and headache. *Journal of the History of the Neurosciences* 10(3): 253–261.

Koehler PJ, Boes CJ (2010): A history of non-drug treatment in headache, particularly migraine. *Brain* 133(8): 2489–2500.

Lagarde A, Michard L (1970): *La Littérature française. 1. Du Moyen Âge à l'âge baroque*. Paris, Bordas-Laffont.

Lardreau E (2012): A curiosity in the history of sciences: The words "megrim" and "migraine." *Journal of the History of the Neurosciences* 21: 31–40.

Lardreau E (2014): *La Migraine: Biographie d'une maladie*. Paris, Les Belles Lettres.

Lindemann (1862): Hemikephalie. *Aerztliches Intelligenz-Blatt (München)* 9: 597.

Marin L (1976): Les corps utopiques rabelaisiens. *Littérature* 21: 35–51.

Ménage G (1750): *Dictionnaire étymologique de la langue françoise*. Paris, Briasson, new edition.

Mongez A (1833): Mémoire sur les animaux promenés ou tués dans les cirques. *Mémoires de l'Institut royal de France: Académie des inscriptions et belles-lettres* 10: 360–460.

Paré G (1947): *Les idées et les lettres au XIIIe siècle*. Montréal, Le Centre de Psychologie et de Pédagogie.

Prévost M (1935): Le dictionnaire. In: *Les Quarante, 1635–1935. Trois siècles de l'Académie française*. Paris, Firmin-Didot et Cie, pp. 115–132.

Rabelais F (1857): *Œuvres, par Burgaud des Marets et Rathery*. Paris, Firmin Didot Frères, Fils et Cie.

Riolan J (1672): *Manuel anatomique, et pathologique, ou abrégé de toute l'anatomie, Et des Usages que l'on en peut tirer pour la Connaissance, & pour la Guérison des Maladies*. Lyon, Antoine Laurens.

Selby G, Lance JW (1960): Observations on 500 cases of migraine and allied vascular headaches. *Journal of Neurology, Neurosurgery and Psychiatry* 23: 23–32.

Simpson JA, Weiner ESC (1989): *The Oxford English Dictionary*. Oxford, Clarendon Press.

Tamin O (1860): *Étude et traitement de l'hémipéricranalgie (migraine)*. Paris, thesis no. 119.

Thorwald J (1966): *Histoire de la médecine dans l'Antiquité*. Paris, Hachette.

Tobler A, Lommatzsch E (1963): *Altfranzösisches Wörterbuch*. Wiesbaden, Franz Steiner Verlag.

Zola E (1972): *La conquête de Plassans*. Paris, Garnier-Flammarion (first edition, 1874).

Zylberstein JC (1996): *Dictionnaire des mots rares et précieux*. Paris, Éditions 10/18.

Phrenology: Scheherazade of etymology

Phrenology belongs to a never-ending trend—sometimes verging on fanaticism (Noel and Carlson 1970, 694)—that, for many centuries, strives to correlate anatomy with behaviors and ultimately with destiny (Kern 1975). This trend aims, whatever the cost, at ascribing behaviors and abilities to limited and specific macroscopical or, more recently (although not really more successful), biological features (Grüsser 1990). As the centuries passed, these presumably-involved features included, among others, the general characteristics of the face (physiognomony: Aristotle, see Fœrster 1893; lavaterism, see Jaton 1988), lines of the forehead (metoposcopy, see Cardano 1658), bumps of the skull (phrenology, see Gall and Spurzheim 1810-1819), and the number of longitudinal frontal gyri (quaternary theory of the frontal lobe, see Benedikt 1879). Some biological features were of a genetic (e.g., supernumerary chromosome, see Jacobs et al. 1965) or molecular (e.g., neuronal nitric oxide synthase, see Nelson et al. 1995) nature.

Although this trend dates back at least to Aristotle, it was still usual during the second half of the eighteenth century on "to assert the existence of a necessary (although much debated) link between the body and the soul" (Pogliano 1990, 144). Unfortunately, this trend, particularly as developed in criminology, has sometimes been used to justify the darkest sides of racial anthropology, whether allegedly scientific or—perhaps even more dangerous—popular. In a letter to his cousin, Marie de Rabutin-Chantal, marquise de Sévigné (1626–1696), dated August 11, 1675, Roger de Rabutin, comte de Bussy (1618–1693), wrote:

> Ne vous souvenez-vous pas, Madame, de la physionomie funeste de ce grand homme (M. de Turenne)? Du temps que je ne l'aimais pas, je disais que c'était une physionomie patibulaire. (Monmerqué 1820, 377)

> [Don't you remember, Madam, the lugubrious physionomy of this great man (M. de Turenne)? At the time I did not like him, I said it was a suspicious-looking physionomy.]

The French adjective *patibulaire* refers to the *fourches patibulaires*, that is:

> (des) piliers de pierre, au haut desquels il y a une pièce de bois posée en-travers sur deux de ces piliers, à laquelle pièce de bois on attache les criminels qui sont condamnés à être pendus & étranglés. Soit que l'exécution se fasse au gibet même, ou que l'exécution ayant été faite ailleurs, on apporte le corps du criminel pour l'attacher à ces fourches, & l'y laisser exposé à la vûe des passans. (Diderot and d'Alembert 1757, 224)

> [stone pillars, at the top of which there is a piece of wood, put crocked on two of these pillars: the piece of wood to which are tied people sentenced to be hanged & strangled. Whether the execution takes place at the gibbet itself, or the execution has been conducted elsewhere, one

brings the body of the criminal to be tied to these forks & to be left at the sight of the passersby.]

To have a *physionomie patibulaire* therefore means that your *physionomie* shows your evil tendencies. Despite the fact that, according to some authors, "neurobiology has given up ...looking for any 'centre' or neuronal system which would be the generator of ... aggressiveness" (Karli 1987, 28–29), old habits die hard, and many people keep on mistrusting someone merely looking suspicious.

Let us briefly summarize the origins of the terms "metoposcopy," "physiognomony," and "lavaterism" before tackling the topic of this article: the amazingly complex meanings of the term *phren* at the roots of the term phrenology.

Metoposcopy

Metoposcopy, from the Greek μέτωπον (*metopon*: forehead) and σκοπέω (*scopeo*: to examine), is "l'art de connaître les hommes par les rides du front" [the art of knowing humans by the lines of the forehead] (Collin de Plancy 1863, 458). Although to be found as far back as 1615 in Samuel Fuchs's (1588–1630) *Metoposcopia & Ophthalmoscopia*, and 1626 in Ciro Spontone's (ca. 1552–ca. 1610) *La Metoposcopia ouero Commensuratione delle Linee della Fronte* (see Spontone 1626), the term metoposcopy was quite likely coined by Italian physician and polymath Girolamo Cardano (1501–1576), sometimes referred to as a "forerunner of Lombroso" (Ore 1967, 889). Although the Latin first edition of Cardano's *Metoposcopia libris tredecim* was published in 1658 (a French translation by Claude Martin de Laurendière was made available in the same year), this book had been written during the author's stay in Milan in 1550 (Hirsch 1884, 663) and, hence, prior to both above-mentioned publications. Surprisingly, the French Renaissance writer François Rabelais (between 1483 and 1494–1553) used the term *métaposcopie* (underlining by authors) in his 1546 *Tiers livre* (Rabelais 1546, 181, chapter 25, line 29). Yet we could not find any etymology or satisfying explanation for this term.

Physiognomony and lavaterism

The term "physiognomony," from the Greek φύσις (*phusis*: nature) and γνώμων (*gnomon*: one who knows, who detects), is sometimes dated back to Aristotle (384–322 BCE; Zucker 2006, 2), who taught, "It will be possible to infer the character from the features of the face" (Aristotle, cited in Froment 2013, 126). We could find five variant spellings of the term physiognomony: *physonomia* in Lucas Brandis's 1473 edition of the *Lapidarius* (Hain 1826, 220, no. 1777; Osler 1923, 52, no. 30), *physionomia* in Arnold ther Hoernen's 1474 edition of the *Tractatus de pomo* (Hain 1826, 221, no. 1786; Osler 1923, 60, no. 48; Klebs 1938, 51, no. 94.1), *physiognomia* in Joan Paquet's 1611 edition of the *Physiognomonica* (Krivatsy 1989, 42, no. 394), *physiogno-monica* in Gottlob Emanuel Richter's 1780 edition of the *Scriptores Physiognomoniae* (Osler 1969, 22, no. 243), and *physiognomica* in the Immanuel Bekker's 1831–1870 edition of *Aristotelis Opera* (Schwab 1967, 6, no. 15).

The term was taken up by Italian scholar Giovanni Battista Della Porta (1535–1615) in 1586 and later by Swiss theologian Johan Kaspar Lavater (1741–1801) in 1772 (see Della Porta 1586; Lavater 1772), leading to a new (quasi-)synonym for physiognomony: "lavaterism." We could not find who coined the term lavaterism, but it was already being widely used before Lavater's death on January 2, 1801. For example, we found this term in a postscript of a letter dated December 20, 1777, from Dutch philosopher and writer François Hemsterhuis (1721–1790) to Princess Adelheid Amalie Gallitzin (1748–1806; see van Sluis 2011, 235). Shortly afterward, in a letter written on March 25, 1785, to her friend—and soon-to-be first editor of her *Memoirs* (Cornut-Gentille 2004, 31)—Louis-Augustin Bosc d'Antic (1759–1828), the famous revolutionary Manon Roland (1754–1793) wrote,

> Mais, à propos, dites-moi donc quelque chose du lavatérisme [...] Vous espérez donc exercer votre science sur ma figure? (Dauban 1864, lxxvii)

> [But, incidentally, tell me something about lavaterism [...] So, you intend to practice your science on my face?]

We could also find the term "lavaterism" in a letter dated August 21, 1791, from a Mr. Brand to English writer Mary Berry (1763–1852; see Lewis 1865, 351).

Phrenology

The term "phrenology" was coined by physician, medical educator, and philanthropist Benjamin Rush (1746–1813) in his November 21, 1805, *Lectures Upon the Mind*. He wrote, "Very different is the state of phrenology, if I may be allowed to coin a word, to designate the science of the mind" (Rush 1811, 271). These *Lectures* are among the 39 documents and archives Rush bequeathed to the Library of The College of Physicians of Philadelphia (Hirsch 1983, no. 917, 189–190). Importantly, Rush's definition of phrenology encompassed much more than:

> Die Lehre, welche sich damit beschäftigt, den Charakter aus der äusseren Form des Schädels (in Verbindung mit den Temperamenten) zu beurteilen. (Ullrich 1898)

> [The teaching which aims at judging the character from the outer morphology of the skull (in connection with the temperament).]

At first sight, the etymology of the term phrenology might look simple: It derives from the Greek φρήν (*phren*: mind) and λόγος (*logos*: knowledge). But appearances can be deceptive: The many meanings of *phren* (Sullivan 1988, 1997, 13–94), as well as the links between the diaphragm and the mind, are both highly complex issues.

The polysemy of *phren*

The meaning, and therefore the translation of the Greek terms "phren" and its derivation *phresin* "*pose de nombreux problèmes, souvent discutés*" [raises many problems, often debated] (Chantraine 1977, 1227). They may refer to intelligence (Stappers 1885, no. 2693, 352), *chœur* [chorus] (Pradier 1997, 45), physical localization of the *thūmos* (to be understood as the concept of spiritedness) for "in some Homeric contexts, *thūmos* is used as a synonym of *phrenes* " (Nagy 2013, 282). They were also used to designate some parts—anatomical or spiritual—of the human body: the diaphragm (see below); the lungs—or, more broadly, the viscera contained in the upper part of the body (Onians 1951, 23–42); and the âme végétative [the vegetative soul] (Magnien 1927, 122).

The situation becomes even more complicated with the two occurrences of the term "phresin" in the New Testament (First Epistle to the Corinthians 14: 20):

Ἀδελφοί, μὴ παιδία γίνεσθε ταῖς φρεσίν: ἀλλὰ τῇ κακίᾳ νηπιάζετε, ταῖς δὲ φρεσὶν τέλειοι γίνεσθε. (Nestle 1923, 450)

[Brothers and sisters, stop thinking like children. In regard to evil be infants, but in your thinking be adults.]

In its successive translations, the biblical meaning of *phresin* has been "sage, sans malice" [reasonable, without malice] (D'Allioli 1884, 510),"mûrs" [mature] (École biblique de Jérusalem 1961, 1420), and"*en adulte*" [like an adult] (Grosjean 1971, 559), to name a few.

From phren to *metaphren*

Etymologically, the term "metaphren" (or *metaphrenon*) refers to something located near to the phren—that is, near to the putative seat of the mind. Its first mention probably goes back to Homer's *Iliad* (Pierron 1884, 177) in which metaphrenon refers to "le dos et les épaules" [the back and the shoulders] (Flacelière 1955, XVI–791, 386). Since its spreading in scientific vocabulary during the sixteenth century (Adrados 2005, 276), its meaning has varied considerably. It referred to the back and/or the 12 thoracic vertebrae (Vassé 1555, 90; Paré 1633, 164), the region located "entre les deux épaules" [between both shoulders] (James 1746, col. 17), the part of the back opposite the breast (Duverney 1761, 8; Taylor 1809, 438; Rabelais 1823, 494), the "dorsum" [whole back] (Dunglison 1868, 616), the region behind the diaphragm (Tecusan 2004, 333), and even the region about the kidneys (Friel 1974, 945).

From phren to frenzy

Frenzy (or its archaic variant "phrenzy") shares the same etymology as phrenic. Both spellings can even be found in the first edition of the early *Dictionnaire de l'Académie françois*, which lists *frénésie* in the index for Volume 1, but *phrénésie* in the index for Volume 2 (*Dictionnaire de l'Académie françoise*, 1694).

The term "frenzy" has been defined as "Unsinnigkeit, Taubsucht" [foolishness] (Frisius 1723, 519), "forte et violente alteration d'esprit" [strong and brutal deterioration of the mind] (Joubert 1738, 863), and "égarement d'esprit, alienation d'esprit, fureur violente" [distraction of the mind, insanity of the mind, brutal fury] (*Dictionnaire de l'Académie Françoise* 1765, 547). *The etymological connection between the diaphragm and some kinds of mental derangement therefore rests on the hypothesis of a so-called "psychical idea" of the diaphragm muscle (Petit 1922).*

The diaphragm and the mind

There are many diaphragms in anatomical terminology: *diaphragma bulbi, oris, pelvis, secundarium* Luschka, *sellae,* and *urogenitale,* among others (Terra 1913, 107), all of them referring to a structure of septal nature and/or function. The diaphragm in question here is, of course, the "thoraco-abdominal" diaphragm (Dumas 1797, 128–129).

Although sometimes attributed to Galen (Lauth 1815, 211), the term "diaphragm" might have been coined by Plato from the verb διαφράσσω (*diaphrasso*: to separate; Furetière 1727;

Morin 1809, 278; Stappers 1885, no. 2692, 352). Indeed, Plato considered the diaphragm as "a septum which should isolate in the abdomen the lowest soul and prevent it from too severely disturbing the superior soul" (trans. fom Joly 1961, 448).

Rufus of Ephesus (ca. 70–ca. 110), "probably the first author to have submitted an anatomical nomenclature" (Olry 1989, 92), confirmed this etymology, although with an emphasis on thoracic rather than abdominal, viscera: "On le nomme diaphragme (cloison) parce qu'il sépare les viscères contenus dans le thorax de ceux qui sont au dehors" [It is called diaphragm (septum) because it separates the viscera contained in the thorax from those which are outside] (d'Éphèse 1879, 178). Chinese medicine also refers to *Huang* (one of the terms for diaphragm) as "a thin membrane located above the diaphragm … which prevents the ascent of troubled breath towards the upper heater" (Huchet 2006, 214).

Since the 1895 *Basle Nomina Anatomica*, the adjective phrenic has replaced diaphragmatic in anatomical terminology (His 1895, 72). Thus, all structures—10 in number—related to the diaphragm are now referred to as phrenic (Federative Committee on Anatomical Terminology 1998, 270). The notion of septum has therefore been cast aside in favor of the notion of mind. But why?

Denis Diderot (1713–1784) helps us answer this question. In his 1769 *Le Rêve de d'Alembert*, French physician and anatomist Théophile de Bordeu (1722–1776) explained to his friend Julie de Lespinasse (1732–1776): "Qu'est-ce qu'un être sensible? Un être abandonné à la discrétion de son diaphragme" [What is a sensitive being? A being abandoned at the discretion of his diaphragm] (Assézat 1875, 171; Siess 1990, 190).

A putative link between the diaphragm and troubles of the mind was raised by many anatomists. Jean Riolan (1577–1657) wrote, "il est souvent cause de la phrénesie" [It is often cause of frenzy] (Riolan 1672, 323), whereas Bernardo Santucci thought that the inflammation of the diaphragm produces a "*continos delirios*" [relentless delirium] (Santucci 1739, 380–381). Isbrand van Diemerbroeck (1609–1674) provided more details:

> Parce que quand il (le diaphragme) est offensé, l'esprit & les sens sont troublés par communication, & que c'est dans son inflammation qu'arrive cet [sic] espèce de délire qu'on nomme Paraphrénesie. (Diemerbroeck 1695, vol. 2, 43)

> [because when it (the diaphragm) is offended, the mind and the senses become troubled by communication, and that it is in its inflammation that the kind of delirium one refers to as parafrenzy happens.]

It is therefore because it was believed to be involved in the soul/mind/mood disorders that the diaphragm shared the Greek root phren with phrenology.

So, why did we call phrenology the "Scheherazade of etymology"? Because one could easily spend a thousand and one nights studying all the meanings and interpretations of the term phren!

Disclosure statement

No potential conflict of interest was reported by the authors.

References

Adrados F. R. 2005. *A history of the Greek Language. From its origin to the present.* Leiden, Boston: Brill.

Assézat J. 1875. Le Rêve de d'Alembert. In *Œuvres complètes de Diderot revues sur les éditions originales*, vol. 2, 122–81. Paris: Garnier frères.

Benedikt M. 1879. *Anatomische Studien an Verbrecher-Gehirnen für Anthropologen, Mediciner, Juristen und Psychologen bearbeitet.* Wien: Wilhelm Braumüller.

Cardano G. 1658. *Metoposcopia libris tredecim, et octigentis faciei humanae eiconibus complexa. Cui accessit Melampodis De naevis corporis tractatus, Graece & Latine nunc primum editus. Interprete Claudio Martino Laurenderio ....* Lutetiae Parisiorum, Apud Thomam Jolly.

Chantraine P. 1977. *Dictionnaire étymologique de la langue grecque. Histoire des mots*, vol. IV-1. Paris: Klincksieck.

Collin de Plancy J. 1863. *Dictionnaire infernal.* 6th ed. Paris: Henri Plon.

Cornut-Gentille P. 2004. *Madame Roland. Une femme en politique sous la Révolution.* Paris: Perrin.

D'Allioli J. F. 1884. *Nouveau commentaire littéral, critique et théologique avec rapport aux textes primitifs sur tous les livres des divines écritures*, vol. 7, 8th ed. Paris: Louis Vivès.

d'Éphèse R. 1879. *Œuvres. Texte collationné sur les manuscrits (...) publication commencée par le Dr Ch. Daremberg, continuée et terminée par Ch. Émile Ruelle.* Paris: à l'Imprimerie nationale.

Dauban C. A. 1864. *Étude sur madame Roland et son temps.* Paris: Plon.

Della Porta G. B. 1586. *De humana physiognomonia libri IIII.* Vici Aequensis, apud I. Cacchium.

Dictionnaire de l'Académie françoise. 1694. Paris: chez la veuve de Jean Baptiste Coignard et chez Jean Baptiste Coignard.

Dictionnaire de l'Académie françoise, vol. 1. 1765. Paris: Chez les libraires associés, nouvelle édition.

Diderot D., and J. L. R. d'Alembert, eds. 1757. *Encyclopédie, ou Dictionnaire raisonné des sciences, des arts et des métiers*, vol. 7. Paris: Briasson, David, Le Breton, Durand.

Diemerbroeck I. D. 1695. *L'anatomie du corps humain.* Lyon: Anisson & Posuel.

Dumas C. L. 1797. *Système méthodique de nomenclature et de classification des muscles du corps humain.* Montpellier: Bonnariq, Avignon et Migueyron.

Dunglison R. 1868. *A dictionary of medical science.* Philadelphia, PA: Henry C. Lea.

Duverney J. G. 1761. *Œuvres anatomiques*, vol. 1. Paris: Charles-Antoine Jombert.

École biblique de Jérusalem, ed. 1961. *La Sainte Bible.* Montréal: Les Éditions Leland Ltée.

Federative Committee on Anatomical Terminology. 1998. *Terminologia Anatomica. International anatomical terminology.* Stuttgart: Thieme.

Flacelière R., ed. 1955. *Iliade. Odyssée*, vol. 115. Paris: Gallimard, Bibliothèque de la Pléiade.

Fœrster R., ed. 1893. *Scriptores Physiognomonici et Latini*, vol. 2. Lipsiae: in acdibus B.G. Teubneri.

Friel J. P., ed. 1974. *Dorland's illustrated medical dictionary.* 25th ed. Philadelphia, PA: W.B. Saunders.

Frisius J. 1723. *Dictionarium Latino-Germanicum nec non Germanico-Latinum.* Coloniae Agrippinae: Sumptibus Wilhelmi Metternich.

Froment A. 2013. *Anatomie impertinente. Le corps humain et l'évolution.* Paris: Odile Jacob.

Fuchs S. 1615. *Metoposcopia & Ophthalmoscopia.* Argentinae, excudebat Theodosius Glaserus, sumptibus Pauli Ledertz.

Furetière A. 1727. *Dictionnaire universel, contenant généralement tous les mots François, tant vieux que modernes ... Nouvelle edition par ... Basnage de Beauval ... Brutel de la Rivière*, vol. 1. La Haye, Pierre Husson, Thomas Johnson, Jean Swart, Jean van Duren, Charles Le Vier, la Veuve Van Dole.

Gall F. J., and G. Spurzheim. 1810-1819. *Anatomie et physiologie du système nerveux en general, et du cerveau en particulier, avec des observations sur la possibilité de reconnoitre plusieurs dispositions intellectuelles et morales de l'homme et des animaux, par la configuration de leurs têtes*, vol. 4 umes and atlas. Paris: F. Schoell.

Grosjean J. 1971. *La Bible. Nouveau Testament.* Paris: Gallimard. Bibliothèque de la Pléiade 226.

Grüsser O. J. 1990. Vom Ort der Seele. Cerebrale Lokalisationstheorien in der Zeit zwischen Albertus Magnus und Paul Broca. *Aus Forschung Und Medizin* 5 (1):75–96.

Hain L. 1826. *Repertorium bibliographicum in quo libri omnes ab arte typographica inventa usque ad annum MD*. Stuttgartiae: sumtibus J.G. Cottae.

Hirsch A. 1884. *Biographisches Lexikon hervorragenden Aerzte aller Zeiten und Völker*, vol. 1. Wien und Leipzig: Urban & Schwarzenberg.

Hirsch R., ed. 1983. *A catalogue of the manuscripts and archives of the library of the college of physicians of Philadelphia*. Philadelphia: University of Philadelphia Press, Francis Clark Wood Institute, College of Physicians of Philadelphia.

His W. 1895. Die anatomische Nomenclatur, Nomia anatomica, Verzeichniss der von der Commission der anatomischen Gesellschaft festgestellten Namen, eingeleitet und im Einverständniss mit dem Redactionsausschuss erläutert. *Archiv Für Anatomie Und Physiologie* (Supplement-band).

Huchet A. 2006. Geshu (17V), étymologie et indications. *Acupunture & Moxibustion* 5 (3):213–20.

Jacobs P. A., M. Brunton, M. M. Melville, R. P. Brittain, and W. F. Clemont. 1965. Aggressive behaviour, mental subnormality and the XYY male. *Nature* 208:1351–52. doi:10.1038/2081351a0.

James R. 1746. *Dictionnaire universel de médecine*, vol. 2. Paris: Briasson, David l'aîné, Durand.

Jaton A. M. 1988. *Jean Gaspard Lavater*. Lucerne, Lausanne: Éditions René Coeckelberghs.

Joly R. 1961. Platon et la médecine. *Bulletin De l'Association Guillaume Budé: Lettres D'humanité* 20:435–51. doi:10.3406/bude.1961.4200.

Joubert J. 1738. *Dictionnaire françois et latin, tiré des auteurs originaux et classiques de l'une et l'autre langue*. Lyon: Louis et Henry Declaustre.

Karli P. 1987. *L'homme agressif*. Paris: Odile Jacob.

Kern S. 1975. *Anatomy & destiny. A cultural history of the human body*. Indianapolis: The Bobbs-Merrill Company, Inc.

Klebs A. C. 1938. *Incunabula Scientifica et Medica*. Bruges: The Saint Catherine Press Ltd.

Krivatsy P. 1989. *A catalogue of seventeenth century printed books in the national library of medicine*. Bethesda, MD: National Library of Medicine.

Lauth T. 1815. *Histoire de l'anatomie*, Vol. 1. Strasbourg: F.G. Levrault.

Lavater J. C. 1772. *Von der Physiognomik*. Leipzig: Weidmanns Erben.

Lewis T. 1865. *Extracts of the journals and correspondence of Miss Berry from the year 1783 to 1852*, vol. 1. London: Longmans, Green and Co.

Magnien V. 1927. Quelques mots du vocabulaire grec exprimant des opérations ou des états de l'âme. *Revue Des Études Grecques* 40 (184–188):117–41.

Monmerqué L., ed. 1820. *Lettres de madame de Sévigné, de sa famille et de ses amis*, vol. 3. Paris: J.J. Blaise.

Morin J. B. 1809. *Dictionnaire étymologique des mots françois dérivés du grec*, vol. 1, 2nd ed. Paris: de l'Imprimerie Impériale.

Nagy G. 2013. *The ancient Greek hero in 24 hours*. Cambridge, MA: Harvard University Press.

Nelson R. J., G. E. Demas, P. L. Huang, F. C. Fishman, V. L. Dawson, T. M. Dawson, and S. H. Snyder. 1995. Behavioural abnormalities in male mice lacking neuronal nitric oxide synthase. *Nature* 378:383–86.

Nestle E. 1923. *Novum Testamentum Graece et Latine. Editio septima*. Stuttgart: Privilegierte Württembergische Bibelanstalt.

Noel P. S., and E. T. Carlson. 1970. Origins of the word "Phrenology". *The American Journal of Psychiatry* 127 (5):694–97.

Olry R. 1989. Histoire des nomenclatures anatomiques. *Documents pour l'Histoire du Vocabulaire Scientifique du CNRS* 9:91–98.

Onians R. B. 1951. *The origins of European thought about the body, the mind, the soul, the world, time, and fate*. Cambridge, UK: Cambridge University Press.

Ore O. 1967. Cardano, Geronimo. In *Encyclopedia Britannica*, vol. 4, 889–90. Chicago, IL: William Benton.

Osler W. 1923. *Incunabula medica. A study of the earliest printed medical book 1467-1480*. Oxford, UK: Oxford University Press.

Osler W. 1969. *Bibliotheca Osleriana. A Catalogue of books illustrating the history of medicine and science*. Kingston and Montreal: McGill-Queen's University Press.

Paré A. 1633. *Les Œuvres*. 9th ed. Lyon: chez la veuve de Claude Rigaud et Claude Obert.

Petit G. 1922. Sur la conception ancienne – Anatomique, physiologique et psychique – Du muscle diaphragme. *Bulletins et Mémoires de la Société d'Anthropologie de Paris* 3:48–54.

Pierron A. 1884. *L'Iliade d'Homère. Texte grec. Chants XIII-XXIV*. 2nd ed. Paris: Hachette et Cie.

Pogliano C. 1990. Entre forme et fonction: Une nouvelle science de l'homme. In *La fabrique de la pensée*, ed. P. Corsi, 144–57. Milano: Electa.

Pradier J. M. 1997. *La Scène et la fabrique des corps. Ethnoscénologie du spectacle vivant en Occident (Ve siècle av. J.-C. – XVIIIe siècle)*. Bordeaux: Presses Universitaires de Bordeaux.

Rabelais F. 1546. *Tiers liure des faictz et dictz Heroïques du noble Pantagruel*. Paris: Cheftien wechel.

Rabelais F. 1823. *Œuvres complètes*, Vol. 8. Paris: Dalibon.

Riolan J. 1672. *Manuel anatomique et pathologique*. new ed. Lyon: Antoine Laurens.

Rush B. 1811. *Sixteen introductory lectures, to courses of lectures upon the institutes and practice of medicine, with a syllabus of the latter*. Philadelphia: Bradford and Innskeep.

Santucci B. 1739. *Anatomia do corpo humano*. Lisboa Occidental: Antonio Pedrozo Galram.

Schwab M. 1967. *Bibliographie d'Aristote*. New York: Burt Franklin (reprint of the 1896 edition).

Siess J. 1990. Lespinasse, ou l'ancienne Julie, petite étude à plusieurs voix, à propos d'une edition récente des Lettres à Condorcet. *Recherches Sur Diderot Et Sur l'Encyclopédie* 9:190–91.

Spontone C. 1626. *La Metoposcopia ouero Commensuratione delle Linee della Fronte*. Venetia: Evangelista Deuchino.

Stappers H. 1885. *Dictionnaire synoptique d'étymologie française*. Bruxelles: Merzbach & Falk.

Sullivan S. D. 1988. *Psychological activity in homer: A study of Phren*. Ottawa: Carleton University Press.

Sullivan S. D. 1997. *Aeschylus' use of psychological terminology. Traditional and new*. Montreal & Kingston: McGill-Queen's University Press.

Taylor T. 1809. *The history of animals. Aristote and his treatise on physiognomony*, vol. 5. London: Printed for the Translator.

Tecusan M. 2004. *The fragments of the methodists. Volume one: Methodists outside Soranus*. Leiden: Brill.

Terra P. D. 1913. *Vademecum anatomicum. Kritisch-etymologisches Wörterbuch der systematischen Anatomie*. Jena: Verlag von Gustav Fischer.

Ullrich M. W. 1898. Phrenologie (Schädellehre). In *Nachdruck anlässig der 18. Göttinger Neurobiologentagung "Gehirn – Wahrnehmung – Kognition"*, ed. N. Elsner. Göttingen: Juni 1990, unpaginated.

van Sluis J. ed. 2011. *François Hemsterhuis. Ma toute chère Diotime. Lettres à la princesse de Gallitzin, 1775-1778*, 234–35. Berltsum: van Sluis, letter 1.196.

Vassé L. 1555. *Tables anatomicques du corps humain universel: Soit de l'homme, ou de la femme*. Paris: Jean Foucher.

Zucker A. 2006. La physiognomonie antique et le langage animal du corps. *Rursus* 1:1–24.

Index

Note: Bold page numbers refer to tables; *italic* page numbers refer to figures and page numbers followed by "n" denote endnotes.

Adhesio interthalamica 49
Age of Enlightenment 157
Akira, T. 150
Altmann, F. 46
Alytes obstetricans 42
Ambelain, R. 88
ambiguus 12–13
Ammon's horn 5
André, N. 115
ansa cervicalis 30–31
Anthony, R. 55
Apert syndrome 39
arachnoidea 20, 21
Arachnophobia 20–21
Araneae telarum 20
Arantius, J. C. 5
arctic hysteria 134
Ariëns Kappers, C. V. 10
Arnold, F. 86
array 156
Aubry, J. 52
autovampirism 89
Avellis syndrome 39

Bach, C. E. 30, 31
Baer, K. E. von 112
Bailey, P. 81
barbes du calamus 72
Barbey d'Aurevilly, J. A. 28–29
Barker, L. F. 9, 10, 36
Barrie, J. M. 27
Bartholin, T. 55, 68, 79, 111
basal cerebellar nuclei *see* deep
  cerebellar nuclei
Bascl 1, 4
Batujeff, N. 45
Bauer-Jokl, M. 18
Bausch, J. L. 114
Bayle, A. L. F. 23
Bell, B. 124
Belzung, E. 78
Bergmann, G. H. 72, 76

Bernard, J. 28
Berry, M. 162
Bettelheim, B. 146
"biceps" 116
Bichat, X. 26, 52
Bidder, H. F. 33
Bidloo, G. 21
Bimet, C. 96
Blasius, G. 20
Blatty, W. P. 132, *132*
Bleuler, P. E. 131
Bloch, O. 139
Bochdalek, V. 5
Bodin, J. 134
Bombina bambina 42
Bombina orientalis 42
Bonin, G. von 81
Bosc d'Antic, L. -A. 162
Bourbon, A. de 96
Boyer, A. 79
Boyle, F. 96
Brash, J. C. 49
Broca, P. 1, 55
Broca's limbic lobe 55
Broc, P. -P. 30, 79
Brodal, A. 1–2, 13
Brodmann, J. 81
Brodmann, K. 81–83, *82*
Brookover, C. 7
Broome, W. 58
Bruecke, E. W. von 64
Bruzen de la Martinière, A. -A. 96
"*Buffonia*" 123
Burdach, K. F. 23, 85, 128
Bürger, G. A. 60
Burke, W. 124
Bussy, comte de 161
Byron, L. 28

Cadogan, W. 102
calamus scriptorius 71, 72
Cardano, G. 161

170 INDEX

carotid arteries 128
"*cauda equina*" 100, *101*, 102
Cavalerie, M. 39
central nuclei 36
cerebellar deep nuclei *see* deep cerebellar
   nuclei
cerebral mythology 5–6
cervical intersegmental arteries 46
Cetto, A. M. 102n1
Champier, S. 140
Charcot, J. -M. 64, 134
Charcot's disease 40
Chase, R. T. 90
Chastenay, L. -M. -V. de 129
Chatterton, T. 97
Chaussier, F. 111
chief 156
Choulant, L. 100
ciliary ganglion 93
circumventricular organs 17
Clancier, G. -E. 97
Clarke, J. A. L. 13
Clark, G. 81
claustrum 23–24
Cloquet, J. 30, 71
cluster headache 157
Coincy, G. de 156
Colladon, T. 100
Colombo, M. R. 67
coma carus 128
conduit scalicoïde 79
confluence of sinuses 51–52
confluens sinuum *see* sinus confluens
Conway, J. H. 117
Cooper, A. 124
corpora restiformia 9
corpus psalloides 75
costé 156
Count of Buffon 123
cranial nerve 7–8
criminology 90
Crosby, E. C. 36
Cruveilhier, J. 23

d'Albret, J. 96
Dante Alighieri 54
Darkschewitsch, L. O. 92
Debierre, C. 12
Dechambre, A. 52
deep cerebellar nuclei 36–37
deep globus pallidus 37
deep gray masses 36
Dejerine, J. 12, 13, 141
delirium 133
Della Porta, G. B. 161
demoniacs 134, 135
demonic possession 132
demonization 135
demonolatry 135
demonomania 135

demonopathology 135
demonopathy 135
demonophobia 135
demonosis 135
Dendy, A. 18
Deschamps, E. 156
Deschanel, P. 57, 58
"devil's stair" 131
diaphragm 163–164
Diderot, D. 164
Diebitsch-Peary, J. 134
Diemerbroeck, I. van 21, 68, 79, 105, 112, 164
dorsal ependymal column 18
Dow, R. S. 10
Doyle, A. C. 138
Dream Ghost 108
Dressler, M. 79
"*Dreybeyn*" 116
Drieu la Rochelle, P. E. 123
Du Laurens, A. 100, 102
Dunglison, R. 9
Du Verney, J. G. 124

Ebers, P. 156
Ecker, A. 3
Edinger, L. 1, 9, 10, 36, 71–72
Ellermeier, F. 76
Elpenor's syndrome 57–58
endymalis 129
Endymion 129
énergumène 134
ependymal organs *see*
   circumventricular organs
epithalam 96
"éponymes confusionnants" 39
eponyms 39–41
erythromelalgia 26
Estienne, C. 86
etymology 127
Eunicke, J. 148
Eustachi, B. 75

facial torture 114
Falcon, J. 139
Falloppio, G. 75, 116
Fehr, J. M. 114
Fenton, E. 58
Ferrari, V. De 45
Fimmler, J. C. 139
Fliess, W. 64
Flynn, R. E. 46
Forel, A. H. 12
fornix 3–4
fornix transversus 76
Forst, J. J. 93
Fort, J. A. A. 67, 85
Fothergill, J. 115
"Fothergill's neuralgia" 115
fourches patibulaires 161
Foville, A. -L. 71

INDEX

frenzy 163
Freud, S. 64
Fritsch, G. 7
Fuchs, L. 20

Galen 51
Gallitzin, A. A. 162
Ganser, S. J. M. 92
Garcin, J. 139
Garengeot, R. J. C. de 5
Gasser, J. L. 93, 117
gawi nulim 108
gemellus 117
Geoffroy Saint-Hilaire, E. 1
Gerald, B. 46
Gesner, C. 145, 158
ghosts 106
Giacomini, C. 55
Gilliland, K. 123
Ginzburger, B. W. 102
Giraudoux, J. 147–148, *148*
Goelicke, A. O. 20
Golgi, C. 15
Grignan, F. -M. de 134
Grimm, J. L. C. 111
Grimm, W. C. 111
Guidon 139, 140
Guilbert, C. 124
guillotine 123
Guillotin, J. -I. 123
Gull, W. W. 140–141
Gunz, J. G. 48
Gurdjian, E. S. 128
Guy, R. K. 117
gyrus founicatus 3–4

Haan, B. B. de 131
Haarman, F. 90
Haën, A. de 93
Hahay 156
Haigh, J. G. 90
Haller, A. von 5, 14, 86
Hallervorden, J. 121, 122
Hallervorden-Spatz disease 121–124
Hare, W. 124
Hassler, R. 129
Heister, L. 21, 68
Hemsterhuis, F. 162
Herophilus' press 51–52
Herrick, C. J. 7, 36
Hewish, A. 92
Hidayat 105
Hidetada, T. 150
Hieronymus, K. F. 60–61
Hildebrandt, G. F. 21
Hiragana 150
Hirsch, A. 140
Hirsch, A. B. R. 93, 117
Hirschfeld, L. 49
His, W. 1, 71

Hoffmann, E. T. A. 148
Holl, M. 31
Holmes, S. 141
Huber, G. 46
Hugo, V. 83
Hunter, J. 124
Hunter, W. 124
hypoglossal artery 45
Hyrtl, J. 52, 71, 117

Iemitsu, T. 150
Ieyasu, T. 150
inferior cerebellar peduncle 9–10
Inferno 54
intercolumnar tubercle 17
interthalamic adhesion 48–49
interthalamic connexus 49

Jamain, A. 48
Jäschke, G. F. 93
Jaus, F. J. 93
Jiro, S. 150
Johnson, S. 105
Johnston, J. B. 7, 36, 128
Jones, E. G. 33, 65, 82
Joubert, L. 100
Joukowsky, P. von 144
Jourdan, A. 155
Jouvet, L. 147

kanashibari 105–108, *107*
Kaplan, R. 96
katakana 150
Kissen 128
Knox, R. 124
Kölliker, A. von 14
Kondziella, D. 122
Krause, W. J. F. 15
Kupffer, K. W. von 33
Kürten, P. 90
Kutschin, O. 33

LaBarre, W. 134
La Fayette, M. de 127
Lagrelette, P. A. 93
lakwat 114
La Motte-Fouqué, de F. *146*, 146–147
Landau, E. 23, 24
Langdon, F. W. 21
lapis specularis 112
Lasègue, E. C. 93
Lashley, K. S. 81
Lasthénie de Ferjol's Syndrome 28–29
Latarjet, A. 117
lavaterism 161–162
Lavater, J. K. 161
Legait, E. -J. 34
Legait, E. J. 18
Leiber, B. 122
Lemos, A. 26

172 INDEX

Lena 4
Lespinasse, J. de 164
Lesueur, L. 57
Lewes, G. H. 26
Lhermitte, J. 133
Lie, T. A. 45
limbic system 54
limbus 54–55
Linières, L. -M. T. de 123
Linné, C. von 123
Litoria aurea 42
locus niger crurum
  cerebri 86
Locy, W. A. 7
Lou Gehrig's disease 40
Lucarelli, S. 45
luciferase 131
Luminet, J. -P. 96
'Lungen-Magennerv' 12
Luys, J. B. 27
lyra 75

Macedo 49
Machiavelli, N. 122
MacLean, P. D. 54, 55
Malleri, C. D. 102
Mallery, K. van 102
Malpighi, M. 15
Martorell syndrome 39
mass 48
Masse, J. N. 23
"Matthew effect" 92–94
Mazzoni, V. 15
McKusick, V. A. 40, 41
Meadow, R. 60
Meckel, J. F. 12, 117
Meissner, G. 14
Ménage, G. 157
Méredieu, A. de 147
Merkel, F. S. 15, 79
Merton, R. K. 92
metaphren 163
metoposcopy 161
Metzger, G. B. 114
Meynert, T. 64
Michel, A. 105
migraine 155–158
migrayne 156
Milton, J. 141
Mitchell, S. W. 26, 27
Mongez, A. 158
Montgomery, R. 123
Morgagni, G. B. 48
Morton, L. T. 14
moyamoya 150–152, *151*, **151**
Munchausen syndrome 60–61
Münchhausen, B. von 60–61
Murayama, K. 46
musketeers 7–8
Mutel, M. 1, 55

Nabeshima 21
Nakajima, T. 42
Nannapaneni, R. 146
neuralgia 116
neuropeptides 42–43
neurosis 133
neurotransmitters 42–43
Nicaise, E. 140
Nicholls, G. E. 18
Nicolas, C. 133
Noll, R. 89
Nomina anatomica 1, 4
nucleus niger 86
"Nucleus X" 92
Nue 108

Obersteiner, H. 12, 36
The Odyssey 58
Oedipus complex 63–65
Oertel, C. 45
Olbert, T. 122
olonism 134
Ondine's curse 144
osphrencephalon 1
otic artery 46
Ozeray, M. 147

Pacini, F. 14
Pagel, J. L. 100
Paracelsus 145
Paré, A. 51
Parhon, C. 31
Parkinson, D. 46
Parkinson, J. 40
Parkinson's disease 39–40
patibulaire 161
Pavie, V. 148
Peary, R. E. 134
Peckham, J. 20
Peletier, J. 96
Pelletier, N. -J. 123
Pernkopf, E. 121
Petromyzon fluvialis 33
phantom limb 26–27
Phillips, E. 141
phrenology 162
Phyllomedusa rohdei 42
Phyllomedusa sauvagei 43
physiognomony 161–162
Pibloktoq 134
Piccolomini, A. 86
pineal gland 68
Pines, L. 17, 18
Pinkus, F. 7
Pinstein, M. L. 46
"Plexus hypoglossocervicalis" 30
Polle syndrome *see* Munchausen syndrome
Polster 128
polysemy of phren 162–163
Pope, A. 58

INDEX 173

Pope Gregory IX 123
possession 133
Pribytkov, G. I. 92
Prins, H. 89
proatlantal artery 45
prosopalgia 115
psalterium 75
psychosis 133
pulvinar 128

"quadriceps" 116

Rabelais, F. 161
Rabutin-Chantal, M. M. de 134, 161
Rabutin, R. de 161
Radeau, A. 57
Rana pipiens 42
Ranson, S. W. 10
Ranvier, L. A. 15
Raspe, R. E. 60
Regimen sanitatis Salernitanum 96
Reil, J. C. 23, 85
Reissner, E. 33
Reissner's fibre 33–34
Remak, R. 140
Renfield, R. M. 88
Renfield's syndrome 88–90
Retzius, G. 1, 72
rhinencephalon 1–2, 54
rhomboid fossa 71–73, *72*
Richer, P. 134
riechcentrum 1
Ringstetten, H. von 147
Riolan, J. 68, 79, 112, 156, 164
Rivarol, A. de 127
Rizzolatti, G. 112
Robertson, A. 138
Rogers, D. 61
Roland, M. 162
Rolfinck, W. 124
Romari, A. 140
Ronsard, P. de 96, 145
Ruffini, A. 15
Rush, B. 162
Ryff, W. H. 78

Sabatier, R. B. 20
sacrosanct one-sidedness 155–156
Salzmann, G. F. 46
Santorini, G. D. 85
Santucci, B. 68
Sappey, P. C. 23, 75, 85, 86
"Satan's bolete" 131
scarlet 157
Schacher's ganglion *see* ciliary ganglion
Scherer, J. 122
Schlegel, A. W. von 147
Schmidt, E. 114
Schwalbe, G. 55
Scott, W. 28

Sébire, G. 135
Seitelberger, F. 122
septum verum 111
Sévigné, M. de 161
Seward, J. 88, 89
Shunsen, T. 108
sinus confluens 52
Skeat, W. W. 139
Smith, C. U. M. 33
Soemmering, S. T. von 7, 116
Spatz, H. 121
Spenser, E. 96
Spiegel, E. 17
"Spinal Marrow" 141
Stein, S. A. V. 127
Stilling, B. 85
Stoker, B. 88
straight sinus 52
striae medullares 72
subfornical and subcommissural organs
    17–18
substantia ferruginea 86
superficial cerebellar nuclei *see* deep
    cerebellar nuclei
Swanson, L. W. 128
Swieten, G. van 93, 157
Szasz, T. S. 131

tabes dorsalis 140–141; definition 141;
    etymology and lexicology 138–139;
    historical and bibliographical roots
    139–140; nonsyphilitic tabes 141
Tarin, P. 117
Terra, P. de 1, 21
tertia cerebri meninge 20
Thorwald, J. 156
"*tic douloureux*" 115
Tilney, F. 10
Tonnô, K. 107
torcular 51
torqueo 51
tortura faciei 114
transversa lamina cinerea *see* interthalamic
    adhesion
"triceps" 116
trigeminal artery 45–46
trigeminal neuralgia 114–117
Trousseau, A. 115
tubercula thalamorum 48
Tulp, N. 157
Turner, W. 1
tympanic membrane 75

Undine 148
Uperoleia rugosa 42

vague 12–13
vampirism 89
Varolius, C. 20
Vater, A. 14

174 INDEX

Vater-Pacini 14–15
Verdier, C. 68
Verheyen, P. 67, 68, 79
vermis 78
vertebrobasilar arterial systems 45
Vigny, A. de 97
Viller, R. 48, 49
Vincent, J. -D. 6, 55
Vos, M. de 76
vulva 68

Wagner-Meissner 14–15
Wagner, R. 15, 144, *145*, 148
Warnasuriya, C. 106
Wartburg, W. von 139
Wepfer, J. J. 115

Wertheimer, P. 117
Wierix, H. 102
Wihje, J. W. van 7
Willis, T. 3
Winslow, J. -B. 5, 48, 75, 79, 102, 116
Wohlfart, G. B. 114
Wolf-Heidegger, G. 102n1
Wollschlaeger, G. 93
Wollschlaeger, P. M. 93

Yamachichi 107, 108
Yasuhara, T. 42

Zola, E. 155
zoophagia 89
Zuckerkandl, E. 1, 55